HTML5

20 Lessons to Successful Web Development

Robin Nixon

New York   Chicago   San Francisco
Athens   London   Madrid   Mexico City
Milan   New Delhi   Singapore   Sydney   Toronto

Library of Congress Cataloging-in-Publication Data

Nixon, Robin, 1961–
   HTML5: 20 lessons to successful web development / Robin Nixon.
      pages   cm
   ISBN 978-0-07-184155-9 (alk. paper)
   1. HTML (Document markup language)   2. Web sites—Design.   3. Web site development.
I. Title.
   QA76.76.H94N587   2015
   006.7'4--dc23   2014045732

McGraw-Hill Education books are available at special quantity discounts to use as premiums and sales promotions, or for use in corporate training programs. To contact a representative, please visit the Contact Us pages at www.mhprofessional.com.

HTML5: 20 Lessons to Successful Web Development

1234567890   DOC DOC   10987654

ISBN   978-0-07-184155-9
MHID   0-07-184155-5

Sponsoring Editor	**Technical Editor**	**Composition**
Brandi Shailer	Albert J. Wiersch	Cenveo Publisher Services
Editorial Supervisors	**Copy Editor**	**Illustration**
Jody McKenzie, Patty Mon	Margaret Berson	Cenveo Publisher Services
Project Manager	**Proofreader**	**Art Director, Cover**
Kritika Kaushik, Cenveo® Publisher Services	Mary Demery	Jeff Weeks
	Indexer	**Cover Designer**
Acquisitions Coordinator	Ted Laux	Jeff Weeks
Amanda Russell	**Production Supervisor**	
	Jean Bodeaux	

To Julie

Contents at a Glance

Contents

Acknowledgments

Once again I would like to thank the amazing team at McGraw-Hill Education, with whom it is always a real pleasure to work on new book projects. In particular I would like to thank my Sponsoring Editor Brandi Shailer, Amanda Russell for overseeing the project's development, Editorial Supervisor Jody McKenzie, Production Supervisor Jean Bodeaux, Copy Editor Margaret Berson, and Jeff Weeks for the excellent cover design. Thanks also goes again to Albert Wiersch (whom I have had the pleasure of working with on a number of occasions) for his meticulous eye for detail during technical review.

Introduction

Why This Book?

The concept for this book grew out of Robin's extremely popular online courses in which thousands of students are enrolled. From their feedback, it became evident that the reason for this popularity was that students love the way the material is broken up into easy-to-digest lessons, each of which can be completed in an hour or less. They also like the no-nonsense, jargon-free, and friendly writing style.

Now, working together, Robin and McGraw-Hill Education have further revised, updated, and developed his HTML5 course into this book, which not only will teach you everything you need to learn in 20 lessons (of less than an hour each), but it also includes an average 15-minute detailed video walkthrough for each lesson—almost five hours of footage in total. Watch the videos after reading the lesson to reinforce key concepts, or use the video as a primer to working through each print lesson. Together, the book and videos make learning HTML5 easier than it has ever been, and they are the ideal way for you to add HTML5 skills to your web development toolkit.

Access the videos by going to mhprofessional.com/nixonhtml5/.

Who Should Read This Book

Each chapter is laid out as a lesson in a straightforward and logical manner, with plenty of examples written using simple and clear HTML. Before moving on to each subsequent lesson, you have the opportunity to test your new knowledge with a set of 10 questions about what you have just learned. You can also work along with every lesson by watching its accompanying video tutorial.

Even if you don't already know the previous version of HTML (version 4.1), you will still learn quickly, because the first part of the book contains a comprehensive primer—great for beginners, or useful for revising before moving on to the new features.

To save you typing them in, all the example files from the book are saved in a freely downloadable zip file available at the companion website: *20lessons.com*.

What This Book Covers

This book covers every aspect of HTML and HTML5, starting with how to lay out an HTML document; handling fonts, colors, and images; creating lists and tables; and building forms. Then, after teaching some elementary JavaScript, it explains how to use the HTML5 canvas as a drawing tool, shows how you can access a user's geolocation information, presents the latest updates to web forms, reveals how to make use of local storage on the user's device and, after illustrating how easy it now is to add audio and video to your pages, also details how to make offline web apps, and run background JavaScript tasks.

How to Use This Book

This book has been written in a logical order so that each lesson builds on information learned in the previous ones. If you have never used HTML before, you should begin at Lesson 1 and then work sequentially through the book, proceeding to the next lesson only when you can correctly answer the self-test questions in the previous one.

If you already use HTML4.1, you can jump right into the HTML5 section, but I recommend you at least browse through the earlier lessons to refresh your memory of all the available features, many of which have been updated in HTML5.

How Is This Book Organized?

Although this book has three parts, they consist of just two approaches. The first deals with teaching all the HTML4 elements and how they go together to make up an HTML document, while the second explains the enhancements that have been added to HTML5.

In Part I, "Basic HTML," the lessons include: An Introduction to HTML4; the Layout of an HTML Document; the HTML Document Body; Fonts, Colors, and Images; Creating Lists and Tables; Links, Forms, and Frames; and Using the Remaining HTML4 Tags.

Part II, "HTML5 and the Canvas," includes these lessons: What's New in HTML5; Accessing the Canvas; Creating Rectangles, Fills, Gradients, and Patterns; Writing Text to the Canvas; Drawing Lines, Paths, and Curves; Manipulating Images, Shadows, and Pixels; Compositing, Transparency, and Transformations.

Part III, "Advanced HTML5," includes these lessons: Supporting Geolocation; Building Advanced Forms; Implementing Local Storage and Cross-document Messaging; Playing Audio; Displaying Video; and Working with Microdata, Web Workers, and Web Applications.

The Appendix lists all the answers to the self-test questions in each chapter.

PART I

Basic HTML

1

An Introduction to HTML

 To view the accompanying video for this lesson, please visit mhprofessional.com/
nixonhtml5/.

In his famous play for radio, *Under Milk Wood*, the poet Dylan Thomas chose to start
with the words "To begin at the beginning," and that seems also the appropriate place
to start this book on HTML5, because many of you will be new to HTML, while others
will be seasoned professionals who wish to add the new skills of HTML5 to your toolkit.

If you are new to web development, simply work your way through the entire
book, or if you already use HTML, I still recommend that you browse through these
early lessons as a refresher before moving on to the HTML5 elements (often called
tags). So let's start at the beginning and look at what HTML is all about.

Each lesson includes examples and screen grabs to illustrate the techniques being
explained, and you can download the example files from the companion website, at
20lessons.com. There is a *.zip* archive file downloadable from the front page in which
each lesson has its own folder, within which you will find the example files and
associated content. For example, the examples from this lesson are all in the *lesson01*
folder.

What Is HTML?

HTML stands for *HyperText Markup Language*, and it was invented by Sir Timothy
Berners-Lee in the early 1990s to solve the problem of quickly and efficiently
distributing documents between scientists around the world who were working with
experimenters at CERN (the European Laboratory for Particle Physics, where the
Large Hadron Collider is now also situated).

The Internet was already in place and there were tens of thousands of computers connected to each other using it, but there was no easy means of publishing content for all to see, and in which references to other documents could be easily followed. So Berners-Lee created a hyperlinking framework he called the *Hyper Text Transfer Protocol*, or HTTP (the same set of letters at the front of a web address). He also created a language to use this protocol, which he called HTML (for Hyper Text Markup Language). To utilize both these new inventions, he also wrote the world's first web browser, of which Figure 1-1 is a screenshot.

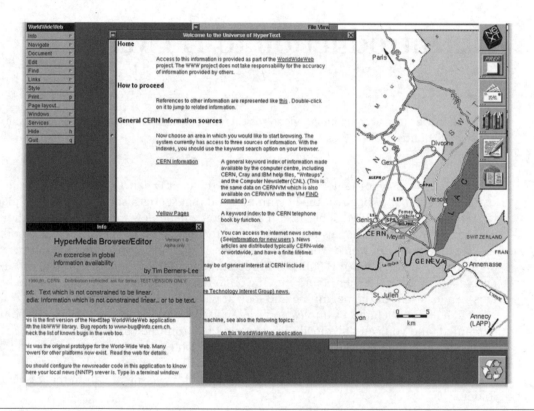

FIGURE 1-1   Berners-Lee's original NextEditor browser

This was a remarkable invention and was widely hailed in the computer press of the time as heralding a new age of communication. Until then the best connectivity computer users had experienced was dialing in to a local bulletin board, usually with only one, or at the most just a few, phone lines attached. You could then upload or download files and read and leave messages, but then you had to log off again to allow other people to take your place. Occasionally these bulletin boards would swap messages every few days with other boards, so users could interact with people further away, but only with a huge delay.

But right away HTML changed everything because now there was a way for all these bulletin boards and, in fact, any computers to stay in touch with each other, and documents could be stored in a multitude of places, which now were only ever a click away. People all over the world could connect to a local Internet host and immediately be in touch with any other person logged in to any other web-connected computer. It's hard to feel that way about it now that we've had the internet for so long, but at the time it was revolutionary, and within the course of a few years, there were three major graphical browsers and more than five million Internet users—while today that has mushroomed into over two billion people who regularly use the Web!

HTTP and HTML Basics

Let's look more closely at these two acronyms, starting with HTTP, which is the communication standard used for controlling the requests and responses that occur between a web browser running on your computer and a web server, and stands for HyperText Transfer Protocol.

The job of the web server is to accept a request from a client such as a web browser and then to reply to it in the most meaningful way it can, generally (as far as you are concerned) by simply returning the contents of a requested document, but in the process many other requests and responses also take place. This returning of a web page is called *serving*, which is why the web server is so named.

In between a client and server there can be a multitude of other computers and devices such as routers, gateways, and proxies. A web *router* chooses the best route to use in order to transfer data as fast as possible between the client and server. *Gateways* are nodes on the edge of one network that act as a connection from it to another, and *proxies* support indirect connections by acting as if they are the destination (or server), and then fetching the data you request and returning it to you, often employing a cache in which commonly requested documents are stored to save fetching them repeatedly.

These devices generally use an Internet protocol suite called TCP/IP for sending all this information flying across the Web, although there are other protocols that could be used to send HTML data (but which generally aren't, and are therefore beyond the scope of this book).

Unlike the bulletin boards mentioned earlier, which supported only one user for each connected telephone line, web servers can use a single Internet connection to allow dozens, hundreds, or even thousands of simultaneous users at a time (depending on the power of the server).

Each web server spends much of its time simply listening for incoming requests. When one arrives, the server returns a response to confirm safe receipt of the request. It does this by sending a status message such as the following back to the client:

```
HTTP/1.1 200 OK
```

After this the server then sends its own message, which generally will be the document that was requested by the client, or it could be an error message if the document was not found.

If a document is returned, it can be in any format such as audio, video, images, or, most commonly, HTML, which consists of a simple text file within which the text is separated into different sections using a special set of markup tags, and which commonly will have the extension *.htm* or *.html* (although any extension is acceptable, as long as the server knows about it). To indicate that this type of file is being sent to the client, a web server will begin the document with a header telling the client about it, which will look like this:

```
Content-Type: text/html; charset=utf-8
```

Here the type of document is clearly specified to be HTML, and the character encoding used by the file is set to utf-8. But other header types could also be sent. For example, if the requested document has been moved to a new location, the web server might, instead, return the following headers:

```
HTTP/1.1 301 Moved Permanently
Location: http://myserver.com/newlocation.html
```

The first header tells the client that the document has moved and, instead of sending the document, the second line states where the document can now be found. Then it's the client's job to go off and request the document from the new location, which could be on the same or a different web server.

As you might imagine, there are many more different types of headers and information that can be sent back and forward between web servers and clients, of which the most common one you may encounter is the following:

```
HTTP/1.0 404 Not Found
```

After sending this header, the web server will then serve up a page explaining why the document could not be found. Because of the header response code of 404, these pages are often referred to as "404" pages.

The Request/Response Sequence

Following is an example of a web client talking to a web server from which it is requesting a file:

1. You enter a URL such as *http://myserver.com* into your browser.

2. Your browser looks up the IP address for myserver.com.

3. Your browser issues a request for the home page from myserver.com.

4. The request crosses the Internet and arrives at the myserver.com web server.

5. The web server looks for the web page on its hard disk.

6. The web page is retrieved by the server and returned to the browser.

7. Your browser displays the web page.

In Step 1, the user enters a URL (Uniform Resource Locator), also known as a web address, into the browser's input field. In this instance the root document (or home page) is being requested. Once the browser receives the request, then in Step 2, it makes a request to a set of servers on the Internet known as domain name servers. These translate sequences of letters such as myserver.com into an IP address, which consists of four groups of numbers separated by periods, like this: `74.125.224.72`. In fact, all websites reside at IP addresses and you can demonstrate this by entering *http://74.125.224.72* into a web browser, which should take you to Google's website.

However, it's difficult to remember such groups of numbers (and is even more so since IPV6 was introduced!). Therefore a system called DNS (Domain Name System) was invented, which simply stores domain names alongside their IP addresses, so that all you need to do is enter *http://google.com*, rather than an obscure set of numbers. Your browser then performs a DNS lookup, discovers that the IP this domain refers to is `74.125.224.72` and then initiates discussions directly with the web server at that address, as shown in Step 3.

In Step 4, the request your browser makes to the web server traverses the Internet and arrives at the destination server where, in Step 5, the page requested (in this instance the home page), is fetched from the server's file system. In Step 6, the web server then transmits that page (preceded by a header) back to your web browser, which then displays the page in Step 7.

If the page was not found then in Step 6, an appropriate error header will be returned to the web browser. Also, web server scripting languages such as Perl and PHP may first manipulate the document and its contents by adding, removing, or changing contents according to any embedded scripting commands. Such documents are generally recognizable by their commonly used file extensions of *.pl* and *.php*.

The Difference Between Get and Post Requests

When requesting a document, it is possible for the web client (or browser) to request additional information or send information to the web server using either Get or Post requests. In a Get request, data is appended to the tail of a URL in the form of a query string, like this:

```
http://google.com/search?q=html5
```

This URL directly sends the search lookup string of `html5` to the Google web servers by passing it as a string value in the argument q. When Google sees this request, it knows to return to you all the pages it thinks are relevant to the request. A longer such request might look like the following, in which the + symbol is used in place of spaces:

```
http://google.com/search?q=html5+course
```

Here the search string `html5 course` is passed to Google.

In a Post request, however, the additional information is passed from the client to the server in the headers, which is neater as far as the user goes, because it does not appear as part of the URL. Both get and post requests are discussed in detail later in this book.

HTML Tags

HTML documents are simply text files in which extra tags have been added within angle brackets, like this: `<head>`. So, for example, the tag `<i>` tells the web browser that all following text should be displayed using an italic font. And when a `</i>` is encountered, the preceding slash (/) character tells the browser to disable the italics. Therefore you frequently find HTML tags in pairs. For example, in the following line of HTML the word fox will appear in bold face, and dog in italics:

```
The <b>fox</b> jumps over the <i>dog</i>.
```

The result looks like this:

```
The fox jumps over the dog.
```

Tag Attributes

There is a whole lot more to HTML, though, than simply markup tags, because many of the tags either support or require the use of attributes. These are arguments that you pass alongside the tag to provide further information to the web browser. Generally an attribute consists of an attribute name followed by the = sign and then either single or double quotation marks enclosing a value.

For example, to create a hyperlink that the user can click to navigate to another document, you use the `<a>` tag (which stands for anchor), like this:

```
<a href='http://google.com'>Visit Google</a>
```

In a web browser this displays simply as:

```
Visit Google
```

> **Note** In HTML tags you can generally use the single or double quotation marks interchangeably. Therefore `<a href="http://google.com">` is equivalent to `<a href='http://google.com'>`. Wherever possible, though, I tend to use single quotes because they don't require pressing the Shift key to type them in. Also there are sometimes occasions when you need two levels of nested quotes, where I would then choose double quotation marks for the outer string, and then apply single quotes within it, like this: `<p style="font-family:'Times New Roman';">`.

In this element the `href` part (which stands for hypertext reference) is the attribute name, and the string `http://google.com` is the attribute value. The content between the opening and closing parts of this tag is the text Visit Google, which is simply displayed, and if default styling is applied, it will be shown in underlined blue (although this is easy to change with HTML or CSS—there's more on this later in the book). The final `</a>` closes the tag, ready for displaying in the browser.

There are several different types of attributes available, with different tags supporting different attributes, but to give you an overview, here are some of the more common ones you will encounter and use:

- **id**   This attribute is used to give a name to the object referred to by the tag so that it can be accessed using Cascading Style Sheets (CSS) or JavaScript. For example, `<h1 id='Header1'>` provides the name or id of `Header1` to the `<h1>` tag. Nothing happens to the contents of the tag (also known as an object) unless either CSS or JavaScript acts upon it to, for example, apply a particular font styling.
- **class**   This attribute lets you supply a group name that may apply to this and other objects. For example `<p class='indent'>` applies the class name `indent` to the `<p>` tag, which might be used by a style sheet (with a suitable rule) to indent the first line of all objects using it.
- **style**   This attribute lets you apply a CSS style to an object by putting it within the quotation marks. For example, to apply the Arial font to a paragraph object, you could use the `style` attribute like this: `<p style='font-family:Arial'>`.
- **title**   Any HTML element may be given a title, which most browsers will use to display as a tooltip when the mouse passes over it. For example, the following anchor displays a tooltip when the mouse passes over it: `<a href='/' title='Go to the Home page'>`.

 CSS stands for Cascading Style Sheets, a way to separate styling from the textual content of a web page, and JavaScript is a language used within the browser to achieve dynamic effects. Both of these are beyond the scope of this book, although occasionally snippets of their use may appear within it. For further information on all aspects of web development, I recommend my other books in the 20 Lessons to Successful Web Development series on CSS & CSS3, JavaScript, and PHP.

Summary

Now that you understand the basics of what HTML is about, in the next lesson I'll introduce the different parts of an HTML document and their associated tags, such as the `<html>`, `<head>`, and `<body>` sections.

Self-Test Questions

Test how much you have learned in this lesson with these questions. If you don't know an answer, go back and reread the relevant section until your knowledge is complete. You can find the answers in the appendix.

1. What does the acronym HTML stand for?
2. What is the difference between a web browser and a web server?

3. What does the acronym HTTP stand for?

4. What does a web proxy do?

5. What file extension is often used by HTML documents?

6. What is a 404 page more commonly known as?

7. What is the difference between an IP address and a domain name?

8. What is a query string?

9. What is an HTML tag?

10. What is a tag attribute?

The Layout of an HTML Document

 To view the accompanying video for this lesson, please visit mhprofessional.com/nixonhtml5/.

Don't worry too much if Lesson 1 has left you scratching your head. If any of it is unclear right now, you will soon understand it as I take you section by section through a typical HTML document, and show you how it is laid out. If you've never used HTML before, I think you'll be pleasantly surprised because it's actually very straightforward.

In this lesson, I explain the different parts of an HTML document such as the `<!DOCTYPE>`, headers, scripts, CSS, meta tags, and the body. You will gain an understanding of how a document is put together and the things it may contain.

 Note The examples from this and all the lessons in this book are freely downloadable at 20lessons.com.

The `<!DOCTYPE>` Declaration

All well-formatted HTML pages begin with a line that tells the browser information about the type of content to expect. This line consists of the `<!DOCTYPE>` declaration, along with some arguments if the version of HTML used is less than 5. There are a number of different arguments available for this declaration, which are listed at *doctype.org* and fully explained at wikipedia.org/wiki/Doctype. For example, a typical HTML 4 document will begin with the following line, which declares the document to be an HTML 4.01 transitional document:

```
<!DOCTYPE HTML PUBLIC '-//W3C//DTD HTML 4.01 Transitional//EN'
  'http://www.w3.org/TR/html4/loose.dtd'>
```

The tag can be spread over more than one line if it would wrap around in your HTML editor, as shown in the example. In HTML5 documents, the declaration has been simplified so that you only need to use the following line:

```
<!DOCTYPE html>
```

You are unlikely to need or very often see the former declaration because all the latest versions (and some older ones too) of all major browsers will render pages either in standards mode if they do not support HTML5, or using HTML5 styling if they do. Either way, you can probably ignore older-style <!DOCTYPE> declarations except when working with legacy pages that have not been updated.

Internet Explorer Tweak for Local Documents

Because Microsoft's Internet Explorer places local documents in a trusted security zone, when you open a web page containing any active content such as JavaScript, you have to click a couple of different things to confirm that you wish to grant the web page access to your computer.

Obviously this is quite annoying when you are simply testing a document prior to uploading it to the Internet or using it in an app. Fortunately, there's a simple solution, which is to tell IE that the document was saved from the Internet (even though it wasn't), so that it then automatically assigns the correct security restrictions without being prompted. Therefore, you can add the following IE-only tag after the <!DOCTYPE> line if you will be accessing local documents using IE:

```
<!-- saved from url=(0014)about:internet -->
```

Don't worry about leaving it in your documents because it is within comment tags (see the "Inserting Comments" section in Lesson 3), and so all browsers other than IE will ignore this line. You can even leave it in place when you upload documents to the Web, because that is the same restricted zone that the command is setting anyway. But, of course, if you won't be using any active content in your web pages (such as JavaScript), or using the Internet Explorer browser, it can be omitted.

The <html> Tag

This tag notifies the web browser that a section of HTML follows. The end of the section should be noted with a matching </html> tag to indicate closure. Any content outside of these tags will be treated simply as text by most browsers unless it is within other tags or comments (explained in Lesson 3).

Many browsers are forgiving and do their best to display a page well, even with missing or misplaced `<html>` or other tags. But it's best to get things in the right order to ensure that all browsers display your content properly.

Within a pair of `<html>` tags, there are generally two other tags used to contain the header and body text of the document. These are `<head>` and `<body>`.

The `<head>` Tag

The `<head>` tag indicates that the HTML within it and its closing `</head>` tag contains further information about the document such as its title, metadata, style sheets, and JavaScript. At its simplest the head section of an HTML document may look like this:

```
<head>
  <title>Welcome to my website</title>
</head>
```

Creating a Document Title

As you saw in the previous example, setting the title of your document is as easy as enclosing it within a pair of `<title>` and `</title>` tags. The title will appear at the top of the browser in the title bar and will be used by search engines such as Google for indexing your website. Therefore, make sure the title is clear, precise, succinct, and contains relevant keywords to the page's contents. Therefore, if your website is about right-handed widgets (for example), a better title might be something like this:

```
<title>
  RH Widgets Inc: Suppliers of Right-Handed Widgets
</title>
```

 Using phrases such as "Welcome to..." was great in the 1990s when the Internet was new and there were few websites. But in the modern age when a user might browse dozens of sites in a single session, these phrases are superfluous "noise" that most people ignore. In my view it's far better to get down to the point immediately, before the user surfs off to a competitor's site.

Including Style Sheets

Cascading Style Sheets (CSS) are not really covered in this course, but you need to know about them. If you don't already know, they are sets of rules used to describe the layout and presentation of an HTML document, which are kept separately from the content. This is done to free the content from its layout and presentation so that different designs can easily be swapped in according to need. For example, a web page can be restyled with basic CSS to make it more suitable for printing, and some CSS rules can be used to help page readers read out a web page to visually impaired people.

More than that, you can change the entire look and feel of a website by altering a few simple CSS rules; something that is very time-consuming to accomplish if the styling is embedded within the web page's contents.

There are different ways of incorporating CSS rules in a document, including embedding them within the text, or as a set of rules within the <head> section of an HTML document using <style> and </style> tags, like the following (which tells the browser to display all Level 1 headings—explained later—in red):

```
<style>
  h1 { color:red; }
</style>
```

Or, by saving all the CSS rules in a separate document, you can simply include a single line in the <head> of a document to include them. The latter is the preferred method of most developers, and you perform it using the <link> tag, like this:

```
<link rel='stylesheet' href='styles.css' type='text/css'>
```

 Since this book only uses a little CSS in passing, it will not be discussed in further detail, but you may be interested in reading my book *CSS & CSS3: 20 Lessons to Successful Web Development*, for a comprehensive introduction.

Incorporating JavaScript

This course is also not about JavaScript, although some elements of HTML5 require the use of JavaScript. Generally JavaScript is included within a web page by either including a section within <script> and </script> tags, or by adding an src attribute to the <script> tag to load in an external file.

For example, the following HTML specifies a script that is embedded within <script> tags (the result of running this code is shown in Figure 2-1):

```
<script>
  alert('This is a JavaScript pop-up alert')
</script>
```

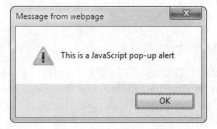

FIGURE 2-1   A JavaScript alert window

Like all JavaScript, the preceding example can be placed almost anywhere within an HTML document, but you will most often find scripts in the `<head>` section of web pages, so that they load in and execute before the body of a document. If scripts are longer than a few lines, they will often be saved as external files that are then loaded in as follows:

```
<script src='ProgramCode.js'></script>
```

The file *ProgramCode.js* is then loaded in from the current folder and its contents are executed as if all its commands were contained within the `<script>` tags. However, the JavaScript examples in this course are short and for ease of comprehension are always inserted alongside the HTML elements upon which they act.

JavaScript `<script>` tags allow you to specify the type of script as being JavaScript (for example: `<script type='text/javascript'>`), but all major browsers allow you to omit this and I generally do so to save on typing. However, if you find yourself with a strict program editor or your programming styles at your company require it, then you'll need to use the full string, as you should when writing HTML4 documents, for which the `type` attribute is required.

You may also see instances of `<script language='javascript'>` if you view the source of some websites, but this was deprecated in HTML4 and is now obsolete in HTML5, and should not be used.

Passing Metadata

It is possible to provide additional information to an HTML document that the browser can use (if it understands it). Such data is sent using the `<meta>` tag. For example, you can tell a browser to exchange the current page for another one after a set length of time, like this:

```
<meta http-equiv='refresh' content='10; url=http://othersite.com'>
```

This `meta` command uses the `http-equiv` attribute with the value of `refresh` to tell the browser that a refresh is being requested. The content attribute has the value `10; url=http://othersite.com`, which states that after 10 seconds the web page at *http://othersite.com* should replace the current one. Note that this is an empty tag (known as a void element) that contains no content and does not make use of a `</meta>` tag to close it.

Other uses of the `<meta>` tag include setting the width of the document for portable browsing hardware such as phones and tablets. This is done using the `viewport` value, and a common width you see used is 960 pixels. However, such documents are not restricted to only devices of at least that width because all this setting does is say how many pixels of width your document uses. Devices of differing resolutions will then render at that width but then zoom in or out, or rescale as necessary to enable your pages to display at their best.

So, for example, to specify a document width of 960 pixels, you might use the following tag:

```
<meta name='viewport' content='width=960'>
```

With both these tags applied, a head section of HTML might look like this:

```
<head>
  <title>The Best Website Ever</title>
  <meta http-equiv='refresh' content='10; url=http://othersite.com'>
  <meta name='viewport' content='width=960'>
</head>
```

However, as a beginner, on the whole you will probably mostly use only the `<title>` tag in the `<head>` section until you become more proficient at HTML, with the possible exception of two other versions of the `<meta>` tag for declaring keywords and a description for a web page, like this:

```
<meta name='keywords' content='keyword1,keyword2,keyword3,etc'>
<meta name='description' content='Description of web page'>
```

These used to be very important for search engine ranking, and while less so these days due to smarter web crawlers, they *are* used by some search engines and indexers, and may be worth including on your web pages.

 The `<meta>` tag is an unusual use of HTML (particularly for newcomers) but you need to be aware of it even if you don't use it, as it often crops up containing a variety of different metadata.

The `<body>` Tag

You place the contents of an HTML document inside a pair of `<body>` and `</body>` tags. Web browsers then know to display everything they find in there, and the HTML you need can be as simple as this:

```
<body>
  This is the body of the document.
</body>
```

As you will learn in Lesson 3, there are dozens of tags you can use within the body of a document, but by default you can simply place some text and it will be displayed in your browser's default text font and size.

Summary

When all the parts I have described so far are brought together, including only the document's title in the `<head>` (without JavaScript or metadata, and so on), a basic HTML document might look something like this:

```
<!DOCTYPE html>
<html>
  <head>
    <title>The Web Page's Title</title>
  </head>
  <body>
    This is the body of the document.
  </body>
</html>
```

As you can see, it's quite simple really and nothing to be frightened of. Each section, such as `<head>` or `<body>`, is closed with a matching `</head>` or `</body>` tag, and the enclosing `<html>` tag is closed right at the document end with a `</html>` tag.

In the following lesson I'll delve more deeply into the `<body>` tag and show you how to use the various tags it supports.

Self-Test Questions

Test how much you have learned in this lesson with these questions. If you don't know an answer, go back and reread the relevant section until your knowledge is complete. You can find the answers in the appendix.

1. What declaration should appear right at the start of every HTML5 document?
2. Which tag is used to specify that it contains HTML contents?
3. What is the purpose of the `<head>` tag?
4. How do you title a document?
5. Where in an HTML document should the `<title>` tag appear?
6. How do you denote the body of an HTML document?
7. Where is the place to put CSS (Cascading Style Sheet) rules?
8. How else can you include a style sheet in an HTML document?
9. How do you embed JavaScript into an HTML document?
10. How can you run an external JavaScript file from an HTML document?

The HTML Document Body

 To view the accompanying video for this lesson, please visit mhprofessional.com/ nixonhtml5/.

Having introduced you to HTML and explained the different sections it requires, in this lesson I start to look more closely at the body section of an HTML document, which resides within <body> and </body> tags.

The <body> section of HTML is where you place all the elements that the web browser should display. At its simplest you can place plain text in this section and the browser will display it for you. However, no matter how many spaces, paragraph returns, or other characters you place within this text, browsers will ignore them and just display the text in one long string. So let's look at how you can format this text to start making it look much more interesting.

Inserting Comments

To start with, let's kick off with comments, probably the simplest type of HTML formatting, and something you place in a document to be seen only in the source, and which is not displayed by the browser. To do this you place your comment between the opening <!-- and closing --> markers or tags.

Comments are useful for detailing the author of a document and explaining how a document develops. To allow this, comments may be as long as you like and include as many lines as you wish. They close only when the --> tag is encountered, so the following is an example of a legal comment string:

```
<!--
  Created by Joe Brown on July 27th 2014.
  Updated Sept 15 2015 by JB: Improved Ad display.
  Updated  Jan 12 2016 by PB: Updated login script.
-->
```

You can also use comments to temporarily remove sections of HTML that you don't want to display, perhaps because you are highly organized and have written something in advance of a product release, so that you only need to uncomment it on release day. Comments are also useful for hiding sections from displaying so you can concentrate on debugging only those sections that you may be having a problem with.

 Although I have waited until this lesson to discuss comments, you should know that you can apply them to any section of HTML, not just the body of a document. This means you can comment out sections in the head or even an entire `<html>` ... `</html>` section if you wish. Also, you should remember that comments may not contain pairs of hyphen characters within them, nor can they end with a hyphen, as this may confuse the browser's HTML parser.

The HTML 4.01 Tags

HTML 4.01 (HTML4 for short) supports almost 100 different elements (also called tags), but since this is a book on HTML5, I will not go into all of them in detail. Rather, in this lesson I concentrate on some of the different types of HTML4 tags and how you use them, and then briefly list the less frequently used ones and the attributes they have.

This includes various text formatting tags, for headings, paragraphs, text emphasis, and lists. Then there are the tags for changing text and background colors and font faces, as well as tags for embedding media such as images, creating hyperlinks, building tables and forms, and much more. So you will get a good grounding in HTML4 before moving on to the new features in HTML5.

The `<div>` and `<span>` Tags

The `<div>` and `<span>` tags were created to help with combining elements into groups. Their main purpose is to enable the contained elements to be manipulated as a group from style sheets. The `<div>` tag creates what is called a block element in that by default its width stretches all the way to the browser's right-hand edge, forcing any following elements onto the next line. Therefore all `<div>` elements have four sides and are rectangular.

On the other hand, the `<span>` tag creates an inline element that flows with the text, and it is therefore particularly suited for applying styles to sections of text. Although this book doesn't teach CSS, style sheets are inextricably entwined with HTML and so, from time to time, I may employ either `<div>` or `<span>` tags with suitable CSS styling where standard HTML does not provide the solution required.

You use the tags as follows:

```
<div>This is some text in a div element</div>
<span>This is some text in a span element</span>
```

The main practical difference between the two that you will usually notice is that <div> elements by default force a line break before and after them, whereas <span> elements do not. You will see how to add CSS styles to them in the "Text Emphasis" section, a little further on.

Simply think of each of these two types of elements as invisible containers in which text and/or other elements are placed, and which can be styled with CSS. Remember that <div> elements are rectangular, while <span> elements go with the flow of text, line by line along and down the screen.

Headings

Let's now look at some of the commonly used tags, those for formatting text, starting with headings. To specify headings in HTML documents, you must enclose them in any one of six different pairs of tags, from <h1> to <h6>, and their counterpart closing tags </h1> to </h6>. The <h1> heading is the largest, and <h6> is the smallest. Headings are also generally formatted in bold to help them stand out from the body even more.

Here are examples of each heading type, and the result of using them is shown in Figure 3-1:

```
<h1>This is a level 1 heading</h1>
<h2>This is a level 2 heading</h2>
<h3>This is a level 3 heading</h3>
<h4>This is a level 4 heading</h4>
<h5>This is a level 5 heading</h5>
<h6>This is a level 6 heading</h6>
```

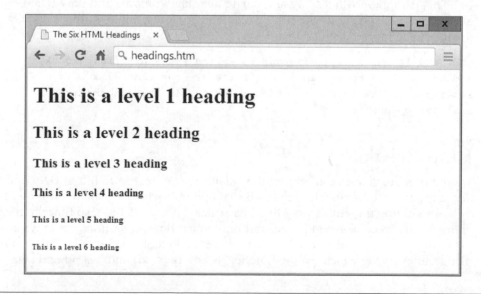

FIGURE 3-1   The six types of HTML headings

Interestingly, the fifth- and sixth-level headings are by default displayed smaller than standard body text. However, most writers will agree that if you need to go any deeper than four levels, you are probably overcomplicating the subject and should consider reworking your content. For this and the previously mentioned reason of small size, I rarely use <h5> and <h6>.

Once you have split a web document with suitable headings inserted in appropriate places using these tags, it is much easier for your readers to comprehend and quickly read it. This is because it is easier on the eye with more whitespace, and each separate topic has its own heading, making it easier to focus in on what interests the reader.

Paragraphs

Each of your paragraphs should be enclosed within <p> and </p> tags so that web browsers know how to handle them. By default it will ensure the correct spacing between each paragraph and, with the addition of CSS, you can further modify styling by, for example, indenting the first line of each, or by choosing ragged or full justification, and so on.

Here is an example of a simple paragraph taken from Matthew 7:7-8 in the Bible (I prefer to use the Bible, Shakespeare, Dickens, and so on, rather than using Lorem Ipsum text), and formatted as an HTML paragraph:

```
<p>Ask, and it shall be given you; seek, and you
shall find; knock, and it shall be opened unto you:
For every one that asks receives; and he that seeks
finds; and to him that knocks it shall be opened.</p>
```

This paragraph will display as a single line that wraps around only when the text encounters the edge of its containing element. So, for example, it might display like the following ragged justified text:

```
Ask, and it shall be given you; seek, and you shall find; knock,
and it shall be opened unto you: For every one that asks
receives; and he that seeks finds; and to him that knocks it
shall be opened.
```

Line Breaks

What a line break does is interrupt the default flow of text from left to right and then down to the next line (or right to left if that option has been enabled, either with CSS or by modifying the <html> tag like this: <html dir='rtl'>), so that the next element displayed is forced to the start of the next line. Sometimes you have a reason for sending a line break to the browser before the end of a paragraph. This is done using the <br> tag which, you will notice, is empty (void) and has no end tag.

Even though in HTML5 the value supplied to `dir` can be either uppercase (for example RTL) or lowercase (for example `rtl`), because XHTML doesn't support uppercase, you should stick with the lowercase style so that your content can be easily repurposed as XHTML (such as in an RSS feed).

So, if you need to make sure some text (or any sequence of HTML elements) displays exactly the way you want, you can force its formatting, for example, as with the following reformatting of the quotation from Matthew:

```
<p>Ask, and it shall be given you;<br>
seek, and you shall find;<br>
knock, and it shall be opened unto you:<br>
For every one that asks receives;<br>
and he that seeks finds;<br>
and to him that knocks it shall be opened.</p>
```

This HTML will display as follows—as long as its containing element is wide enough:

Ask, and it shall be given you;
seek, and you shall find;
knock, and it shall be opened unto you:
For every one that asks receives;
and he that seeks finds;
and to him that knocks it shall be opened.

Whatever is next in your HTML to be displayed, whether an image, a video, or some text, the <br> will always force it down to continue on the next line. There is also a special case of this tag, which is used to clear any temporary left or right alignment. For example, it is possible to display an image with left alignment so that text flows down along its right-hand side (there's more on how to do this later in the section "Displaying Images" in Lesson 4). But if you have insufficient text to fill in all the space to the right of the picture before the next paragraph or heading, then that would also appear beside it.

In such cases you can use the <br> tag to clear any alignment and force further text (or other elements) to appear not just down a line, but under the image or other object around which the text has been flowing. There are three versions of the tag to do this, for clearing left alignment, right alignment, and all alignments respectively, as follows:

```
<br clear='left'>
<br clear='right'>
<br clear='all'>
```

The `clear` attribute is not part of HTML5 (even though your browser may still support it), and so you are recommended to create this type of alignment using CSS instead, since there is a good chance that this attribute will stop working sometime soon.

Text Emphasis

There are many different ways you can change the emphasis of text in HTML, each with an accompanying tag. For example you can bold, italicize, underline, and strike through text, and you can also display text in superscript or subscript.

Following are the most common HTML tags you will use for this, the results of using which you can see in Figure 3-2. Some of these tags are obsolete in HTML5, which means that they have been removed from HTML5. However, the practicality of billions of web pages already employing them means that support for them in browsers is unlikely to end, otherwise too many websites would break. Even so, you should avoid using obsolete elements in new documents.

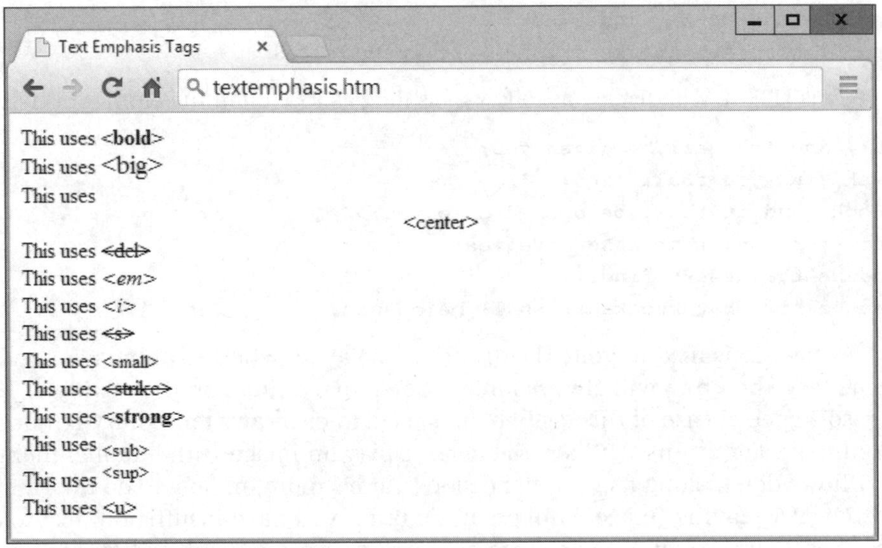

FIGURE 3-2 The text emphasis tags and how they display

`<b> ... </b>`

Text within these tags will appear in bold face. This is the same as using the `<strong>` tag, but it is possible to style this tag differently than `<strong>` with CSS. HTML5 considers there to be a semantic difference between these tags, though, in that `<b>` should be used only for formatting in bold.

`<big> ... </big>` (Obsolete)

Text within these tags will be bigger than that outside. This tag is obsolete in HTML5.

`<center>` ... `</center>` (Obsolete)

Text within these tags will appear centered. However, these tags are obsolete in HTML5 and you are recommended to use CSS in their place. Note how in Figure 3-2 you can see that by using this tag, if the text within it is not already at the start of a line, then a line break will automatically be issued first. A line break is also issued after closing this tag, so beware of adding one yourself, which would result in a double line break.

`<del>` ... `</del>`

Text within these tags will appear with a strikethrough line through it. This is the same as using the `<s>` and `<strike>` tags (although `<strike>` is obsolete in HTML5). It is possible to style this tag differently than `<s>` and `<strike>` with CSS. In HTML5 `<del>` represents a removal from the document.

`<em>` ... `</em>`

Normally text within these tags is displayed in italics, and so it is the same as using `<i>`, but it is possible to style this tag differently than `<i>` using CSS. In HTML5, `<em>` is meant for adding emphasis to text (it just happens to italicize by default).

`<i>` ... `</i>`

Text within these tags will appear in italics. This is the same as using the `<em>` tag, but it is possible to style this tag differently than `<em>` with CSS. The `<i>` tag should be used only for italicizing in HTML5.

`<s>` ... `</s>`

Text within these tags will appear with a strikethrough line through it. These tags were deprecated in HTML4 but restored in HTML5, and are the same as using `<strike>` (which is now obsolete in HTML5). The `<s>` tag is similar to the `<del>` tag, but in HTML5 it is intended for indicating something that is no longer accurate or relevant.

`<small>` ... `</small>`

Text within these tags will be shown smaller than that outside.

`<strike>` ... `</strike>` (Obsolete)

The same as `<s>`, although it is obsolete in HTML5, and so either `<s>` or `<del>` is recommended instead. It is possible to style this tag differently than `<s>` and `<del>` using CSS.

`<strong>` ... `</strong>`

Normally text within these tags is displayed in bold face, and so it is the same as using `<b>`, but it is possible to style this tag differently than `<b>` using CSS. In HTML5 `<strong>` is intended for text that is especially important, such as a key point to learn.

`<sub> ... </sub>`

Text within these tags will appear subscripted.

`<sup> ... </sup>`

Text within these tags will appear superscripted.

`<u> ... </u>`

Text within these tags will appear underlined. This tag was deprecated in HTML4 but restored in HTML5, and is intended to represent text that should be stylistically different from normal text, such as misspelled words.

When you wish to create emphasis, it is often best to use CSS. One way is to add the CSS inline, as with the following example, which creates italic and strikethrough text:

```
<span style='font-style:italic;'>italic</span>.
<span style='text-decoration:line-through;'>strike through</span>.
```

An even better way is to separate the styling from the content by creating a class containing a rule, and then applying the class. Doing so in detail is beyond the scope of this book, but the following snippet shows one way of doing this using a period symbol in front of the class names in the `<style>` section:

```
<head>
  <title> CSS Text Emphasis</title>
  <style>
    .italic { font-style     :italic; }
    .strike { text-decoration:line-through; }
  </style>
</head>
<body>
  This is <span class='italic'>italic</span>.<br>
  This is <span class='strike'>strikethrough</span>.
</body>
```

Figure 3-3 shows the preceding example being displayed in a web browser.

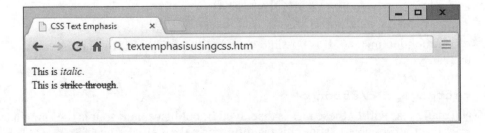

FIGURE 3-3 Using CSS to create text emphasis

Summary

Armed with the tags you have learned so far, you can already create some quite impressive HTML documents, but in the following lesson I add even more tools to your kit by showing how to change font face and color, and embed images in your documents.

Self-Test Questions

Test how much you have learned in this lesson with these questions. If you don't know an answer, go back and reread the relevant section until your knowledge is complete. You can find the answers in the appendix.

1. How can you place a comment in an HTML document?
2. What is the difference between a <div> and a <span> element?
3. What are the six pairs of tags you can use to create different levels of headings?
4. Which tags do you use to denote the start and end of a paragraph?
5. How can you issue a line break in an HTML document?
6. How can you format HTML text in bold without using CSS?
7. Which HTML tag can be used for displaying italic text?
8. What is one way to display text in italics with CSS?
9. How can you make an element display as line-through using CSS?
10. What does the term *deprecated* mean?

LESSON 4

Fonts, Colors, and Images

 To view the accompanying video for this lesson, please visit mhprofessional.com/nixonhtml5/.

So far you have learned about the structure of an HTML document, and how to format and emphasize text to present it well.

In this lesson, I show you how to change the font face and size of any text, as well as how to add coloring to the text foreground or background, and how to load and display images in a document, including on-the-fly resizing.

Changing Font Face and Color

Even without using CSS, there are many ways you can use HTML to change the way a font displays by passing different attributes to the `<font>` tag. However, the use of this tag (and another called `<basefont>`) has been deprecated in HTML4 and made obsolete in HTML5. This means that at some time in the future they could be removed entirely from HTML, but I seriously doubt this will ever happen since they are so widely used on billions of pages worldwide, which would all break if this happened. Nevertheless, you should avoid using them on any new web pages.

It's true that CSS is a better way to manage colors, but this is a book on HTML, and so I will show you what you can achieve with it. Once you've mastered HTML, though, I strongly advise you to learn CSS if you haven't already.

Anyway, let's start off this lesson with the `<font>` tag.

`<font color='…'> ... </font>`

The color of the text is changed to the value in the quotation marks. This value may be a color name (see the following section, "The Named Colors") or a color number (see the "Coloring by Numbers" section). For example:

```
<font color='red'>This is red text</font>
```

`<font face='…'> ... </font>`

The font face of the text is changed to the value in the quotation marks. This value should be the name of a font available to the browser. If the font is not found, a replacement will be selected. For example:

```
<font face='Arial'>This text is in the Arial font</font>
```

`<font size='…'> ... </font>`

The font size of the text is changed to the value in the quotation marks. This should be a value between 1 and 7 (from smallest to largest size font, with a default of 3). The value may be preceded with a + or – symbol to indicate a relative rather than absolute change of size. For example:

```
<font size='5'>This is font size 5</font>
```

You may combine any or all of the `color`, `face`, and `size` attributes in a single `<font>` tag, for example, like this:

```
<font color='red' face='Arial' size='5'>
  This is red, size 5 text, in the Arial font
</font>
```

`<basefont>`

Additionally you can use the global tag `<basefont>`, which has the same attributes as the `<font>` tag but is used to change the default font values for an entire document. In particular, if the size is changed, then any use of the `<font>` tag with + or – values will change the font's size relative to the value specified for the basefont.

Note Headings are not affected by the `<basefont>` tag, and on some browsers, tables do not use this tag's values either.

`<body bgcolor='…'>`

You can change the default background color of a web page by specifying your choice of color as an attribute to the `<body>` tag, like this, which sets it to cyan:

```
<body bgcolor='cyan'>
```

The Named Colors

All browsers support 16 main color names for the color attribute values, including: `aqua`, `black`, `blue`, `fuchsia`, `gray`, `green`, `lime`, `maroon`, `navy`, `olive`, `purple`, `red`, `silver`, `teal`, `white`, and `yellow`.

Modern browsers support many more color names (up to 147), but those names are not part of the HTML standard. Among other options, you can often add the words dark or `light` before a color name, but do check that all browsers you intend to support work with these color names. Here are some examples:

```
<body bgcolor='lightgreen'>
<font color='darkblue'>
<font color='navajowhite'>
```

See Table 4-1 for the full list of color names supported by all web browsers (and their equivalent hex string values). If you need a wider choice of colors, you should really use hexadecimal color numbers, which allow very precise color selection, as explained in the following section.

TABLE 4-1 The 140 cross-browser color names and their hex values *(Continued)*

Color	Value	Color	Value	Color	Value
AliceBlue	#F0F8FF	GhostWhite	#F8F8FF	NavajoWhite	#FFDEAD
AntiqueWhite	#FAEBD7	Gold	#FFD700	Navy	#000080
Aqua	#00FFFF	GoldenRod	#DAA520	OldLace	#FDF5E6
Aquamarine	#7FFFD4	Gray	#808080	Olive	#808000
Azure	#F0FFFF	Green	#008000	OliveDrab	#6B8E23
Beige	#F5F5DC	GreenYellow	#ADFF2F	Orange	#FFA500
Bisque	#FFE4C4	HoneyDew	#F0FFF0	OrangeRed	#FF4500
Black	#000000	HotPink	#FF69B4	Orchid	#DA70D6
BlanchedAlmond	#FFEBCD	IndianRed	#CD5C5C	PaleGoldenRod	#EEE8AA
Blue	#0000FF	Indigo	#4B0082	PaleGreen	#98FB98
BlueViolet	#8A2BE2	Ivory	#FFFFF0	PaleTurquoise	#AFEEEE
Brown	#A52A2A	Khaki	#F0E68C	PaleVioletRed	#DB7093
BurlyWood	#DEB887	Lavender	#E6E6FA	PapayaWhip	#FFEFD5
CadetBlue	#5F9EA0	LavenderBlush	#FFF0F5	PeachPuff	#FFDAB9
Chartreuse	#7FFF00	LawnGreen	#7CFC00	Peru	#CD853F
Chocolate	#D2691E	LemonChiffon	#FFFACD	Pink	#FFC0CB
Coral	#FF7F50	LightBlue	#ADD8E6	Plum	#DDA0DD

TABLE 4-1 The 140 cross-browser color names and their hex values

Color	Value	Color	Value	Color	Value
CornflowerBlue	#6495ED	LightCoral	#F08080	PowderBlue	#B0E0E6
Cornsilk	#FFF8DC	LightCyan	#E0FFFF	Purple	#800080
Crimson	#DC143C	LightGoldenRodYellow	#FAFAD2	Red	#FF0000
Cyan	#00FFFF	LightGray	#D3D3D3	RosyBrown	#BC8F8F
DarkBlue	#00008B	LightGreen	#90EE90	RoyalBlue	#4169E1
DarkCyan	#008B8B	LightPink	#FFB6C1	SaddleBrown	#8B4513
DarkGoldenRod	#B8860B	LightSalmon	#FFA07A	Salmon	#FA8072
DarkGray	#A9A9A9	LightSeaGreen	#20B2AA	SandyBrown	#F4A460
DarkGreen	#006400	LightSkyBlue	#87CEFA	SeaGreen	#2E8B57
DarkKhaki	#BDB76B	LightSlateGray	#778899	SeaShell	#FFF5EE
DarkMagenta	#8B008B	LightSteelBlue	#B0C4DE	Sienna	#A0522D
DarkOliveGreen	#556B2F	LightYellow	#FFFFE0	Silver	#C0C0C0
DarkOrange	#FF8C00	Lime	#00FF00	SkyBlue	#87CEEB
DarkOrchid	#9932CC	LimeGreen	#32CD32	SlateBlue	#6A5ACD
DarkRed	#8B0000	Linen	#FAF0E6	SlateGray	#708090
DarkSalmon	#E9967A	Magenta	#FF00FF	Snow	#FFFAFA
DarkSeaGreen	#8FBC8F	Maroon	#800000	SpringGreen	#00FF7F
DarkSlateBlue	#483D8B	MediumAquaMarine	#66CDAA	SteelBlue	#4682B4
DarkSlateGray	#2F4F4F	MediumBlue	#0000CD	Tan	#D2B48C
DarkTurquoise	#00CED1	MediumOrchid	#BA55D3	Teal	#008080
DarkViolet	#9400D3	MediumPurple	#9370DB	Thistle	#D8BFD8
DeepPink	#FF1493	MediumSeaGreen	#3CB371	Tomato	#FF6347
DeepSkyBlue	#00BFFF	MediumSlateBlue	#7B68EE	Turquoise	#40E0D0
DimGray	#696969	MediumSpringGreen	#00FA9A	Violet	#EE82EE
DodgerBlue	#1E90FF	MediumTurquoise	#48D1CC	Wheat	#F5DEB3
FireBrick	#B22222	MediumVioletRed	#C71585	White	#FFFFFF
FloralWhite	#FFFAF0	MidnightBlue	#191970	WhiteSmoke	#F5F5F5
ForestGreen	#228B22	MintCream	#F5FFFA	Yellow	#FFFF00
Fuchsia	#FF00FF	MistyRose	#FFE4E1	YellowGreen	#9ACD32
Gainsboro	#DCDCDC	Moccasin	#FFE4B5		

Coloring by Numbers

Instead of providing color names to HTML tags, you can be much more precise by passing numeric values instead. To do this you start with a # symbol and follow it with six hexadecimal numbers consisting of three pairs, which represent the primary colors of red, green, and blue.

For example, numbers in hexadecimal go from 0 through to F, rather than the 0 to 9 we are used to in decimal notation. Therefore a single hexadecimal digit can represent any of 16 different values (instead of 10). This means that two hexadecimal digits together can represent 256 values (16 × 16, between 00 and FF), and therefore it is possible to create a color out of any one of 256 levels of red, 256 green, and 256 blue—over 16 million colors (256 × 256 × 256).

This is done by following the # symbol with six hexadecimal digits, like this, for example: #006699, which indicates a color consisting of 00 red, hexadecimal 66 (102 decimal) of green, and hexadecimal 99 (153 decimal) of blue. Therefore the value #000000 specifies the color black because it assigns values of 00 to red, 00 to green, and 00 to blue. On the other hand, a value of #FFFF00 specifies the color yellow because it assigns values of FF to red, FF to green, and 00 to blue (on a computer, combining red and green results in the color yellow).

For example, the following tag changes the font color to orange:

```
<font color='#FF8800'>This is orange text</font>
```

 You may use either the lowercase letters a–f, or the uppercase A–F, or a combination in hexadecimal color values. Also, in some browsers, if you are prepared to sacrifice the availability of over 16 million possible colors for a more limiting 4,000 or so, you can use a single hexadecimal digit for each primary color in a value, rather than two of them, like this: #000, or #148. The former is the color black, while the latter is shorthand for the color #114488—only use this format if your web pages won't be accessed with Internet Explorer. However, color values of either length (three or six hexadecimal digits) are accepted by CSS rules (as opposed to HTML) in all browsers.

Font Faces

There are a number of fonts available to a web browser, depending upon the availability of fonts in the underlying operating system. Therefore, when you choose a font name, you are permitted to select alternative, or second-best fonts, in order of preference so that a web page will degrade gracefully according to your font preferences.

For example, as a backup in cases where a computer may not have the Arial font installed, you might choose to ask the browser to choose the best sans-serif font it can find by using the following syntax:

```
<font face='Arial, sans-serif'>
  This is Arial, or sans-serif if unavailable
</font>
```

Following is a list of all the main fonts that are likely to be available on most PCs, Macs, Linux boxes or other modern computers, along with one or more suitable substitutes where the chosen font isn't available. Simply enter the entire string as the value of the `face` attribute of a `<font>` tag to select it.

- `"Arial, sans-serif"`
- `"'Arial Black', sans-serif"`
- `"'Arial Narrow', sans-serif"`
- `"'Avant Garde', sans-serif"`
- `"Bookman, 'Bookman Old Style', serif"`
- `"'Century Gothic', sans-serif"`
- `"Copperplate, 'Copperplate Gothic Light', serif"`
- `"'Comic Sans MS', cursive"`
- `"Courier, monospace"`
- `"'Courier New', monospace"`
- `"Garamond, serif"`
- `"'Gill Sans', 'Gill Sans MT', sans-serif"`
- `"Georgia, serif"`
- `"Helvetica, sans-serif"`
- `"Impact, fantasy"`
- `"'Lucida Grande', 'Lucida Sans Unicode', sans-serif"`
- `"'Lucida Console', monospace"`
- `"Palatino, 'Palatino Linotype', serif"`
- `"Tahoma, sans-serif"`
- `"Times, serif"`
- `"'Times New Roman', serif"`
- `"Trebuchet, sans-serif"`
- `"Verdana, sans-serif"`

For example, for the Lucida Grande font, enter the string shown, like this:

```
<font face="'Lucida Grande', 'Lucida Sans Unicode', sans-serif">
  This is Lucida Grande, or Lucida Sans Unicode, or sans-serif
  if both are unavailable.
</font>
```

Figure 4-1 shows how these font strings display on a standard Windows computer using Internet Explorer.

 The single quotation marks are required within the double quotes to enclose font face names that contain spaces in them.

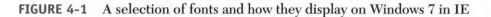

FIGURE 4-1   A selection of fonts and how they display on Windows 7 in IE

You can also use these strings without the double quotes (but keeping the single ones) as part of CSS declarations for changing a font face, like this:

```
<span style="font-family:Palatino, 'Palatino Linotype', serif;">
  This is Palatino, or Palatino Linotype, or serif
  if both are unavailable.
</span>
```

Or, better still, employ a CSS class that you create in a separate CSS style sheet or within <style> … </style> tags in the <head> of your document. For more on using CSS, you may wish to refer to my book, *CSS & CSS3: 20 Lessons to Successful Web Development*.

Displaying Images

Images are easily displayed in a web page and various image types are supported, mainly including *.jpg*, *.gif,* and *.png*. Each of these has different features and drawbacks.

For example, *.gif* images can be animated, but display fewer colors; *.jpg* images display more colors but may employ a lossy compression technique that introduces distortions; while *.png* images offer the best of both worlds, but can be larger.

You include an image in your HTML using the `<img>` tag (note that this void tag is empty and has no matching `</img>` tag), accompanied by one or more of the following attributes:

- **src**   This value tells the browser where to fetch the image from. If it is preceded by the string `http://` (or `https://` on secure servers), then the image will be downloaded from the website at the domain following the `http://`. Otherwise the image is assumed to be on the current website (or on the local disc) and is loaded from the current folder there.

- **alt**   Some browsers do not display images, or their display may have been disabled, so you can use this attribute to provide alternate text describing the image. This is also useful in cases where an image is slow or fails to load, as shown by the fourth image in Figure 4-2, in which the alternate text is displayed due to the image not being found.

- **width and/or height**   By default web browsers will look up an image's dimensions and display it using them. But sometimes you may wish to display an image using a different width and height, which you can specify using one or both of these attributes. If only one attribute is used, the browser will compute the other dimension such that the image will stay in proportion. Another reason to specify an image's width and height is to ensure that page layout is correctly aligned even before the image is loaded. If you specify these values in advance, the browser will allocate the space required for the image right away.

- **border**   Using this attribute you can specify the width of border (if any) to apply to an image. It accepts the value 0 or any positive number. Unless this setting is modified by CSS, if an image has a border and is placed with an anchor, the border color will change when the mouse passes over it. The three images that could be loaded in Figure 4-2 have no border, a one-pixel border, and a five-pixel border respectively. This attribute is obsolete in HTML5 and CSS is recommended instead.

- **align**   With this attribute you can position an image vertically by aligning it within the current line using any of the values `top`, `middle`, `bottom`, `absmiddle`, or `absbottom`. You can also align it to the left or right of the current line using the values `left` or `right`. This attribute is obsolete in HTML5 and CSS is recommended instead.

FIGURE 4-2   Four images displayed using the `<img>` tag, with one missing

The lines of HTML used to create Figure 4-2 are as follows:

```
<img src='image1.png' border='0' width='200' height='150' alt='Image 1'>
<img src='image2.jpg' border='1' width='200' height='150' alt='Image 2'>
<img src='image3.gif' border='5' width='200' height='150' alt='Image 3'>
<img src='image4.png' border='1' width='200' height='150' alt='Image 4'>
```

In Lesson 3, I introduced the `<br>` tag, which is used for creating a line break, and mentioned that it also had a secondary purpose, which is to clear left or right alignment. Well, here's how that works.

Figure 4-3 shows an image being displayed using left alignment with some text flowing to its right. It was created with the following HTML:

```
<img src='image1.png' align='left'>

<p>An island or isle is any piece of sub-continental land
that is surrounded by water. Very small islands such as
emergent land features on atolls can be called islets, cays
or keys.</p>

<p>An island in a river or lake may be called an eyot or
holm. A grouping of geographically or geologically related
islands is called an archipelago.</p>
```

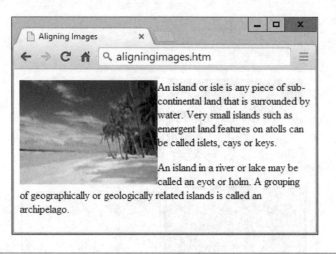

FIGURE 4-3   A left-aligned image with text flowing to the right

Disregarding (for now) the fact that the text butts right up against the image, it also seems rather messy because the second paragraph probably should begin under the image. To fix this the `<br clear='left'>` tag is used (although `clear='all'` would also work in this instance) prior to closing the first paragraph, as follows, with the result shown in Figure 4-4:

```
<img src='image1.png' align='left'>

<p>An island or isle is any piece of sub-continental land
that is surrounded by water. Very small islands such as
emergent land features on atolls can be called islets, cays
or keys. <br clear='left'></p>

<p>An island in a river or lake may be called an eyot or
holm. A grouping of geographically or geologically related
islands is called an archipelago.</p>
```

Although better, this display could still do with a little more cleaning up, so in Figure 4-5 I have added a 1-pixel border to the image, a heading to the text, and created a 15-pixel blank margin to the right of the image using a CSS declaration, as follows:

```
<img src='image1.png' align='left' border='1' style='margin-right:15px;'>

<h1>All About Islands</h1>

<p>An island or isle is any piece of sub-continental land
that is surrounded by water. Very small islands such as
emergent land features on atolls can be called islets, cays
or keys.<br clear='left'></p>
```

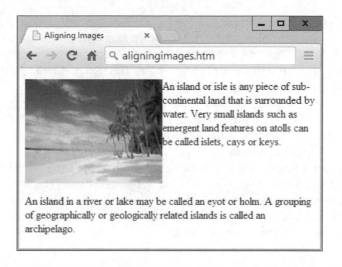

FIGURE 4-4   The left alignment is cleared before the start of the second paragraph.

```
<p>An island in a river or lake may be called an eyot or
holm. A grouping of geographically or geologically related
islands is called an archipelago.</p>
```

 Ideally, the CSS styling should be removed from within the body of the web document and into an external style sheet using a class name, which can then be applied to any left-aligned object. Please refer to your favorite CSS book or website for full details on using CSS.

FIGURE 4-5   Now a border, heading, and margin have been added.

By default, images will line up next to each other unless you use CSS styling or tags such as <br> to force a line break, or <p> to start a new paragraph. Text will also line up next to an image, but starting only at the bottom-most possible line, and then wrapping around to the next line. So use the align attribute to force a full left (or right) align to allow text to flow from the top-most position.

If you choose to right-align an image (or any element, in fact), things are just the same, except that text will flow to its left, and you should use either the clear='right' or clear='all' attributes of the <br> tag if you wish to turn off the wrapping prior to reaching the bottom of the image.

Remember, though, that the clear attribute (like align) has been made obsolete in HTML5 and, even though it still works in all major browsers (for backward compatibility reasons), you should learn to use CSS to achieve the same effect for all new documents—because one day deprecated and obsolete attributes may be removed altogether, which will break pages that use these attributes.

Summary

Now that you have mastered managing fonts, colors, and images, in the next lesson I will turn to building lists and tables.

Self-Test Questions

Test how much you have learned in this lesson with these questions. If you don't know an answer, go back and reread the relevant section until your knowledge is complete. You can find the answers in the appendix.

1. What HTML tag is used to manipulate fonts?
2. Which attribute affects the color of text?
3. Which attribute changes the font face?
4. Which attribute changes a font's size?
5. How can you change the background of a document without using CSS?
6. What colors do the following hexadecimal number values represent: #FF0000, #FFFFFF, #888888?
7. How can you change font face using CSS?
8. Which HTML tag can you use to display images?
9. How can you left-align an image without using CSS?
10. What is the CSS way of left-aligning an element?

Creating Lists and Tables

To view the accompanying video for this lesson, please visit mhprofessional.com/nixonhtml5/.

B y now you should be really appreciating the power of HTML, and we've only covered a subsection of HTML 4.01, but bear with me if you are new to HTML, because you need this background in order to prepare you for all the goodies that have been added in HTML5.

And even if you are experienced with HTML, it may still be a good idea to continue browsing through these early lessons to give yourself a quick refresher on the subject.

Building Lists

HTML supports a wide variety of different list types, including bulleted, numbered, and definition lists. Numbered lists are known as *ordered lists*, and list items can be denoted with letters of the alphabet or roman numerals as well as with numbers, and bulleted lists can use squares, or filled or outlined circles.

Figure 5-1 shows every possible type of list, all on a single web page, including both the upper- and lowercase forms that are available.

A typical ordered list can be created with HTML, such as the following:

```
<ol>
  <li>Apple</li>
  <li>Pear</li>
  <li>Banana</li>
  <li>Plum</li>
  <li>Orange</li>
</ol>
```

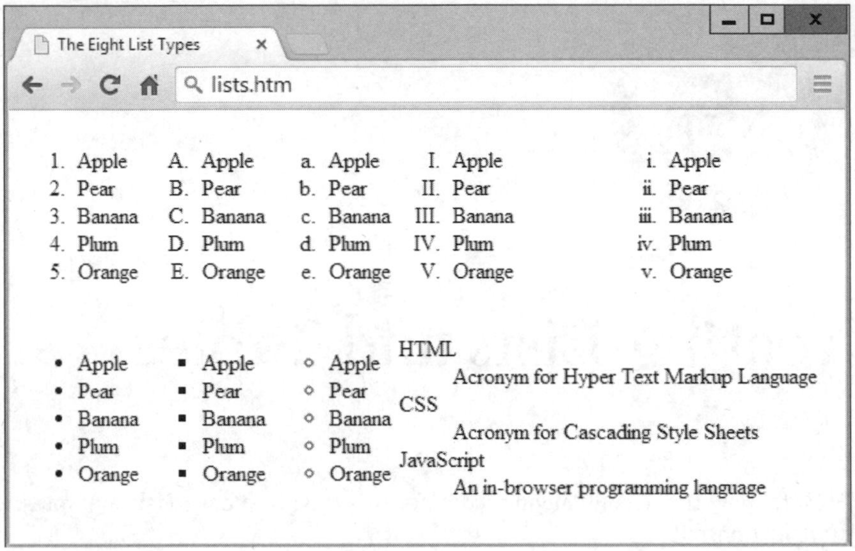

FIGURE 5-1 The eight different HTML list types

As you can see, lists are a little more complex than the tags we've used so far because they consist of more than one tag. To start with there are the enclosing `<ol>` and `</ol>` tags, which indicate that the content between the tags is a list. Then each item of the list is itself enclosed in `<li>` and `</li>` tags. The preceding example displays as the first list in row one of Figure 5-1.

An unordered (or bulleted list) using the default of filled circles could be created like this (which displays as the first list in row two of Figure 5-1):

```
<ul>
  <li>Apple</li>
  <li>Pear</li>
  <li>Banana</li>
  <li>Plum</li>
  <li>Orange</li>
</ul>
```

Lists may also contain sublists (and so on), like this:

```
<ul>
  <li>Apple
    <ul>
      <li>Bramley</li>
      <li>Cox</li>
      <li>Golden Delicious</li>
    </ul>
  </li>
  <li>Pear</li>
```

```
    <li>Banana</li>
    <li>Plum</li>
    <li>Orange</li>
</ul>
```

In this example the sublist of `Bramley`, `Cox`, and `Golden Delicious` will appear with an open circle symbol. This is because the default order of rotation between bullets is filled circle (the outer list level), open circle, filled square, and then back to filled circle, and so on. In HTML these three shapes are referred to using the values `disc`, `circle`, and `square`.

Overriding the Defaults

You can obtain greater control over your lists by overriding the default values and specifying values of your own, out of the following attributes:

- **start**   By default ordered lists start with the number 1 and each additional item in the list is prefaced by the next number in sequence, but you can choose any other starting value, both positive and negative, or zero. This attribute is not used by unordered lists, which always display the same character before each item.
- **type**   Ordered lists preface digits before each list item by default, but you can change this behavior to displaying upper- or lowercase letters, or upper- or lowercase roman numerals by giving this attribute a value of one of the following: 1, A, a, I, or i, respectively. Unordered lists require any of three words as values for this attribute, out of `disc`, `square`, and `circle`, the default being the same as specifying `disc`. The `type` attribute for `<ul>` lists (but not for `<ol>` lists) is obsolete in HTML5.

So, for example, to use the square bullet (in place of the default disc) in a list, you can use HTML such as this (which displays as the second list in the bottom row of Figure 5-1):

```
<ul type='square'>
  <li>Apple</li>
  <li>Pear</li>
  <li>Banana</li>
  <li>Plum</li>
  <li>Orange</li>
</ul>
```

Or, for example, to use uppercase roman numerals, you could use code such as this (which displays as the fourth list in the top row of Figure 5-1):

```
<ol type='I'>
  <li>Apple</li>
  <li>Pear</li>
  <li>Banana</li>
  <li>Plum</li>
  <li>Orange</li>
</ol>
```

Or, to begin an ordered list at a specified number, you could use code like this (which will commence numbering from the digit 5, instead of 1):

```
<ol start='5'>
  <li>Apple</li>
  <li>Pear</li>
  <li>Banana</li>
  <li>Plum</li>
  <li>Orange</li>
</ol>
```

Definition Lists

HTML also supports another kind of list known as a *definition list*. This type of list is used in places where it is not appropriate to use either ordered or bulleted lists, for example, when giving definitions of words, which look better if the word being defined is used as the bullet.

In definition lists the first part of each list element is referred to as the *term*, and the second as the *definition*, which gives rise to the HTML tags of <dl> and </dl> for enclosing a definition list, <dt> and </dt> for denoting a term, and <dd> and </dd> for denoting the term's definition, as shown in the following example:

```
<dl>
  <dt>HTML</dt>
  <dd>Acronym for Hyper Text Markup Language</dd>
  <dt>CSS</dt>
  <dd>Acronym for Cascading Style Sheets</dd>
  <dt>JavaScript</dt>
  <dd>An in-browser programming language</dd>
</dl>
```

This HTML will display as follows:

```
HTML
     Acronym for Hyper Text Markup Language
CSS
     Acronym for Cascading Style Sheets
JavaScript
     An in-browser programming language
```

Creating Tables

HTML tables are great for presenting tabular data in a clear and concise way and have also been used for many years as an aid to layout, even though there are more efficient ways of creating good layouts using CSS. However, for knocking together a quick and dirty example, or for laying out rows and columns of data, tables are great.

You create a table using the `<table>` and `</table>` tags, which support the following attributes:

- **align**   This attribute supports values of `left`, `right`, or `center` to align the table according to the surrounding text, although the attribute is now deprecated and use of CSS is recommended instead.
- **bgcolor**   Using this attribute you can set the background color of a table. However, CSS is recommended for this as the attribute is now deprecated.
- **border**   With this attribute you can specify a border around the table of 0 or any positive number of pixels.
- **bordercolor**   With this attribute you can specify the color of the border using standard color names or hexadecimal number values.
- **cellpadding**   This attribute specifies the number of pixels space between cell walls and their content, which can be a value of 0 or any higher number.
- **cellspacing**   This attribute specifies the number of pixels space between cells and the outer table border, which can be a value of 0 or any higher number.
- **height** and / or **width**   With these attributes you can specify the width and height of a table. When these attributes are unspecified, the browser will resize the table to the best fit for its contents.

 In HTML5 all of these attributes are obsolete, and should be avoided in new documents—use CSS instead.

For example, the following HTML creates a table that is 450 pixels wide, 200 pixels deep, has a 1-pixel border, 5 pixels of padding inside each cell, 5 pixels of spacing outside the cells, and a background color of cyan:

```
<table border='1' bgcolor='cyan' width='450' height='200'
  cellpadding='5' cellspacing='5'>
  <!-- Table contents -->
</table>
```

Table Rows and Columns

Within each table there must be at least one row and one column. These are created using the `<tr>` (for table row) and `<td>` (for table data) tags. In the following example, two rows of three columns each are created:

```
<table border='1' bgcolor='cyan' width='450' height='200'
  cellpadding='5' cellspacing='5'>
  <tr>
    <td>Row 1, Col 1</td>
    <td>Row 1, Col 2</td>
    <td>Row 1, Col 3</td>
  </tr>
```

```
<tr>
   <td>Row 2, Col 1</td>
   <td>Row 2, Col 2</td>
   <td>Row 2, Col 3</td>
</tr>
</table>
```

The <tr> and </tr> tags are used twice for the two rows, while there are six instances of <td> and </td> for the six cells (two rows of three). Both these types of tags also accept the bgcolor, height, and width attributes that <table> itself does (with the exceptions noted below).

 The <tr> tag accepts bgcolor in HTML4, but not height and width, while the <td> tag accepts all three attributes (but only in HTML4).

Therefore, the following HTML creates the same table but sets the top row of the table to green and the bottom to yellow. It also sets the first column width to exactly 200 pixels and then the remaining two columns to 25 percent each (by using the % symbol) of whatever width remains (in this case 250 pixels, leaving 125 pixels each), as shown in Figure 5-2.

```
<table border='1' bgcolor='cyan' width='450' height='200'
   cellpadding='5' cellspacing='5'>
   <tr bgcolor='green'>
      <td width='200'>Row 1, Col 1</td>
      <td width='25%'>Row 1, Col 2</td>
      <td width='25%'>Row 1, Col 3</td>
   </tr>
   <tr bgcolor='yellow'>
      <td>Row 2, Col 1</td>
      <td>Row 2, Col 2</td>
      <td>Row 2, Col 3</td>
   </tr>
</table>
```

 Because the widths have already been specified in the first row, there is no need to do so again for the second.

If you want the top row of your table to be a header, you can use CSS styling or HTML tags to format the headings in bold and otherwise change them, or you can

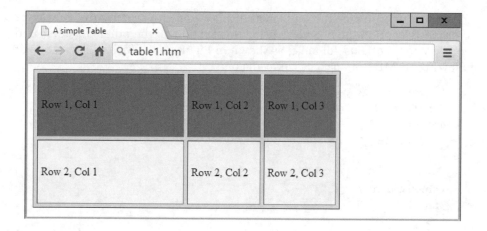

FIGURE 5-2   A simple table with two rows and three columns

use the `<th>` and `</th>` tags (for table heading), in a similar fashion to the `<td>` and `</td>` tags, like this:

```
<tr bgcolor='cyan'>
  <th width='200'>Heading 1</th>
  <th width='25%'>Heading 2</th>
  <th width='25%'>Heading 3</th>
</tr>
```

As you can see from Figure 5-3 (in which this additional HTML has been inserted before the green and yellow rows), the use of these tags is identical to `<td>` and `</td>`, with the only exception being in the way the cell content is displayed; it is bold and centered.

FIGURE 5-3   A heading row of cells has been added to the table.

To further enhance the way tables display, you can also use the <caption> tag to properly caption them. So let's bring this tag and all the others together into a real-world example of a useful table, as shown in Figure 5-4, which was created with the following HTML from data at wikipedia.org:

```
<table border='2' cellpadding='5' cellspacing='1'
  width='250' bgcolor='lightgreen' bordercolor='blue'>
  <caption>
    <i> Browser Share Spring 2014</i>
  </caption>
  <tr>
    <th>Browser</th>
    <th>Share</th>
  </tr>
  <tr>
    <td>Google Chrome</td>
    <td>44%</td>
  </tr>
  <tr>
    <td>Internet Explorer</td>
    <td>23%</td>
  </tr>
  <tr>
    <td>Mozilla Firefox</td>
    <td>19%</td>
  </tr>
  <tr>
    <td>Apple Safari</td>
    <td>9%</td>
  </tr>
  <tr>
    <td>Opera</td>
    <td>1%</td>
  </tr>
  <tr>
    <td>Others</td>
    <td>4%</td>
  </tr>
</table>
```

Extending Rows and Columns

With HTML tables, you are not limited to a fixed number of rows and columns because you can make some cells extend over more than one column and/or more than one row using the colspan and rowspan attributes. For example, in the

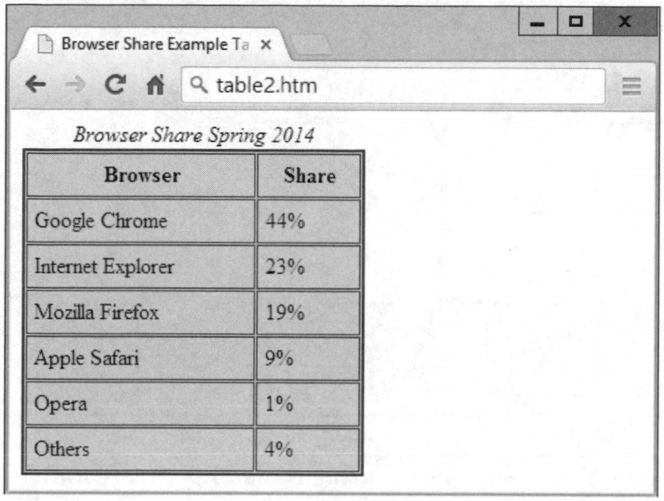

FIGURE 5-4   A table detailing browser market share for March 2014

following very simple table, the numbers 1 through 10 are displayed in a table of three rows by four columns, as shown in Figure 5-5. This means that there are two extra cells that are not used and which are therefore merged into one and grayed out:

```
<table border='1' width='450' height='200'>
  <tr align='center'>
    <td width='25%'>1</td>
    <td width='25%'>2</td>
    <td width='25%'>3</td>
    <td width='25%'>4</td>
  </tr>
  <tr align='center'>
    <td>5</td>
    <td>6</td>
    <td>7</td>
    <td>8</td>
  </tr>
  <tr align='center'>
    <td>9</td>
    <td>10</td>
    <td colspan='2' bgcolor='lightgray'></td>
    <!-- Cell omitted here -->
  </tr>
</table>
```

FIGURE 5-5 Two cells have been merged using the `colspan` attribute.

> **Note** I have employed a few other interesting features in this table including setting its width to 450 pixels and the width of each column to 25 percent of that, the height of the table to 200 pixels, and using the `align` attribute with a value of `center` to center the contents of each table row. I have also used comment tags to show where the omitted cell would have been.

Because the third cell on the third row is now two cells wide, there is no fourth cell to define in that row, and so none is defined.

You can also extend a cell over two rows, as in the following example, which is modified from the previous one using the `rowspan` attribute (the result of which is shown in Figure 5-6):

```
<table border='1' width='450' height='200'>
  <tr align='center'>
    <td width='25%'>1</td>
    <td width='25%'>4</td>
    <td width='25%'>7</td>
    <td width='25%'>10</td>
  </tr>
  <tr align='center'>
    <td>2</td>
    <td>5</td>
    <td>8</td>
    <td rowspan='2' bgcolor='lightgray'></td>
  </tr>
```

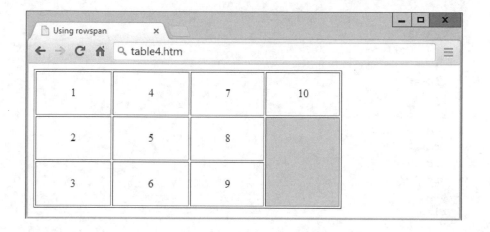

FIGURE 5-6   Two cells have been merged using the rowspan attribute.

```
<tr align='center'>
  <td>3</td>
  <td>6</td>
  <td>9</td>
  <!-- Cell omitted here -->
</tr>
</table>
```

Because the fourth cell on the second row is now two cells deep, there is no fourth cell to define in the bottom row and so, again, the final cell is not defined.

Following is an example of a table that's four rows by four columns that could be used as the basis for a simple board game. It combines both the rowspan and colspan attributes by displaying the numbers 1 through 12 clockwise in small cells, around a larger central cell of double width and height, as shown in Figure 5-7:

```
<table border='1' width='450' height='450'>
  <tr align='center'>
    <td width='25%'>1</td>
    <td width='25%'>2</td>
    <td width='25%'>3</td>
    <td width='25%'>4</td>
  </tr>
  <tr align='center'>
    <td>12</td>
    <td colspan='2' rowspan='2' bgcolor='lightgray'></td>
    <!-- Cell omitted here -->
    <td>5</td>
  </tr>
```

```
<tr align='center'>
  <td>11</td>
  <!-- Cell omitted here -->
  <!-- Cell omitted here -->
  <td>6</td>
</tr>
<tr align='center'>
  <td>10</td>
  <td>9</td>
  <td>8</td>
  <td>7</td>
</tr>
</table>
```

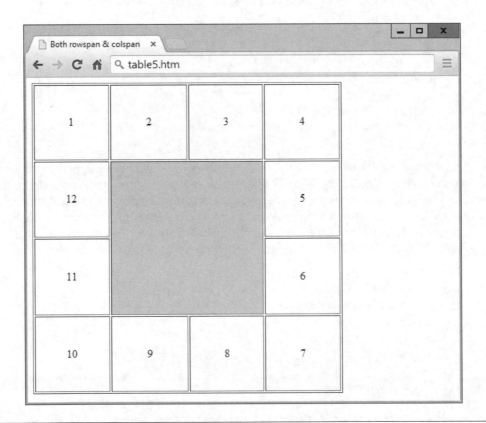

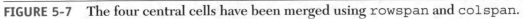

FIGURE 5-7   The four central cells have been merged using `rowspan` and `colspan`.

Summary

Now that you have lists and tables added to your HTML toolkit, you have the ability to really make your web pages stand out. In the next lesson I will show you how to add interactivity to your pages using hyperlinks, forms, and frames.

Self-Test Questions

Test how much you have learned in this lesson with these questions. If you don't know an answer, go back and reread the relevant section until your knowledge is complete. You can find the answers in the appendix.

1. Which HTML tag do you use to begin an ordered list?

2. What tag is used to denote a list item?

3. How do you specify an unordered list in HTML?

4. How can you change the start value of an ordered list?

5. How can you change the bullet type of an unordered list or the case of an alphabetic or roman ordered list?

6. Which three tags are used by definition lists?

7. Which tag is used to create an HTML table?

8. What tags are used for table rows, table cells, and table headings?

9. How can you add a caption to an HTML table?

10. Which two attributes allow cells to spread out over more than one row or column?

6

Links, Forms, and Frames

 To view the accompanying video for this lesson, please visit mhprofessional.com/nixonhtml5/.

The great thing about the Internet is the way documents located anywhere in the world can be linked to each other so that you can navigate to them with a single mouse click. This interconnectedness even extends to the ability to embed pages or portions of pages from the same or any other website, anywhere at all, within the current page.

The same goes for sending data to websites and web pages, which is often achieved using forms. The data in a form can be posted to a web server for processing or, if it is sent in the correct way, a simple JavaScript can receive the data and act on it, without recourse to the web server.

In this lesson I show how all these things work and how you can use them to their best effect.

Using Hyperlinks

To create a link to another document, you must first know where this new document resides; in other words, whether it is on the local server or another one. An external web address (on a different server) uses what is known as an absolute URL (Uniform Resource Locator), which usually begins with http:// (or https:// for secure sites that use encryption), such as:

```
http://bbc.co.uk
```

It can be more complicated than that simple URL, by including the folder structure (and sometimes a filename too) within which a web page resides, like this, which accesses the folder /*weather*:

```
http://bbc.co.uk/weather/
```

Some organizations distinguish different servers by adding a prefix before the domain name, the most common of which is www, like this:

```
http://www.bbc.co.uk
```

Because typing **www.** involves an extra four characters, most good websites allow you to ignore this prefix (but not all). But when it is used, it denotes the organization's main web server. Alternative servers may use prefixes such as news, like this (which leads to the BBC's news service):

```
http://news.bbc.co.uk
```

The Query String

Many websites support the use of a query string, which is a string of data placed after the URL to provide additional information to a web server. For example, the following URL passes the value html5 to the field name q on Google's search page, the result of which is shown in Figure 6-1:

```
https://google.com/search?q=html5
```

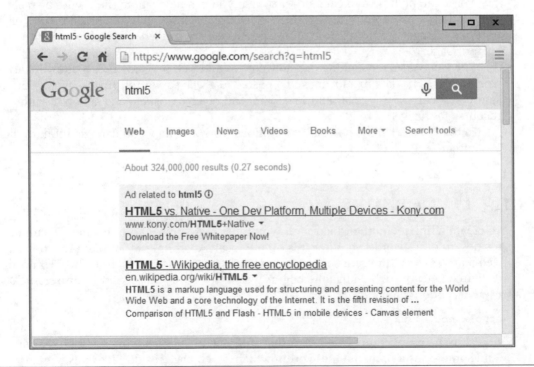

FIGURE 6-1   The Google search engine returning results for "html5"

Query strings begin with a ? character, followed by a field/value pair that is separated by an = sign. Further field/value pairs may follow if preceded by a & character, like this:

```
https://google.com/search?q=html5&hl=fr
```

Here the field name `hl` is set to the value `fr`, which has the result of changing Google's default language for this session to French, as shown in Figure 6-2. I cover query strings in more detail in the section on forms.

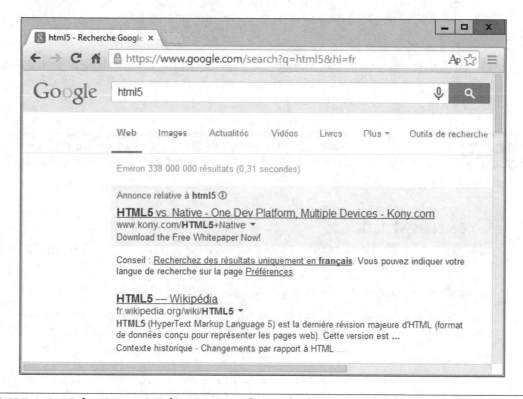

FIGURE 6-2   Like Figure 6-1, but presented in French due to the query string used

Relative URLs

When documents reside on the current server, you can access them more easily and make them more portable by using relative instead of absolute URLs. For example, if you need to link to the file *agenda.htm* in the current folder, you can simply use its name as the URL, like this:

```
agenda.htm
```

Or, if the document is in the subfolder `meetings`, you could refer to it like this:

```
meetings/agenda.htm
```

Alternatively, if the file is in the parent folder of the current one, you can use the special token `../` which simply specifies that the document can be found one directory higher up, like this:

```
../agenda.htm
```

There again, if the file is in a sister folder, perhaps called `misc`, you can easily refer to it by referencing the folder from the parent one, like this:

```
../misc/agenda.htm
```

Finally, to refer to the root, or uppermost, folder of the current drive or web location, you use the `/` symbol. So if the file is in the root folder, it can be accessed like this:

```
/agenda.htm
```

 This form of accessing is not fully relative to the current folder since it includes a jump all the way to the root folder, and the distance between the root and current folder is not indicated in this form of URL.

Creating Links

To create a link within an HTML document, you apply the `<a>` tag, supplying a value to an attribute called `href` (for hypertext reference), like this:

```
<a href='http://google.com'>Visit Google</a>
```

The final `</a>` tag closes the pair of tags, which encompass the text to be displayed for the link, which in the preceding case simply looks like this:

Visit Google

If linking relatively to the file *agenda.htm*, discussed in the previous section, you might use one of the following forms of HTML depending on the file's location:

```
View the agenda <a href='agenda.htm'>here</a>.
View the agenda <a href='meetings/agenda.htm'>here</a>.
View the agenda <a href='../agenda.htm'>here</a>.
View the agenda <a href='../misc/agenda.htm'>here</a>.
View the agenda <a href='/agenda.htm'>here</a>.
```

All of these display in the same way, like this:

View the agenda here.

URLs in Images

In Lesson 4 I showed how to embed images in documents, but assumed that the pictures resided in the current folder. But, in fact, they can reside almost anywhere on the current server, or elsewhere on the Internet, and all of the following are valid HTML for displaying an image located in different places:

```
<img src='image.jpg'>
<img src='meetings/image.jpg'>
<img src='../image.jpg'>
<img src='../misc/image.jpg'>
<img src='/image.jpg'>
<img src='http://aserver.com/folder/extra/image.jpg'>
```

The `target` Attribute

You can specify whether a linked URL should replace the current web page or open in a new one by supplying a value for the target attribute. For example, if you would like a web page to open in a new blank window (or tab, according to how the user's web browser is configured), you can add the specifier `target='_blank'`, like this:

```
<a href='http://google.com' target='_blank'>Visit Google</a>
```

There are three other reserved words you can also supply to the `target` attribute: `_self` to replace the current page (the default), `_parent` to replace the parent page or frame (if the current document resides in a frame), or `_top` to ignore any and all frames and replace the entire contents of the current browser window with the new document.

Additionally, if you have already named a frame, window, or tab using the relevant HTML or JavaScript, you can specify that name as the target in place of one of the four reserved words.

Creating an Anchor

It is even possible to link to a section of a web page by first specifying an anchor using the name attribute of the `<a>` tag, like this:

```
<a name='anchorname'></a>
```

Now you can link directly to that section of the web page using a query string referring to the anchor name, preceded by a # symbol, like this:

```
Click <a href='http://server.com/page.htm#anchorname'>this link</a>
```

When it is passed this URL, the web browser will load in the specified page and then scroll it so that the section beginning with the anchor name is at the top of the browser window. In HTML5 the name attribute has been obsoleted in favor of `id`.

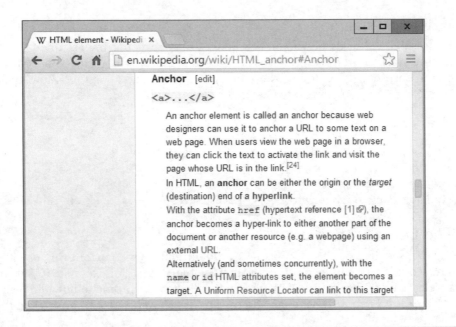

FIGURE 6-3 The Wikipedia Anchor section is itself an anchor.

 A good example of anchors in action is the Wikipedia page on the subject. Go to the website at wikipedia.org and enter the search term **html anchor**. You will then be taken to the Wikipedia HTML Element page, and then scrolled down automatically to the section about anchors, as shown in Figure 6-3.

Building Forms

Web forms are the means with which you can request input from the user of a web page. Historically, web form data has been posted to the web server and then processed, but nowadays form data can be preprocessed using JavaScript to ensure that it is in the form required and all fields are correctly completed. Additionally, through the use of Ajax, a technology whereby JavaScript communicates behind the scenes with a web server, modern forms can check for the availability of a username you prefer, before you even submit a form.

 In fact JavaScript can incrementally submit all parts of a form as you fill it in, avoiding the need to use a submit button at all. And where input is used only to control the current web page (and no interaction is required with the web server), JavaScript can read from and write to form fields, and retrieve data from a query string.

An HTML form begins with the <form> tag and is closed with </form>, and the tag supports three commonly used attributes, as follows:

- **method** There are two values accepted by this attribute: post or get. When you select post, all the form data is sent to the web server invisibly (using headers), but when using get, the data is appended to an HTML request in a query string. This can result in messy-looking URLs but, among other possibilities, it does enable a form to be posted to a JavaScript program rather than a web server.
- **action** This attribute should contain the URL to which the form is to be submitted. If the form is sent using a get request and then a ? followed by the form, data (as a query string) will be tacked onto this value.
- **enctype** This attribute tells the program that will receive the form what type of data to expect, out of: application/x-www-form-urlencoded, multipart/form-data, and text/plain. The first encodes all characters before transmitting the form. The second is used when a file is also (or only) being uploaded to a web server. In the last form, text is transmitted, with spaces converted into + symbols for use in a query string. By default, if no encoding is specified, application/x-www-form-urlencoded is used.

Figure 6-4 shows a range of form elements all incorporated into a single form, using the following HTML:

```
<form method='post' action='program.php'><pre>
  Input type: text     <input type='text'     name='f1' size='26'>
  Input type: password <input type='password' name='f2' size='26'>

  Input type: radio    <input type='radio'    name='f3' value='1'>1
  Input type: radio    <input type='radio'    name='f3' value='2'>2

  Input type: checkbox <input type='checkbox' name='f4' value='1'>1
  Input type: checkbox <input type='checkbox' name='f4' value='2'>2

  Input type: hidden   <input type='hidden'   name='f5'>

  Textarea:  <textarea name='f6' rows='3' cols='20'></textarea>

  Select:    <select name='f7'>
               <option value='1'>First Option</option>
               <option value='2' selected='selected'>
                 Second option</option>
               <option value='3'>Third Option</option>
             </select>

  Button:    <button name= 'f8' value='f8'>Button</button>
```

```
   Label:       <label>
                  <input type= 'checkbox' name= 'agree'
                    value='yes'>I agree
                </label>

   Input type: submit <input type='submit'>
</pre></form>
```

 Note The `<pre>` and `</pre>` tags are used here simply to help space out the form without having to use CSS or several HTML tags. It tells the browser to display all spaces within the tags as it encounters them, and not to treat them as collapsible whitespace.

```
┌──────────────────────────────────────────────────────┐
│ [] Example Form          x                    _ □ X  │
│ ← → C ⌂   🔍 form.htm                            ≡   │
│                                                        │
│     Input type: text      [                  ]        │
│     Input type: password  [                  ]        │
│                                                        │
│     Input type: radio     ○ 1                          │
│     Input type: radio     ○ 2                          │
│                                                        │
│     Input type: checkbox  □ 1                          │
│     Input type: checkbox  □ 2                          │
│                                                        │
│     Input type: hidden                                 │
│                                                        │
│                           ┌──────────────────┐        │
│                           │                  │        │
│                           │                  │        │
│     Textarea:             └──────────────────┘        │
│                                                        │
│     Select:               [Second option ▼]           │
│                                                        │
│     Button:               [ Button ]                   │
│                                                        │
│     Label:                                             │
│                              □ I agree                 │
│                                                        │
│     Input type: submit    [ Submit ]                   │
│                                                        │
└──────────────────────────────────────────────────────┘
```

FIGURE 6-4   A form incorporating a variety of elements

The `<input>` Tag

The code in the preceding section makes use of the following `type` attribute values of the `<input>` tag:

- **text**   This value creates an input field suitable for entering text. You can change the width of the input field with the `size` attribute and limit the number of characters allowed with the `maxlength` attribute.
- **password**   This value creates an input field suitable for entering passwords in that all typed characters are replaced with the `*` character when displayed, but are properly stored internally. You can change the width of the input field with the `size` attribute and limit the number of characters allowed with the `maxlength` attribute.
- **radio**   Each form may have any number of radio buttons, but only one can be active at a time. When another radio button is clicked, the previously selected one is deselected. Radio buttons are round.
- **checkbox**   You use this value to create checkboxes, which are like radio buttons but are square, and more than one may be selected at a time.
- **hidden**   Sometimes you may wish to pass a value in a web form that the user shouldn't see, such as an identifying token or other data, and doing so is accomplished by passing this value. In this case, you will also have to provide the value to be posted in the `value` attribute (see the section "The `value` Attribute").
- **submit**   This value creates a button that will submit the form. By default the button will read *Submit* or *Submit Query*.

The `name` Attribute

When sending data using a form, you need to give each item of data a name so that both your form and the receiving program know which piece of data is for what. To do this you use the `name` attribute, like this:

```
<input type='text' name='firstname'>
```

Here the field's name is `firstname` and therefore it is clear that this will be used for the input of a person's first name.

The `value` Attribute

You can specify a predefined value for any form field by assigning it using the `value` attribute, like this:

```
<input type='text' name='firstname' value='Guest'>
```

Here a default value of *Guest* is given to the input field, which could be useful, for example, if allowing guests to make posts in a guestbook or comment. Such predefined fields can be overwritten or edited by the user, so the value is not fixed.

The `<textarea>` Tag

Sometimes the single line of input supplied by the `<input>` tag is insufficient in size, in which case you can use the `<textarea>` tag, which supports adjustable width and height, over more than one line of input. Unlike the `<input>` tag, however, predefined data is not passed through a `value=` attribute. Instead, whatever you place between `<textarea>` and `</textarea>` tags becomes the predefined input, which can then be edited or replaced by the user.
Therefore the following lines provide an empty and a predefined `textarea` input with a default width of 20 characters and height of two lines:

```
<textarea name='summary'></textarea>
<textarea name='summary'>Replace with a summary</textarea>
```

You can specify the number of rows and columns to use for the `textarea` with the `rows` and `cols` attributes, like the following, which creates an area 30 characters wide and five lines high:

```
<textarea name='summary' rows='5' cols='30'></textarea>
```

The `<select>` Tag

If you need a drop-down list of options from which a user can select one, you can use the `<select>` tag in conjunction with a secondary tag, `<option>`. Together these tags let you create a list of values and names to display, that will pop down when clicked, like this:

```
<select name='icecream'>
  <option value='b'>Banana</option>
  <option value='c'>Chocolate</option>
  <option value='s'>Strawberry</option>
  <option value='v' selected='selected'>Vanilla</option>
  <option value='w'>Walnut</option>
</select>
```

The fourth element in the list has been set as the default by using the attribute `selected='selected'`. When the list is popped down, this option will be the one shown as selected and will stay so, unless the user chooses a different element. If your HTML will not be repurposed in XHTML format, you can omit the `='selected'` assignment, and simply apply the keyword `selected` like this: `<option value='v' selected>Vanilla</option>`.

The `<button>` Tag

This tag displays a clickable button but, depending on your target audience, you may choose not to use it because Internet Explorer versions 7 or lower will submit the contents between the `<button>` and `</button>` tags, while other browsers submit the contents of its `value` attribute. If you are certain your users will be on IE 8 or higher (or another browser), this tag will be safe to use.

The `<label>` Tag

This tag is especially handy for use with radio buttons or checkboxes (which are small) because you can place one of these elements alongside some explanatory text, and if you surround them both with `<label>` and `</label>` tags, the user can click either the text or the radio button or checkbox to activate it. Here's a common example:

```
<label>
  <input type='checkbox' name='agree' value='yes'>
  I agree to these terms and conditions.
</label>
```

This example displays as follows, and clicking any part of it (not just the checkbox) will check or uncheck the box:

☐ **I agree to these terms and conditions.**

Frames and Iframes

There are two ways in which you can embed entire web pages within other pages: frames and iframes. The first way to do this, and the least recommended, is to use frames to split a web page into the multiple parts and then place them all in frames within the `<frameset>` tag, like this (although it is obsolete in HTML5):

```
<frameset rows='20%, *, 20%'>
  <frame src='header.htm'>
  <frame src='body.htm'>
  <frame src='footer.htm'>
</frameset>
<noframes>
  <!-- Alternative content goes here -->
</noframes>
```

 Note the use of the `<noframes>` and `</noframes>` tags in the example to display alternative content to users whose browser doesn't support frames. Although all modern mainstream browsers do support frames, some specialist ones such as audio browsers for blind people, or text-only browsers, may benefit from the use of these tags.

This results in a top frame that takes up 20 percent of the browser height and which is pulled in from the file *header.htm*. Then there's the main frame, which (due to the * attribute in the `rows` attribute) will expand to fit whatever space there is after the fixed-size frames are in place. It is loaded in from the file *body.htm*. And finally the footer frame is loaded in from *footer.htm* and placed in the bottom 20 percent of the web page.

The problem with this method is that the entire web page is made up of frames and there is no content on the page itself. This is obviously not ideal and is not good for ranking in search engines, which will not find such a page very interesting.

Instead I recommend that when you need a frame you use an `<iframe>` tag, as shown in Figure 6-5 (in which a Wikipedia page has been embedded within another web page), because you can drop a frame of any width and height anywhere in a document as easily as if it were an image, like this:

```
<!-- Some HTML content here -->
  <iframe src='anotherpage.htm' width='640' height='300'>
  </iframe>
<!-- More HTML content here -->
```

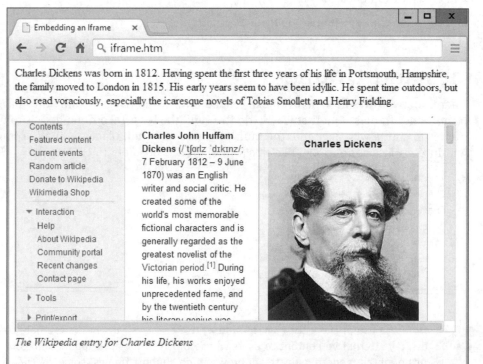

FIGURE 6-5   A Wikipedia page is embedded in another web page.

Summary

This lesson completes most of your introduction to HTML. The following lesson takes you through the remaining HTML 4.01 tags which (combined with this chapter) you can use as a reference if you are new to HTML, or as a refresher if you are a seasoned user.

Self-Test Questions

Test how much you have learned in this lesson with these questions. If you don't know an answer, go back and reread the relevant section until your knowledge is complete. You can find the answers in the appendix.

1. HyperText Transfer Protocol uses the string http:// to preface insecure Internet URLs, but how do you access encrypted, secure URLs?

2. If *http://mydomain.com* calls up the root of a web server, how can you access a subfolder from this root called *folder*?

3. How would you format a link to the website mydomain.com in HTML?

4. Without mentioning a domain by name, what URL will take the user to the root document of a domain?

5. How can you make a destination URL from a hyperlink load into a frame or window other than the current one?

6. How can you hyperlink directly to a section within a web document?

7. What HTML tag is used to create a form?

8. How can you request a single text input line from a user?

9. How can you provide more than a single line of space to input text?

10. What tag can you use to embed another document within the current one?

7

Using the Remaining HTML4 Tags

 To view the accompanying video for this lesson, please visit mhprofessional.com/nixonhtml5/.

At this point in the book you now understand what HTML is and how to use many HTML4 tags. So, in this lesson, to illustrate how you can apply your new knowledge to any and all elements, we'll look at implementing a few of the tags you haven't seen so far.

At the same time you need to know which HTML4 elements have been deprecated or obsoleted in HTML5. Although you can still use them (for now), deprecated and obsoleted tags have been superseded by better methods of achieving the same result, so the developers of the HTML standard are giving us a warning that they reserve the right to remove these tags altogether at some point in the future—therefore you should avoid using them in all new documents.

As well as exploring some of the remaining HTML4 elements, we'll also be looking at how to replicate the functionality of the deprecated HTML4 tags using CSS, or alternate tags.

Conditional HTML for Internet Explorer

The Microsoft Internet Explorer browser makes use of comment tags to create conditional sections of HTML for all versions between 5 and 9. The reason for this is that IE has several different ways of interpreting HTML depending on the version of the browser used, and the workaround Microsoft created to cater for these differences is to allow developers to place several different browser-specific sections of HTML in a single document, processing only those relevant to a particular browser version.

You use IE conditional comments by inserting a pair of square brackets immediately following the opening < ! - - comment marker, placing an if statement inside, like this:

```
<!--[if IE 6]>
  You are using IE 6
<![endif]-->
```

In this instance the text in the comment is displayed only by the IE 6 web browser. All other versions of Internet Explorer and all other browsers will completely ignore the text within the comment tags. There are several possible statement types you can use, as follows.

Simple Comparisons

The previous example is a simple comparison, in which the IE constant is tested to see whether it has a value of 6, indicating that the current browser is IE 6. You can also simply test for the browser being any version of IE by leaving out the numeric value, like this:

```
<!--[if IE]>
  You are using an Internet Explorer browser
<![endif]-->
```

Higher or Lower Values

If, for example, you wish to display some HTML only to versions of Internet Explorer prior to version 9, you can use this form of conditional HTML:

```
<!--[if lt IE 9]>
  You are using IE 5, 6, 7 or 8
<![endif]-->
```

Here the lt stands for *less than*, and so the content of the comment tags is only uncommented if the browser is any version of Internet Explorer up to and including version 8. Another way to achieve the same result is with the lte operator, which stands for *less than or equal to*, like this:

```
<!--[if lte IE 8]>
  You are using IE 5, 6, 7 or 8
<![endif]-->
```

You can also check for a version of IE being greater than a given value, as with the two following conditional comments, both of which only display the contents of the tags if the browser is IE 8 or greater:

```
<!--[if gt IE 7]>
  You are using IE 8 or 9
<![endif]-->
```

```
<!--[if gte IE 8]>
  You are using IE 8 or 9
<![endif]-->
```

The Not Operator

You can also test for the inverse of a comparison using the not operator (which is an exclamation mark), like the following, which displays the contents only if the browser is Internet Explorer, but not version 6. Note the use of brackets to contain the expression that follows the ! symbol.

```
<!--[if !(IE 6)]>
  You are using an Internet Explorer browser, but not IE6
<![endif]-->
```

The Mark of the Web

Internet Explorer also uses comments to stamp what it calls *The Mark of the Web* onto an HTML document, as a way of setting the security zone to which a document applies during development. For example, the following sets the security zone to the local intranet:

```
<!-- saved from url=(0016)http://localhost -->
```

And this comment sets the security zone to the Internet:

```
<!-- saved from url=(0014)about:internet -->
```

For further information, please visit tinyurl.com/motweb.
Let's now take a look at the tags themselves.

<abbr> ... </abbr>

This tag states that the content is an abbreviation. It is most helpful to specialized browsers (such as those for visually impaired people) or search engine web crawlers, and is best used in conjunction with a title attribute so that users can see an explanation when they pass the mouse over it, like this:

```
<abbr title='Sound Navigation And Ranging'>SONAR</abbr>
```

You can also use the <dfn> (for definition) tag in a similar way to achieve the same result.

<acronym> ... </acronym> (Obsolete)

This element denotes an acronym but it is now obsolete and you should use <abbr> instead—it works in the exactly the same way.

<address> ... </address>

This element denotes the contents as containing address data. It is helpful to specialized HTML readers and search engine web crawlers. Simply remember to place the opening and closing tags around any addresses you put in a document to make them more easily machine locatable, like this:

```
<address>
  1600 Pennsylvania Ave NW
  Washington
  DC 20500
  United States
</address>
```

<applet> ... </applet> (Obsolete)

This element used to be one way you could load an external app into a document, but it is now obsolete and you should use <object> instead.

<area>

This element creates an area within an image map, which can then be styled with CSS, or have a hyperlink attached. To use it, you must first load in an image to use as a map, like this:

```
<img src='face.png' width='250' height='320' usemap='#facemap'>
```

With the image loaded, you use the <map> tag to create an image map, and then place one or more <area> tags inside it to define the area(s) you want, like this:

```
<map name='facemap'>
  <area shape='rect'   title='Hair'  coords=' 25, 10,225,130'>
  <area shape='rect'   title='Ear'   coords=' 20,130, 50,200'>
  <area shape='rect'   title='Ear'   coords='200,130,225,200'>
  <area shape='circle' title='Eye'   coords=' 88,145, 15     '
    href='eyes.htm'>
  <area shape='circle' title='Eye'   coords='160,145, 15     '>
  <area shape='rect'   title='Nose'  coords='100,150,145,205'>
  <area shape='poly'   title='Mouth' coords='
    95,230,110,220,130,220,150,230,135,240,110,240'>
</map>
```

The shape attribute can have values of rect, circle, or poly, and the coords attribute must then contain the values specifying the shape. Optionally, you can supply a title attribute for a tooltip, an href to create a hyperlink, and so on.

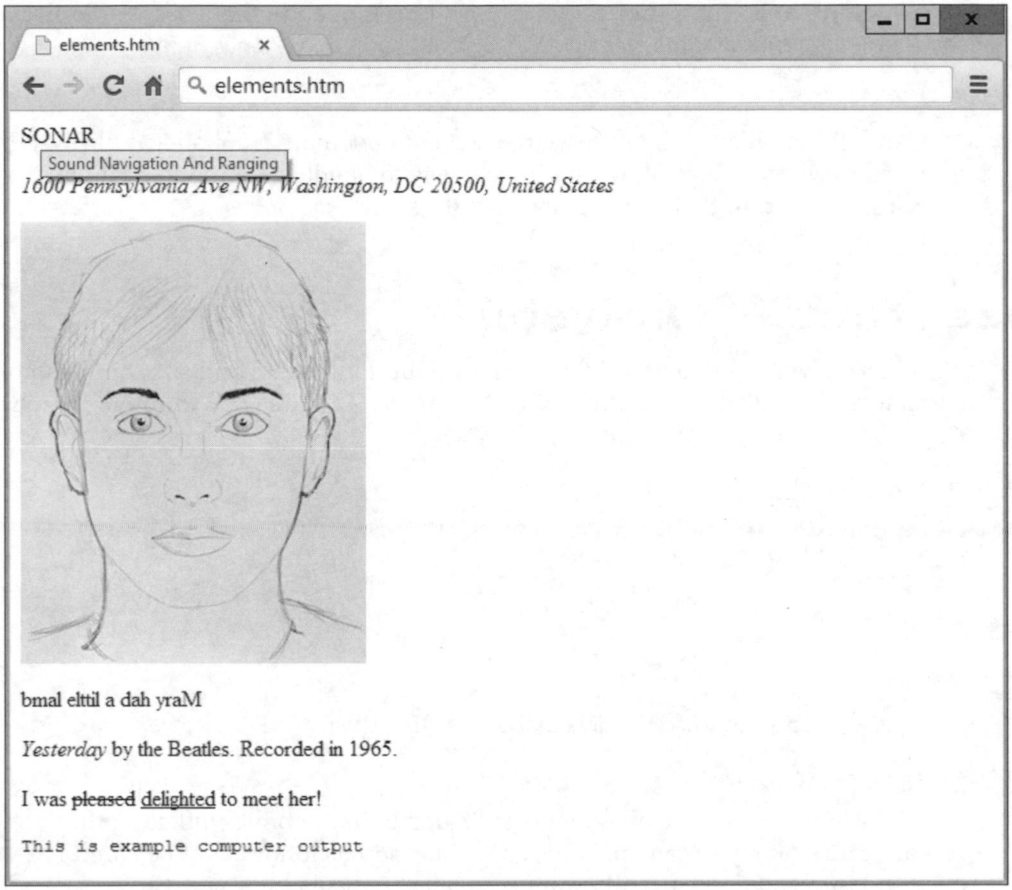

FIGURE 7-1 Several examples from this lesson

Figure 7-1 shows the *face.png* image loaded. The image map areas and tooltips will only be visible when the mouse passes over them.

`<base>`

Use this tag to specify the base destination for all URLs in a document and, optionally, a target window or tab. For example, if you wish all relative links in a document to refer to the base URL *http://mywebsite.com/project/* even if the document is located elsewhere on the Internet, you can make this happen as follows:

```
<base href='http://mywebsite.com/project/'>
```

Now, any hyperlinks that are relative will be applied to that base. For example, the following will now link to *http://mywebsite.com/project/news.htm*:

```
<a href='news.htm'>News</a>
```

This will work even if you serve the current document from a local file system, or from anywhere else, making this a great way to handle documents that have to be relocated away from their original location for some reason.

`<basefont>` (Obsolete)

With this tag you used to be able to set the default font, color, and size, but it is now obsolete and, instead, you are recommended to use CSS, like this example, which sets 12-point text in a blue Arial font:

```
<style>
  .mystyle {
    font-family:Arial;
    font-size  :12pt;
    color      :blue;
  }
</style>
```

And you can then use the `mystyle` class like this:

```
<span class='mystyle'>Some text</span>
```

To assign a CSS rule to all elements in a document's body (emulating the `<basefont>` tag), you can apply a rule to the `body` as follows, but be careful as you may find that you don't actually want *everything* to display the same way:

```
<style>
  body {
    font-family:Arial;
    font-size  :12pt;
    color      :blue;
  }
</style>
```

`<bdo> ... </bdo>`

With this tag you can change the direction in which text flows. It takes two values for the `dir` attribute: `ltr` (the default) for left to right—for displaying most western languages, and `rtl` for *right to left*—for displaying languages such as Arabic. You use it like this:

```
<bdo dir='rtl'>Mary had a little lamb</bdo>
```

Underneath the face image in Figure 7-1, you can see the result of applying this HTML is to display *bmal elttil a dah yraM*.

<big> ... </big> (Obsolete) and <small> ... </small>

The <big> element enlarges the size of text but is obsolete in HTML5, so you should use CSS to achieve the same effect. For example, the following CSS rule (which should be in the <style> section of a document) creates a class called big that doubles text size:

```
.big { font-size:200%; }
```

You can then use the class like this:

```
Normal text. <span class='big'>Big text.</span> Normal again.
```

Opposite to-<big> there is the <small> tag, which is not obsolete in HTML5 because it has been assigned a semantic meaning, but can probably be better achieved with CSS when you just want smaller text rather than to imply something has less emphasis, such as the following to create a new class called small:

```
.small { font-size:50%; }
```

You can then use the class like this:

```
Normal text. <span class='small'>Small text.</span> Normal again.
```

<blockquote> ... </blockquote>

With this element you can specify a large section of text to be a quotation from another source, so that it will be styled differently, like this:

```
<blockquote>
  All the world's a stage, And all the men and women merely players:
  They have their exits and their entrances; And one man in his time
  plays many parts.
</blockquote>
```

To define a shorter quotation you can use the <q> tag as follows, and quotation marks will be placed around it by the browser, as shown in Figure 7-2:

```
Dr. Seuss said, <q>Don't cry because it's over, smile because it happened.</q>
```

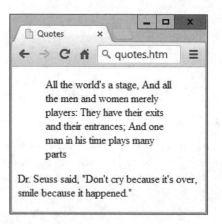

FIGURE 7-2 Using `<blockquote>` and `<q>` elements

`<center>` ... `</center>` (Obsolete)

This tag was used to align text to the center of the browser, but it is now obsolete in favor of using CSS, such as this rule that creates a class called `center`:

```
.center {
  display    :block;
  margin     :auto;
  text-align:center;
}
```

This works because it forces elements to which it is applied to display as block elements (rather than inline), before setting the text alignment to centered. Once the class has been created, just apply it to your HTML, like this:

```
This is some left-aligned text<br>

<span class='center'>This is centered text</span>
```

`<cite>` ... `</cite>`

You can provide a citation for a section of text using this tag, as follows:

```
<cite>Yesterday</cite> by the Beatles. Recorded in 1965.
```

Other than italicizing (or otherwise slightly modifying its display), this tag has no effect. Its main purpose, though, is to provide information to specialist HTML readers and search engine web crawlers indicating the title of a work.

`<code> ... </code>`

When you wish to display some text as if it is programming code, you can use this tag as follows:

```
<p>Here is some JavaScript program code:</p>

<code>
  var n = 1

  search: while (true)
  {
    n += 1

    for (var i = 2; i <- Math.sqrt(n); i += 1)
      if (n % i == 0) continue search;
    postMcooago(n);
  }
</code>
```

However, this tag doesn't cause line feeds to be displayed, and neither does it show the spacing. Instead the preceding example will display all on one line. To overcome this, you should restrict this tag for use on single lines, and probably use the `<pre>` tag instead (as shown in Figure 7-3), which displays text as it finds it—in other words, preformatted.

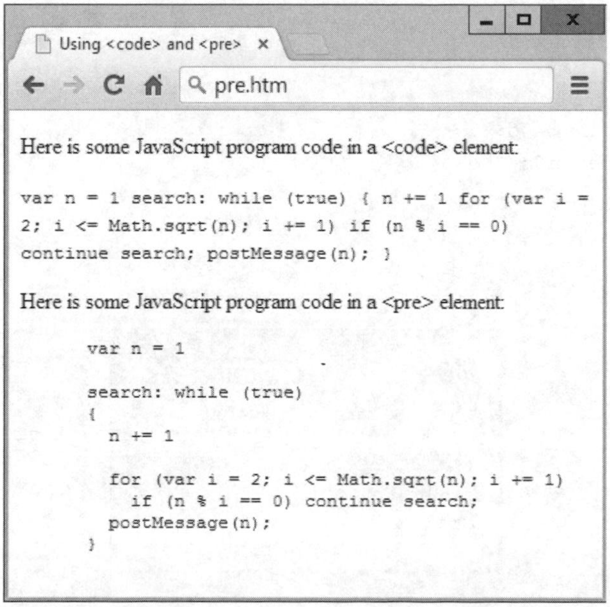

FIGURE 7-3   The difference between `<code>` and `<pre>` elements

The <samp> tag is identical to the <code> tag and can be used in the same way, although they do have different semantic meanings in HTML5. There is also a <tt> tag, which is meant to emulate the output of a teletype machine, and the <kbd> tag, which you can use to make output display as if it has been entered at the keyboard. All have the same formatting drawback that is corrected using the <pre> tag.

Also similar to these is the <dir> tag, which is now obsolete but was intended to make its contents look like a directory listing. Again, however, it did not issue line feeds and would actually wrap several lines if you didn't use a <br> tag after each—so it wasn't very useful anyway. If you encounter this tag when maintaining a web page, you should probably replace it with one of the preceding non-obsolete tags.

<col> and <colgroup>

This tag specifies properties for each column within a <colgroup> section of a table. For example, to change the background colors for the columns of a table, you could use HTML such as this (as shown in Figure 7-4):

```
<table>
  <caption><i>Weight Loss</i></caption>
  <colgroup>
    <col style="background-color:#eee;">
    <col style="background-color:#ddd;">
  </colgroup>
  <tr>
    <th>Month</th>
    <th>Weight</th>
  </tr>
  <tr>
    <td>January</td>
    <td>180 pounds</td>
  </tr>
</table>
```

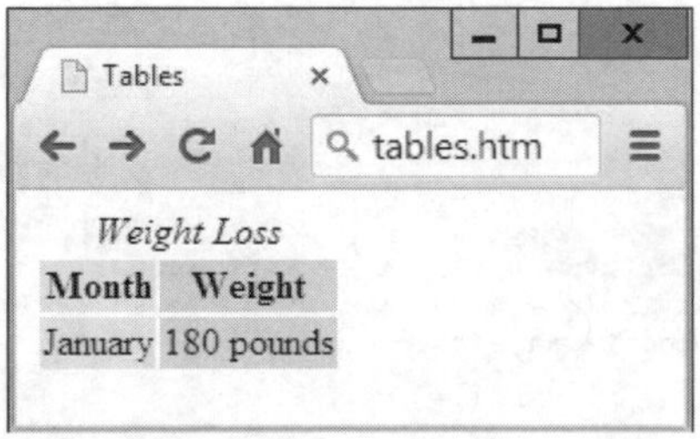

FIGURE 7-4 A table with colored columns

<del> ... </del>

Use this tag to indicate that a section of text should display as if it has been deleted. This tag is often used in conjunction with the <ins> tag to show a modification or correction that has been made (a deletion followed by an insertion), as shown in the second line up from the bottom of Figure 7-1:

```
I was <del>pleased</del> <ins>delighted</ins> to meet her!
```

This tag should also be used in preference to the equivalent <strike> tag, which has been obsoleted in HTML5. You can also use the <s> tag for the same effect, although <s> and <del> have differing semantic meanings in HTML5.

<fieldset> ... </fieldset>

When you need to group a collection of form fields together, you can do so with this tag, which draws a box around the grouped (contained) elements. In conjunction with the <legend> tag, it creates a title that breaks into the box border. Use it like this and the result will look like Figure 7-5:

```
<form>
  <fieldset>
    <legend>Your Name</legend>
    Forename: <input type='text' name='fname'>
    Surname:  <input type='text' name='sname'>
  </fieldset><br>
  Email: <input type='text' name='email'>
  <input type='submit'>
</form>
```

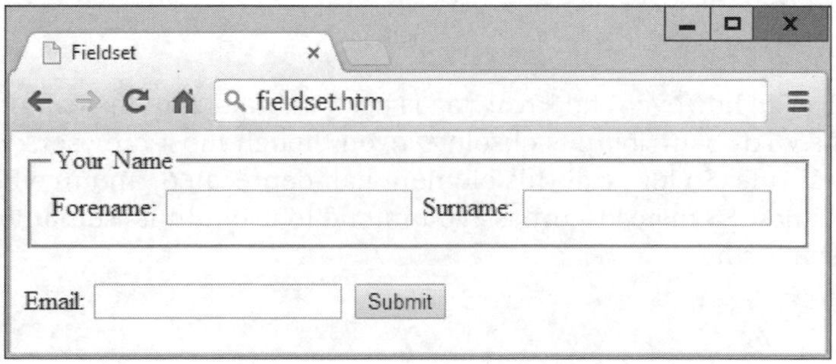

FIGURE 7-5   Using <fieldset> and <legend> elements

`<font>` ... `</font>` (Obsolete)

This obsolete tag used to let you change the font type, size, and color, all things that are better done using a CSS class, like this:

```
<style>
  .offer {
    font-family:'Times New Roman';
    font-size  :14pt;
    color      :green;
  }
</style>
```

And you can then use the `offer` class like this:

```
This product is on <span class='offer'>special offer</span>!
```

`<frameset>` (Obsolete)

In the past you used to use this tag in conjunction with the `<frame>` and `<noframes>` tags to create sets of frames in a web page that contained other documents, but they have now all been removed from HTML5 in favor of using the `<iframe>` tag and CSS.

`<hr>`

With the `<hr>` tag, you can display a horizontal rule with which to separate sections of a document. By default the rule will be the width of the page, but you can change this by supplying different values to its `width` attribute, like this (which creates rules of 100 percent of the parent object, 75 percent, and 100 pixels):

```
<hr>
<hr width='75%'>
<hr width='100'>
```

In HTML5, however, the `<hr>` tag is used thematically instead of as an actual rule, so the `width` attribute is obsolete, even though most browsers will still display a horizontal rule. So let's call this element half-deprecated, and maybe choose to use other tags and CSS instead—unless you intend to use it in its semantic context, in which case it's fine.

`<iframe>` ... `</iframe>`

Using this tag, you can load another document into the current one, displaying it within a frame with dimensions that you supply, like this:

```
<iframe src='http://somesite.com' width='300' height='150'></iframe>
```

For browsers that don't support inline frames, you can place text between the opening and closing tags that only they will display.

`<isindex>` ... `</isindex>` (Obsolete)

This tag used to provide a single-line text-input that would be sent to the server for returning a list of pages matching the query. However, it was almost never used and is now obsolete because you can do the same thing using `<input>` fields as detailed in Lesson 6.

`<menu>` ... `</menu>` (Reserved)

This tag used to specify a clickable menu, but it was deprecated in HTML4 and it is recommended that you use CSS instead, or simply place links in an ordered or unordered list. In HTML5, however, `<menu>` is back to represent a list of commands, but it is not yet supported by any browsers at the time of writing.

`<optgroup>` ... `</optgroup>`

When you wish to create groups of options within a `<select>` element, you use the `<optgroup>` tag, which requires a label attribute to be supplied that gives the group a title. You can then use the `<option>` tag as you normally would to list the options for that group. The left-hand drop-down menu in Figure 7-6 is the result of the following HTML and does not use `<optgroup>`:

```
<select>
  <option value='Apple'>Apple</option>
  <option value='Pear'>Pear</option>
  <option value='Banana'>Banana</option>
</select>
```

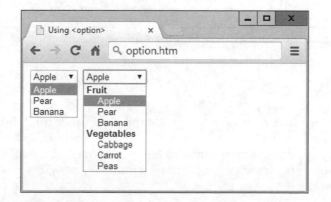

FIGURE 7-6   Using `<option>` tags in a `<select>` element

The right-hand drop-down menu in Figure 7-6 was created with the following HTML, which employs the `<optgroup>` tag twice:

```
<select>
  <optgroup label='Fruit'>
    <option value='Apple'>Apple</option>
    <option value='Pear'>Pear</option>
    <option value='Banana'>Banana</option>
  </optgroup>
  <optgroup label='Vegetables'>
    <option value='Cabbage'>Cabbage</option>
    <option value='Carrot'>Carrot</option>
    <option value='Peas'>Peas</option>
  </optgroup>
</select>
```

`<sub>` ... `</sub>` and `<sup>` ... `</sup>`

With the `<sub>` tag, you can display text in a smaller subscript font, while the `<sup>` tag displays it at the same small size but in a superscript font, like this (as shown in Figure 7-7):

```
Glucose has the formula C<sub>6</sub>H<sub>12</sub>O<sub>6</sub>.<br>
My birthday is May 2<sup>nd</sup>.
```

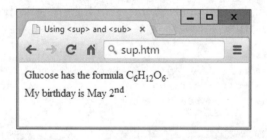

FIGURE 7-7 Using `<sup>` and `<sub>` tags for super- and subscripting

Summary

Congratulations. You have now completed the first part of this book consisting of an introduction to HTML4, and should now either have a basic understanding of what you can do with it, or if you already knew HTML, you have refreshed all its tags in your mind.

In the following lesson we'll start to get into the nitty-gritty of HTML5 and learn exactly what the fuss is all about.

Self-Test Questions

Test how much you have learned in this lesson with these questions. If you don't know an answer, go back over the relevant section until your knowledge is complete. You can find the answers in the appendix.

1. Which HTML tags let you use an image map on an image?

2. How can you denote text as a citation?

3. How can you change the direction of text flow from left-to-right to right-to-left?

4. What is *The Mark of the Web*?

5. Which tag displays text as if it has been deleted?

6. Which tag displays text as if it has been inserted?

7. How can you display text in a superscript font?

8. What HTML tag is a good way to display short quotations?

9. Which HTML tag is best for displaying long quotations?

10. Which HTML tag displays preformatted text?

PART II

HTML5
and the Canvas

What's New in HTML5

 To view the accompanying video for this lesson, please visit mhprofessional.com/nixonhtml5/.

HTML5 is a specification that's still under development (because a number of HTML5 features are still only sparsely implemented in some major browsers) even though the final draft was submitted in 2013. Therefore it's important for you to know about all the tags (both current and future), and how they work on various platforms and browsers, so that you will know just what you can do with HTML5 right now, and also what might become available to you in the future.

But what exactly is HTML5? Is it a new standard different from the previous 4.01 version? Surprisingly, the answer is no, because HTML5 is simply a loose collection of enhancements that have been (or will be) made to the HTML 4.01 specification, covering a wide range of differing areas; it has simply been found convenient to label these additions as HTML5.

This is why I made sure that you had a thorough grounding in HTML 4.01 before beginning this section, because that means that you now actually already have over 75 percent of the full HTML5 specification under your belt. Now you'll start to look at the remaining 25 percent or so that constitutes the HTML5 enhancements.

 When an older browser comes across an HTML5 tag that it doesn't recognize, the tag will simply be ignored, in the same way as if you use made-up tag names such as `<newtagname>` and `</newtagname>`. However, any text or HTML between such tags is displayed. This ensures that backward compatibility is retained for users with older browsers.

The Canvas

The <canvas> element was introduced by Apple to the Webkit rendering engine (the power behind the default iOS and Android web browsers, and also used by Safari, Opera, and Chrome), to provide a means of drawing graphics from within a web page, without having to load a plug-in such as Java or Flash. It was later standardized and has since been adopted by Opera and Gecko-based browsers, as used in the Mozilla Firefox browser, and is also included in Google Chrome and Microsoft Internet Explorer 9.

A *canvas* is a region within a web page that can be drawn on using JavaScript. As there can be more than one canvas in a web page, it is necessary to provide an ID for each so that the drawing commands know which canvas they should apply to. So, to create a canvas, you use HTML such as the following, which creates a 400×300-pixel canvas with the ID canvas1:

```
<canvas id='canvas1' width='400' height='300'>
  This web page uses the HTML5 canvas element,  which is
  available on most modern browsers. If you wish to view
  this page at its best, please upgrade your browser to
  the most recent version.
</canvas>
```

Note   This is a book on HTML5. However, many HTML5 features can only be accessed using JavaScript. Therefore in these lessons I provide illustrations of how to perform certain functions and give examples in JavaScript, but I do not teach the JavaScript language itself. You will be able to use and modify the examples since they are simple and clearly explained, but if you wish to achieve more complex results in JavaScript and other web development technologies, you may wish to read my other books in this series of 20 Lessons to Successful Web Development on CSS, JavaScript, and PHP.

Older browsers that do not recognize the <canvas> tag will ignore it and simply display the text between the opening and closing tag, which, in this instance, provides information to users about upgrading their browser.

The great thing about the HTML5 canvas is that you can now draw anything you like in a web browser, in a similar way to using a plug-in such as Flash, but using simple HTML and JavaScript syntax. This makes your web pages far more dynamic and able to display on a wider range of operating systems and devices. For example, the iOS infrastructure does not support Flash on iPhones and iPads, but does support the HTML5 canvas.

In Figure 8-1 I have created a 400×300-pixel canvas and drawn a square in its center using the following combination of HTML and JavaScript:

```
<canvas id='canvas1' width='400' height='300'>
  This web page uses the HTML5 canvas element,  which is
  available on most modern browsers. If you wish to view
  this page at its best,  please upgrade your browser to
```

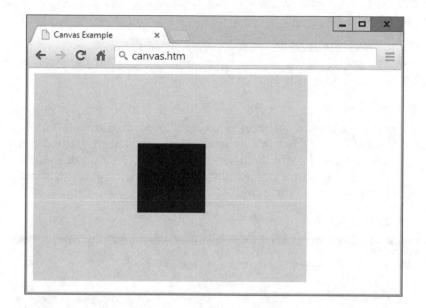

FIGURE 8-1   A 100×100-pixel square in a 400×300-pixel canvas

```
    the most recent version.
</canvas>

<script>
  canvas = document.getElementById('canvas1')
  canvas.style.background = '#ddd'
  context = canvas.getContext('2d')
  context.fillRect(150, 100, 100, 100)
</script>
```

The first part of this example is a repeat of the HTML snippet that creates the <canvas>, and the four lines within the <script> and </script> tags do the work of placing the square on the canvas. Let's look at them in turn, starting with:

```
canvas = document.getElementById('canvas1')
```

This creates a JavaScript object (an element capable of holding different types of information), which refers to the canvas1 canvas. In the following line the background of the canvas is set to a light gray color (#ddd) by altering its CSS style property:

```
canvas.style.background = '#ddd'
```

Next it is necessary to decide the way in which the canvas is to be accessed. For example, in the future it will be possible to access a canvas using 3D, which will make it possible to write professional-looking games. But for now 2D is the only option available, and that is what I have used, as follows:

```
context = canvas.getContext('2d')
```

Finally, a square is drawn on the canvas by using the context and the JavaScript function `fillRect()`. The square has its top-left corner at 150 pixels in by 100 down and has a width and height that are both 100 pixels:

```
context.fillRect(150, 100, 100, 100)
```

As you can see, even if you are not a JavaScript programmer, this is relatively straightforward, and will become more so when I explain the canvas element in more detail in Lessons 9 and 10. In the meantime, Figure 8-2 shows the addition of a circle and some text to the canvas, achieved using the following extra statements added into the `<script>` section of the example:

```
context.arc(60, 60, 50, 0, Math.PI * 2, false)
context.stroke()
context.font = '70px Times'
context.fillText('Hi!', 300, 280, 100)
```

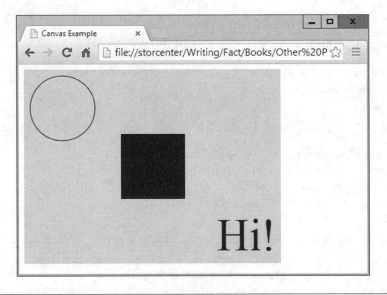

FIGURE 8-2 A circle and some text have been added to the canvas.

Geolocation

Geolocation is a technology that is used to determine the location of a computer or mobile device, which can be returned to the web server in order to provide relevant information. For example, a local map can be displayed, or details of local stores such as restaurants or gas stations can be provided.

Geolocation can also be used to help improve web connectivity by notifying you of nearby Wi-Fi access points, or to alert you of the proximity of friends, acquaintances, or colleagues.

Different methods are used to obtain your location, starting with your IP (Internet Protocol) address, which can reveal which country you are in, and programs that do this can often get very close to your locality. There's nothing you can normally do about this because all websites need to know your IP address in order to send you data. However, there are third-party services that will act as a proxy for you, replacing your IP address with theirs when communicating with a web server.

With HTML5 geolocation, if Wi-Fi is enabled on your computer, it is also possible to send more precise location information by scanning your locally accessible Wi-Fi hotspots to pinpoint your location, using databases containing millions of hotspot names and MAC (Media Access Control) addresses, along with their locations.

Also, if you are using a mobile device, triangulation of the mobile antenna masts you can connect to reveals your location quite accurately. Finally, if your computer has GPS (Global Positioning System) functionality, this can reveal your exact location to within just a few feet, as long as your device is in range of the GPS satellites that orbit the earth.

In Figure 8-3 permission has been granted by the user to return the geolocation data of a device at the location 40.689167, -74.044444, which is a point close to the Statue of Liberty in New York City, USA.

Geolocation is explained in greater depth in Lesson 15, and JavaScript code is supplied, which you can use without needing to learn the entire language.

FIGURE 8-3   A map is displayed as a result of returning geolocation data.

Forms

Forms have been provided with a number of new enhancements in HTML5, and in my view they are long overdue (and still only partially supported by some browsers).

To start with, you can now place <input> tags outside of <form> and </form> tags as long as the new form attribute is used to identify the form ID to which the input refers. Similarly, you can change the method (either Get or Post) of a form with the new formmethod attribute.

There are also enhancements letting you change the encoding type of a form, or create or override the new formnovalidate attribute. You can also use the formaction attribute to change the action (destination) of a form, and you can use formtarget to change the target frame, tab, or window. At the same time, it is now possible to change the height and width of the image type of the <input> tag using height and width attributes.

Two particularly handy new attributes are autocomplete and autofocus. The former allows previously entered values for a field to be offered as suggested values, while the latter is used to tell the browser to automatically focus on a particular form field ready for input. This is what happens when you go to a search engine such as Google (see Figure 8-4), where you can begin to enter your search immediately. In the good old days before the use of these tags and JavaScript, you had to click in a field first before it would obtain focus, and you would not be offered suggestions as you typed.

Data lists can also now be included in a form such that you can create a list of labels and values to which you assign an ID. Then you can use that ID as the value for the new list attribute to easily offer a selection of choices to an input. This is

FIGURE 8-4   Google supports autofocus and autocompletion.

especially useful when you wish to use the same list more than once as it avoids unnecessarily duplicating it.

New `min`, `max`, and `step` attributes have also been added for inputs that contain numbers or dates, and there's a new `multiple` attribute with which you can allow an `<input>` tag to accept multiple values. This is especially useful, for example, when selecting groups of files to upload to a server.

Pattern matching is now supported in forms via the new `pattern` attribute, the `placeholder` attribute lets you display some hint text in a field that disappears once the field is selected, and you can use the `required` attribute to tell a form that a field must be completed.

Several new values are now supported for the `type` attribute, including `color`, `date`, `month`, `time`, `week`, `number`, `range`, `tel`, `url`, and `email`. These allow the browser to check such input fields for proper syntax and sensible data being entered. There's also a powerful search `type` value, which enables a field to provide search suggestions in a similar fashion to the instant results that appear when entering a request into the Google search engine.

All these values and more are fully detailed in Lesson 16.

Local Storage

Before HTML5, the only way that data could be stored on a local device was via the use of *cookies*, which are small bundles of data generally used to help retain the contents of a shopping basket, or more controversially, by advertising websites to track your browsing.

But it has long been realized that the web could be significantly sped up if a local data store were made available that could be used, for example, for storing longer documents as you edit them, prior to them being sent to the server for safekeeping. With HTML5 this is possible, and even large chunks of data (up to 5MB per website) can be stored locally, but only if the user agrees to it, so you retain full control.

What's more, on some browsers local storage can be accessed like a database using Web SQL, providing the possibility of creating advanced local web apps for handling data such as your music collection, or personal exercising and dieting, and so on.

Lesson 17 fully explains what you can and can't do with local storage.

Audio and Video

Possibly the most interesting and popular enhancements in HTML5 (other than the canvas) are the ability to now play audio and video directly from within HTML, with no need to embed Flash or any other type of object as a player.

To do this, the new tags `<audio>` and `<video>` have been provided, but how to use them is still a bit up in the air as it can depend on the browser and operating system being used. In addition there has been a big hoo-ha going on about the use of the H.264 video codec (the software algorithm used to compress all the video data down to a manageable size for the Internet), which is not free for products that encode or decode the video (such as browsers), although it is free for end users.

Because of this, different browsers support different codecs, but there are workarounds and tweaks you can employ to ensure that just about all your users can play HTML5 audio and video, and all of this is explained in Lessons 18 and 19.

The `<embed>` Tag

While on the subject of embedding objects (such as video players) in a web page, the `<embed>` tag, which was officially deprecated in HTML 4.01, has now been restored and made official again. Therefore, for example, you can officially use code such as the following to play a YouTube video in a non-HTML5 browser using Flash:

```
<object width="480" height="385">
  <param name="movie" value="http://www.youtube.com/v/sNdJUL1fELI">
  <param name="allowFullScreen" value="true">
  <param name="allowscriptaccess" value="always">
  <embed src=http://www.youtube.com/v/sNdJUL1fELI
    type="application/x-shockwave-flash"
    allowscriptaccess="always" allowfullscreen="true"
    width="480" height="385">
</object>
```

Code such as this can be inserted between `<video>` and `</video>` tags so that browsers that do not recognize them will use Flash to display a video, as shown in Figure 8-5.

FIGURE 8-5   Embedding a YouTube Flash video

Microdata

Microdata is a subset of HTML designed for making a document have meaning to machines by providing metadata, just as it has meaning to a reader of the document.

What it does is make available the following new tag attributes: `itemscope`, `itemtype`, `itemid`, `itemref`, and `itemprop`. Using them you will be able to clearly define the properties of an item such as a book, providing a range of information that a computer can use to understand, for example, its authors, publishers, contents, and so on. Further information on microdata is in Lesson 20.

Web Workers

Normally, to achieve background processing in JavaScript, you need to set up a timer that is constantly called, supplying slices of processor time to one or more functions, and these functions must then quickly do a small piece of work and return, in order to not slow down the browser and make it seem sluggish.

Web workers are not yet widely implemented but will provide a standard way for browsers to run multiple JavaScript threads in the background that can pass messages to each other, in much the same manner as the threads running in an operating system. You will simply call up a new worker script, which will sit there in the background waiting for messages to be sent to it, which it will then act upon.

On the whole the aim of this is to achieve a speed increase of two to three times over regular background JavaScripts, although getting to grips with programming them is likely to require a steeper learning curve. Lesson 20 discusses web workers in more detail.

Web Applications

The idea of offline web applications is that once you visit a website, it tells your browser about all the files it uses so that the browser can download them all and you can then run the web application locally, even without an Internet connection.

There is a complication with web applications in that they require a web server to set up with the correct MIME types (originally known as Multipurpose Internet Mail Extensions, but the word *Mail* has since been replaced with *Media*), in order for a browser that understands web applications to make use of the feature and fetch the files it needs. Lesson 20 goes into web applications in greater detail.

Still to Come

There are a number of other new HTML5 tags that have not yet been implemented in any browser, and which I therefore won't detail (particularly since their specs could change).

But, for the sake of completeness, these tags are: `<article>`, `<aside>`, `<details>`, `<figcaption>`, `<figure>`, `<footer>`, `<header>`, `<hgroup>`, `<keygen>`, `<mark>`, `<menuitem>`, `<meter>`, `<nav>`, `<output>`, `<progress>`, `<rp>`, `<rt>`, `<ruby>`, `<section>`, `<summary>`, `<time>`, and `<wbr>`. You can get more information on these and all other HTML5 tags at *dev.w3.org/html5/markup*.

Summary

This lesson has introduced you to all the new goodies in HTML5. In the following lessons I will explain each of these main areas in depth so that you can begin to use the tags that have been widely supported in your own web pages, and will be prepared to also include the lesser-supported ones as browsers pick them up.

Self-Test Questions

Test how much you have learned in this lesson with these questions. If you don't know an answer, go back and reread the relevant section until your knowledge is complete. You can find the answers in the appendix.

1. Which tag is used to create an HTML5 canvas?

2. What happens with the canvas in non-HTML5 compatible browsers?

3. Which JavaScript function is used to fetch an object with which to access an element such as a canvas?

4. What does the acronym GPS stand for?

5. Which new HTML5 technology is superior to cookies?

6. Which two new tags have been added to HTML5 to handle multimedia?

7. What HTML tag is used to allow fallback to Flash for playing media?

8. What new HTML5 technology helps provide additional information about the contents of a document?

9. Which new HTML5 technology lets the programmer offload background JavaScript tasks to be handled by the web browser?

10. What did the acronym MIME stand for, and what does it stand for nowadays?

Accessing the Canvas

 To view the accompanying video for this lesson, please visit mhprofessional.com/
nixonhtml5/.

There are no two ways around it. If I'm going to show you how to use the HTML5
canvas, then I'm also going to have to give you an ultra-crash course on JavaScript,
or at least on those aspects of it required for manipulating the canvas.

So here goes (if you already know JavaScript, you can briefly skim the following
section, before moving on to the "Accessing the Canvas with JavaScript" section).

An Ultra-Crash Course in JavaScript

Although I'm going to teach you a few parts of JavaScript, it is by no means the entire
language, but it will be just sufficient for you to complement your use of HTML for
manipulating the canvas. Along the way I also touch upon a few elements of CSS
(Cascading Style Sheets) too.

JavaScript was created to allow you to directly access various parts of the HTML
DOM (Document Object Model). To explain the DOM, take a look at the following
example web page:

```
<html>
  <head>
    <title>Example</title>
    <meta name='robots' content='index, follow'>
  </head>
  <body>
    <a href='http://yahoo.com'>Visit Yahoo!</a>
    <form id='login' method='post' action='form.php'>
      <input name='name' type='text' value='jane'>
```

```
      <input type='submit'>
    </form>
    <img src='dad.jpg'>
  </body>
</html>
```

This is a simple page that displays a link to the Yahoo! website and has a form underneath that submits a username to a PHP script with the filename *form.php*. Beneath that an image is included. In terms of this web page's DOM, it looks something like Figure 9-1, in which the entire content is contained within `<html>` and `</html>` tags.

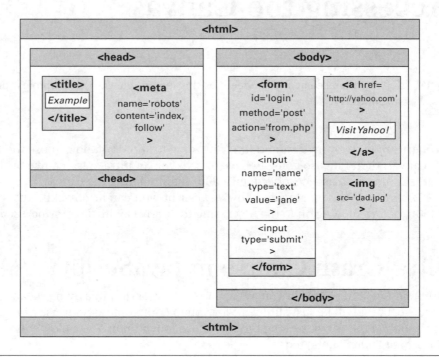

FIGURE 9-1 The DOM of the preceding HTML example

Looking at the `<head>` section in Figure 9-1, you can see that there are two elements. The first is the document's title of *Example*, contained within `<title>` and `</title>` tags, while the second is the meta tag, which tells search engine crawlers that the document may be crawled, its contents indexed, and any links can be followed. This is done by passing the value `robots` to the `name` attribute, and `index, follow` to the `content` attribute. Meta tags are self-closing (empty) so there is no `</meta>` tag. The section is then closed with a `</head>` tag.

To the right of the figure is the body of the document, which is contained within `<body>` and `</body>` tags. There are three elements in this section, a link to *yahoo.com* in `<a>` and `</a>` tags, an embedded image that uses a self-closing `<img>` tag, and a form contained within `<form>` and `</form>` tags.

The form assigns the value `login` to the `id` attribute, `post` to the `method` attribute, and the program name *form.php* to the `action` attribute. This is the program that is to process the form when it is submitted. The opening `<form>` tag is then closed, and inside the form there are two self-closing `<input>` tags. The first passes the value `name` to the `name` attribute, the value `text` to the `type` attribute, and the value `jane` to the `name` attribute. This prepopulates the input field with the word `jane`, but it can be altered by the user.

After this a second `<input>` tag creates a submit button by passing the value `submit` to its `type` attribute. Finally the form is closed with a `</form>` tag.

When opened in a browser, the document looks something like Figure 9-2.

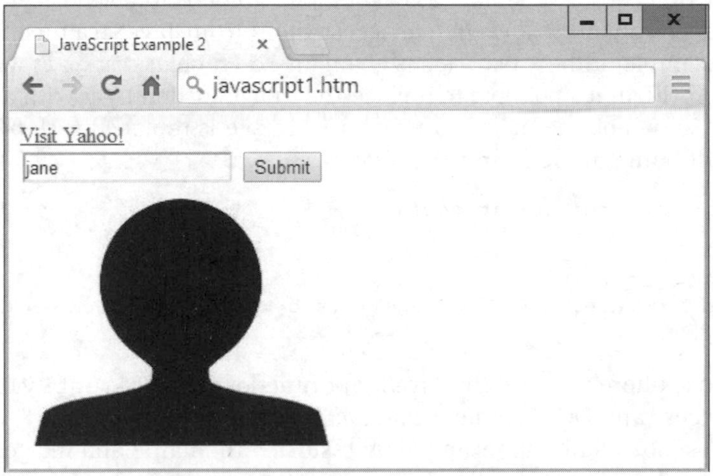

FIGURE 9-2   The result of displaying the example web page

Accessing Form Elements from JavaScript

Now let's look at how these elements can be manipulated from JavaScript, which should always be placed within `<script>` and `</script>` tags. For example, the following code changes the document's title from *Example* to *This is an example web page*:

```
<script>
  document.title = 'This is an example web page'
</script>
```

This has the same effect as if you opened the document and went straight in and edited the title within the `<title>` and `</title>` tags yourself. See how easy JavaScript is?

Similarly the form method type of post is easily changed to get, like this:

```
<script>
  document.forms.login.method = 'get'
</script>
```

Here the JavaScript references first the document, then the forms within that document, then the form with the id of login and its method, which is then modified.

Using the `getElementById()` Function

In the previous two examples I showed you how to access parts of a document by their type, but there's a far, far easier method, which is to give every element in a document a unique id, and then to access them from JavaScript using just those ids.

For example, if the <img> tag is given an id (such as image1) with which it can be identified, it's possible to replace the image loaded by it with another, like the following, in which the male-shaped *dad.jpg* image is replaced with *mom.jpg* to match the default name in the form field of *jane*:

```
<img src='dad.jpg' id='image1'>

<script>
  document.getElementById('image1').src = 'mom.jpg'
</script>
```

The trick here is to use the JavaScript function getElementById(), which will let you access any DOM element that has been given a unique id.

So let's look at another example by restoring the name and image mismatch by altering the default name value. If we were to use the initial example in this section, we would have to access the element via document.forms.login, and so on, but by giving the form field an id (for example of name) and using getElementById(), we can avoid all that and go straight to the element to change it, like this (in which I have shown only the changed <input> tag and not the remainder of the HTML, which remains unchanged):

```
<input name='name' type='text' value='jane' id='name'>

<script>
  document.getElementById('name').value = 'mike'
</script>
```

See how much easier it is than having to remember whether an element is part of a form, an image, or something else? All you have to do is know the name of an element and getElementById() will do the job of finding it for you. Figure 9-3 shows how the web page now displays after these changes. The title is different, the default input value is 'mike', and the image shown is *mom.jpg* (yes, the gender is all confused again).

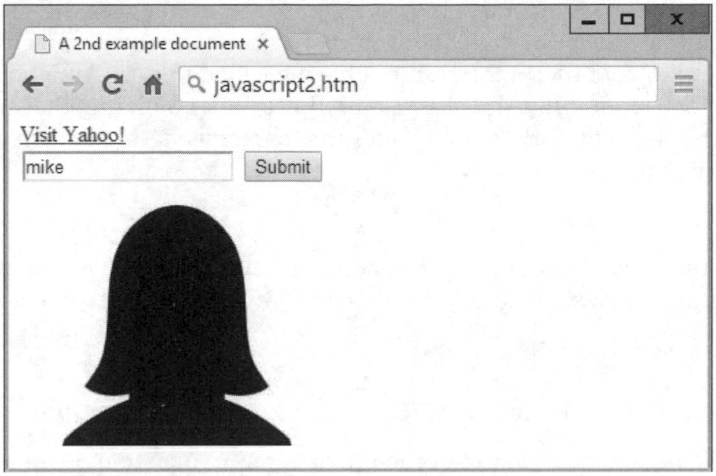

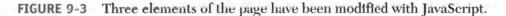

FIGURE 9-3   Three elements of the page have been modified with JavaScript.

The Simpler O() Function

I use the `getElementById()` function so often that I always create a simple function called `O()` (with an uppercase O) to make it easier to type in. The function looks like this and I simply place it anywhere in a section of JavaScript, like this (highlighted in bold):

```
<script>
  O('name').value = 'mike'

  function O(obj)
  {
    if (typeof obj == 'object') return obj
    else return document.getElementById(obj)
  }
</script>
```

Doing this saves 22 characters of typing each time the replacement `O()` function is used instead of the longer one. One reason for the tremendous shortening is that the preceding `document` keyword has also been incorporated into the `O()` function, saving on typing that in too.

Note   In JavaScript tutorials on the Web and in books, you may see functions referred to either by the term *function*, or using the term *method*, but they both mean the same thing: a set of instructions grouped together, which can receive one or more values and then return a value upon completion.

However, there's one further step I like to take that makes the function even more useful and that's to allow the passing to it of either element IDs (which is what it does so far), or an object that is the result of having called the O() function.

Let me explain it like this. Instead of directly manipulating the value of the form input with the id of name directly, let's first create what is called an object from this element, like this:

```
newobject = O('name')
```

Now that I have this object, I can access it several times without ever having to call the O() function again, like this (in which the value is changed on separate occasions):

```
newobject.value ='mike'
  // A few lines of code go here
newobject.value ='fred'
```

Now, whenever I wish to refer to the element in question, I can simply use the object that I created. But now, what if I want to change the style property of an object? Because the S() function I created for this (shown after this paragraph) calls the O() function, and that only supports id names, then the only way to do this is to go back to using a call such as this (to make the input exactly 150 pixels wide):

```
S('name').width = '150px'
```

But I have been using the object newobject, and for the sake of consistency, I would prefer to pass that to the S() function. To enable this, all that's necessary is to allow the O() function to be passed either an object or an id, so the argument passed in obj is analyzed by the code and if it happens to already be of the type object, then the object is simply returned, because it is already an object.

But if it is not of that type, then it must be an id name, in which case it is looked up and returned as an object with a call to getElementById().

 Note   If this confuses you, don't worry. You don't need to learn JavaScript, or (indeed) understand fully the workings of these snippets of code, in order to use the following examples to access the HTML5 canvas.

The Partner S() Function

In a similar fashion to the savings produced by using the O() function, there is one other that I employ frequently because it is also used all the time in JavaScript, and that's the new function S() (with an uppercase S). This is used to enable JavaScript to easily access any style attribute of any element.

For example, if I wish to change the width and height of the image, I can do it like this (which results in Figure 9-4, when the other lines of HTML and JavaScript we've been using are included):

```
<img src='dad.jpg' id='image1'>

<script>
  O('image1').style.width = '150px' // More to type
```

```
S('image1').height      = '120px' // Less to type

function O(obj)
{
  if (typeof obj == 'object') return obj
  else return document.getElementById(obj)
}

function S(obj)
{
  return O(obj).style
}
</script>
```

FIGURE 9-4 The *mom.jpg* image has been reduced in size.

 The // characters create a comment to the end of the line, which I have used in the preceding example to comment each of the final two lines within the script (that the second version of syntax is shorter than the first).

What I've done here is simply make the S() function place a call to the O() function but with an added .style suffix, and now I can use O() for accessing elements by name, and S() for accessing the style attributes of elements by name.

Believe it or not, these two functions alone provide you with a huge amount of scope and power to modify any part of a document, without learning the JavaScript language. All you need to remember to do is include the O() and S() functions somewhere in a script in any document that will refer to them. Then, whenever you need to use these functions, open up a new <script> tag and access them, like this:

```
<script>
  S('image1').width  = '150px'
  S('image1').height = '120px'
</script>
```

This works because you are allowed to enter `<script>` tags as many times as you like in a document—there is no requirement to keep all your JavaScript code within a single set of `<script>` and `</script>` tags, although you may do so if you wish.

Alternatively, if you would like to create an object on the first call to the `O()` function, and then reference that instead, the preceding code might look like this:

```
<script>
  myimage           = O('image1')
  S(myimage).width  = '150px'
  S(myimage).height = '120px'
</script>
```

This code can be quicker as the object is only looked up once, and is therefore a more efficient way to code when an element may be accessed more than once. By the way, the reason `myimage` does not have quotation marks around it is because it is an object, not an `id` value that is a string.

Note   I use the functions `O()` and `S()` extensively throughout this book, so I recommend you get comfortable with them by downloading the examples from the companion website and then playing with them until you feel you have mastered their use.

The `<canvas>` Tag

With that little (but necessary) preamble over, now we can get down to directly manipulating an HTML5 canvas. As you may recall from Lesson 8, the following code creates a canvas and places a square in its center (and results in Figure 9-5):

```
<canvas id='canvas1' width='400' height='300'>
  This web page uses the HTML5 canvas element,  which is
  available on most modern browsers. If you wish to view
  this page at its best,  please upgrade your browser to
  the most recent version.
</canvas>

<script>
  canvas              = O('canvas1')
  S(canvas).background = '#ddd'
  context              = canvas.getContext('2d')
  context.fillRect(150, 100, 100, 100)

  function O(obj)
  {
    if (typeof obj == 'object') return obj
    else return document.getElementById(obj)
  }
```

```
   function S(obj)
   {
     return O(obj).style
   }
</script>
```

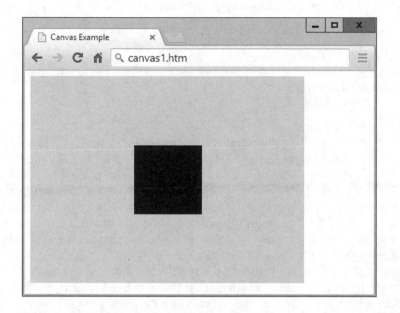

FIGURE 9-5   Drawing a black square on a gray canvas

The <canvas> tag itself supports only two attributes; width and height, as used in the example. And it is important that you provide a unique identifier for each canvas you use, so that you can access them from JavaScript. In the example, the id is given a value of canvas1.

The other thing to remember about the <canvas> tag is that anything between it and the closing </canvas> tag is ignored by all HTML5-compatible browsers, and so is displayed only by browsers that do not recognize it. Therefore this is where you can place text and/or HTML to inform users about what they are missing and perhaps how to upgrade their browser.

Accessing the Canvas with JavaScript

Let's look closely at the code from the previous example, as follows:

```
<script>
  canvas               = O('canvas1')
  S(canvas).background = '#ddd'
  context              = canvas.getContext('2d')
```

```
    context.fillRect(150, 100, 100, 100)

    function O(obj)
    {
      if (typeof obj == 'object') return obj
      else return document.getElementById(obj)
    }

    function S(obj)
    {
      return O(obj).style
    }
</script>
```

Ignoring the opening and closing tags, and the `O()` and `S()` functions, the object `canvas` is created by passing the `id` of the canvas (`canvas1`) to the `O()` function.

Armed with this object, the following line passes it to the `S()` function and then sets its `background` property to a light gray (`#ddd`) color. This is where the power of extending the `O()` function to also support objects comes in (because the `S()` function calls the `O()` function). By virtue of this extension it has been a simple matter to pass the object created from the canvas straight to the `S()` function, allowing for far simpler and more compact coding.

Next, to be able to read from and write to the canvas, a context (with the name `context`) is created with which to access it, using the JavaScript `getContext()` function, which is told to treat the canvas as a two-dimensional workspace.

Then the final line uses this context to create a filled rectangle at an offset of 150 pixels horizontally in from the top-left corner, and 100 pixels vertically down from the same corner. The rectangle is given a width and height of 100 pixels, resulting in a filled, black square.

 From now on, I will be assuming that you have placed the two functions `O()` and `S()` within `<script>` and `</script>` tags somewhere in your document, and will not be showing the code for these functions in any more examples. So please ensure that you have included them before testing any examples, or they will not work.

Converting a Canvas to an Image

Because of the way the canvas is created, it is not possible for users to right-click and save a copy to the desktop, for example. Likewise, you cannot directly use a canvas as an image. But there is a way you can convert a canvas to what is known as a data URL. This displays as an image and can then be copied and/or saved.

Consider the following code in which a canvas is created and then followed by an image, which does not have any `src` attribute:

```
<canvas id='canvas1' width='400' height='300'></canvas>
<img id='image'>

<script>
  canvas                = O('canvas1')
  S(canvas).background  = '#ddd'
  context               = canvas.getContext('2d')
  context.fillRect(150, 100, 100, 100)

  O('image').src = canvas.toDataURL()
</script>
```

What this code does (remember, it assumes you already have the `O()` and `S()` functions listed somewhere) is identical to the previous example, but there is a new line of code at the end that accesses the image using the `O()` function and then attaches a value to its `src` attribute, which is gained by calling the `toDataURL()` function on the `canvas` object.

The `toDataURL()` function extracts the image data from the canvas referred to by the `canvas` object and returns a string of text in which the canvas has been encoded as a displayable image, which is interpreted by the browser and reconstructed into an image.

When the code is loaded into a browser, it displays as Figure 9-6. Notice how the background color of the canvas (which has been applied only to the canvas element and not the contents of the canvas) is ignored by the `toDataURL()` function, so that when the image data is extracted, you see only the central black square.

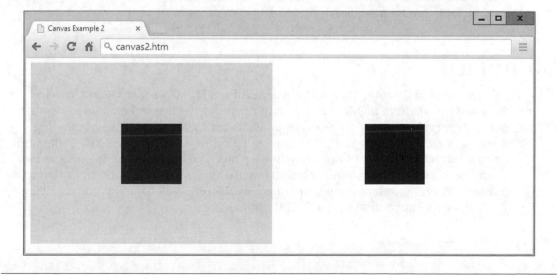

FIGURE 9-6   Displaying a canvas and a copy saved into an image

The `imagetype` Argument

When an image is created from a canvas, you can choose the type of image to use between a *jpeg* and *png* image using the `imagetype` argument, as in the following two examples, which are identical in result since the default image type is *png*.

```
O('image').src = canvas.toDataURL()
O('image').src = canvas.toDataURL('image/png')
```

Or, for a *jpeg* image, you can use code such as the following three examples, which create a very low-quality, medium-quality, and a very high-quality image by passing an additional argument containing a value between 0 (low quality) and 1 (high quality):

```
O('image').src = canvas.toDataURL('image/jpeg', 0)
O('image').src = canvas.toDataURL('image/jpeg', 0.5)
O('image').src = canvas.toDataURL('image/jpeg', 1)
```

 Remember that the `canvas` object is used to call the `toDataURL()` method, not the `context` object. This is because the latter is for applying changes to the canvas using the context rendering assigned, while the former refers to the canvas object itself.

Uses for this feature could be online image manipulation programs that run in the browser (as opposed to on a web server somewhere far away from the browser), and which returns a transformed or newly created image ready for the user to save to their hard disk and use. This means that it is possible to use the HTML5 canvas to create a graphics program, like Photoshop, that runs within a browser and requires no interaction with a web server. Therefore it could also be turned into a web app or even a standalone app for a mobile device like a tablet or phone.

Summary

Now that you understand the basic elements of the HTML5 canvas, and have the tools and information required to use it, in the following lesson I explain in depth how to use each aspect of the features available for writing to a canvas, including drawing lines, rectangles, and circles; changing colors; using pattern and gradient fills; writing text; changing font face; using lines, paths, and curves; applying images to a canvas; adding shadows; direct pixel manipulation; compositing and transparency; transformations and translations, and more. By the time you complete the next lesson, you will be an expert at using the HTML canvas.

Self-Test Questions

Test how much you have learned in this lesson with these questions. If you don't know an answer, go back and reread the relevant section until your knowledge is complete. You can find the answers in the appendix.

1. What is the DOM?

2. What JavaScript command could you use to change a web document's title?

3. How can you create a JavaScript object from an HTML element?

4. What attribute must a canvas be given in order for JavaScript to access it?

5. How can you access an object's style properties from JavaScript?

6. What is the purpose of the O ( ) function in these examples?

7. What is the purpose of the S ( ) function in these examples?

8. What kind of object is needed to be created from a canvas object in order for drawing functions to operate correctly?

9. Which JavaScript function is used to copy canvas data into an image?

10. How can you create a single-line comment in JavaScript?

Creating Rectangles, Fills, Gradients, and Patterns

 To view the accompanying video for this lesson, please visit mhprofessional.com/ nixonhtml5/.

N ow that you've seen how to use JavaScript to access the HTML5 canvas, let's look at all the different functions available for creating different effects, including drawing lines, rectangles, and circles; changing colors; using pattern and gradient fills; writing text; changing font face; using lines, paths and curves; applying images to a canvas; adding shadows; direct pixel manipulation; compositing and transparency; transformations and translations, and more.

Drawing Rectangles

Other than drawing lines (which we'll get to later, since they are handled using paths), rectangles are probably the simplest type of object you can draw on an HTML5 canvas, as you've already seen with the `fillRect()` function used in a couple of examples.

You can also fill a rectangle with a color other than black, and you can create unfilled (or clear) rectangles with different border widths, line styles, and corners.

 Remember that JavaScript functions are also often referred to as *methods*, but as the terms are interchangeable, I have selected to use only the word *function*.

The `fillRect()` Function

We have already explored the `fillRect()` function; it takes four arguments representing the vertical and horizontal offsets of the top left-hand corner of a rectangle from the top-left corner of the canvas, followed by the rectangle's width and height, all of which are in units of pixels, or one screen dot.

The syntax of the function is as follows, which creates a filled rectangle 50 pixels wide and 70 pixels high, at an offset of 20 pixels in from the left edge of the canvas (410 by 170 pixels), and 30 pixels down from its top:

```
<canvas id='example' width='410' height='170'></canvas>

<script>

  canvas              = O('example')
  S(canvas).background = '#ddd'

  context.fillRect(20, 30, 50, 70)

  // The O() and S() functions must be somewhere in the document
</script>
```

This example shows all the bits and pieces needed to set up everything ready to make the call to `fillRect()`, but for simplicity in the rest of this lesson, I will show only the relevant calls required for the function or functions being explained, like this:

```
context.fillRect(20, 30, 50, 70)
```

 Note If you are trying out these examples, you must ensure that you have first created a suitable canvas using the `<canvas>` and `</canvas>` tags and specified a suitable width and height for it (with enough room to display whatever is written to the canvas), have entered the `O()` and `S()` functions within any preceding pair of `<script>` and `</script>` tags (including the current pair), and have created a context for accessing the canvas called `context`.

The default color of a filled rectangle is black, but you will learn how to change this in the next section, or even how to use a gradient or a pattern to fill it later in this lesson.

The `fillStyle` Property

Using the `fillStyle` property, you can set the type of fill color to use, using either short (three-digit) or long (six-digit) hexadecimal colors. For example, to choose red you can pass the values #F00 or #FF0000, like this:

```
context.fillStyle = '#F00'
```

You may also use any of the HTML color names (listed in Lesson 4) such as red, steelblue, and so on, like this:

```
context.fillStyle = 'red'
```

Once selected, the color will apply to all fill operations until it is changed. For example, the following pair of lines will create a red rectangle, rather than a (default) black one:

```
context.fillStyle = 'red'
context.fillRect(20, 30, 50, 70)
```

For more information on using colors, please refer to Lesson 4.

The `clearRect()` Function

If you want to draw a clear rectangle, in which all the RGBA (Red, Green, Blue, and Alpha transparency) values of a pixel are set to zero, you can use the clearRect() function, as follows:

```
context.clearRect(20, 30, 50, 70)
```

This function uses the same arguments as fillRect(), namely the horizontal and vertical offset of the top left-hand corner of the rectangle from the top-left corner of the canvas, followed by the width and height of the rectangle to clear.

The cleared area will be stripped of all color, leaving only any underlying background color that may have been applied to the <canvas> tag (and which therefore is not part of the canvas, but is actually underneath it).

The `strokeRect()` Function

With the strokeRect() function, you can create a rectangle that uses the current strokeStyle, lineWidth, lineJoin, and miterLimit properties to draw the border lines and corners (as detailed in the "Drawing Lines" section in Lesson 12), and is used like this:

```
context.strokeRect(20, 30, 50, 70)
```

The function takes the same arguments as fillRect(), namely the horizontal and vertical offset of the top left-hand corner of the rectangle from the top-left corner of the canvas, followed by the width and height of the rectangle to draw.

It is possible to apply these effects on their own or in combination with others, so the following code (in which I have lined up the columns of arguments for ease of comparison) is valid and results in Figure 10-1, in which a red outer square created using fillRect() has a clear one drawn over it using clearRect() (because it's clear all you see is a thick-lined outer rectangle—the inner area of which has been cleared). Within the clear square is another lined rectangle which was created using the `strokeRect()` function:

```
context.fillStyle = 'red'
context.fillRect(  10, 10, 150, 150)
context.clearRect( 20, 20, 130, 130)
context.strokeRect(30, 30, 110, 110)
```

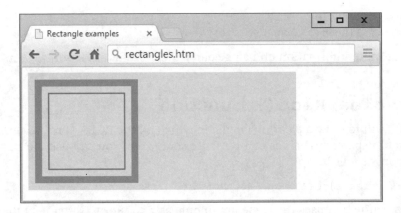

FIGURE 10-1   The three types of rectangle drawn inside each other in red

 I have covered rectangles before lines because they are simpler to draw. As you will see in Lesson 12, lines must be drawn by creating paths of locations that you connect up. Therefore, the properties that are associated with lines and paths are explained in that section, rather than here.

Creating Gradients

You saw how to create a simple, filled rectangle in the previous section, but it's also easy to apply a variety of different types of gradient to both the `fillRect()` function, as you've already seen, and the `fill()` function, which is introduced later on.

The `createLinearGradient()` Function

The simplest type of gradient available with the HTML5 canvas is a default linear gradient. To create a linear gradient, you need to specify the colors to use and the positions at which they should change. For example, in the following statement, the object `gradient` is set to start at the location 55,10 and end at 55,160.

```
gradient = context.createLinearGradient(55, 10, 55, 160)
```

Why these coordinates? Well, you must specify the start and end relative to the entire canvas, not to the object being filled. Therefore, I will be drawing a 90×150-pixel rectangle with its top-left corner at location 10,10, and then I choose a start point of 55,10, which is halfway along the top of the rectangle, and an end point of 55,160, which is halfway along the rectangle's bottom edge.

The reason that the gradient start and end locations are relative to the canvas and not to objects being filled is to allow you greater subtlety and the ability to create a gradient that covers the entire canvas (or as much or little as you like), and of which only the part existing underneath an object being filled is revealed. This, for example, would enable you to create a gradient that represents a sunset and then draw the inside of a car and use the gradient fill on the windows to reveal the correct parts of the outside gradient for the positions of the windows.

Now that the linear gradient object is created, it is necessary to choose the start and end colors, as with the following two lines, which set an initial stop position (as it is known) of the color #FFF (white), and an end of #000 (black). This is achieved using the addColorStop() function, which is fully explained a little further on, as follows:

```
gradient.addColorStop(0, '#FFF')
gradient.addColorStop(1, '#000')
```

What these two calls do is specify with the first argument to each the position at which the color is to be applied (in this case they are 0 and 1 for the start and end), and the second argument sets the color to apply at each of these positions. This gradient is then applied to the current context using the fillStyle property, and then a 90×150-pixel rectangle is drawn using these fill values:

```
context.fillStyle = gradient
context.fillRect(10, 10, 90, 150)
```

The result of these commands looks like Figure 10-2, in which you can see the fill fade linearly from white to black starting at the top and ending at the bottom of the rectangle.

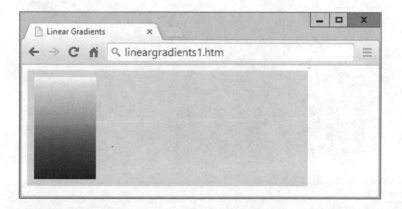

FIGURE 10-2   A vertically aligned linear gradient fill

You can change the start and end coordinates for the fill to any other locations. For example, in Figure 10-3 a second rectangle has been filled from left to right by choosing the following values for the call to `createLinearGradient()`:

```
gradient = context.createLinearGradient(110, 85, 200, 85)
```

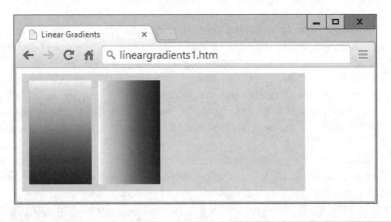

FIGURE 10-3 A horizontally filled rectangular gradient has been added.

These coordinates specify a start point halfway down the rectangle's left edge, and an end that is halfway down its right edge, as used by this `fillRect()` call:

```
context.fillRect(110, 10, 90, 150)
```

In fact, you can choose any start and end location (within or without the area to be filled) as, for example, with this code, which creates a diagonal gradient from top left (210,10) to bottom right (300,160), as shown in Figure 10-4.

```
gradient = context.createLinearGradient(210, 10, 300, 160)
context.fillRect(210, 10, 90, 150)
```

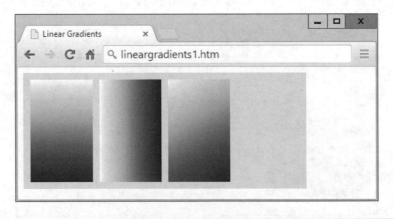

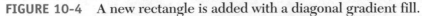

FIGURE 10-4 A new rectangle is added with a diagonal gradient fill.

The `createRadialGradient()` Function

You can also create a gradient that expands radially. That is, it starts at a point and has a certain radius, and then ends focused around another point, with a different (or the same) radius.

For example, the following call to `createRadialGradient()` specifies an initial location at the center of a rectangle and a width of 0 pixels. The second pair of coordinates remains the same, but with a radius of 45 pixels, so that the gradient starts in the center and continues to the left and right edges. As you can see in Figure 10-5, the top and bottom of the rectangle are outside the radius and so are provided with the color applied to the final stop, which is black:

```
gradient = context.createRadialGradient(355, 85, 0, 355, 85, 45)
context.fillRect(310, 10, 90, 150)
```

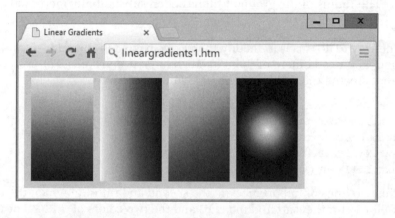

FIGURE 10-5   The fourth rectangle features a radial gradient.

So that you can see the effect of using start and/or end coordinates that are outside the area being filled, I have increased the radius of the second part of the gradient in Figure 10-6 to 150 pixels, so that it extends past all the rectangle's edges, like this (as shown in Figure 10-6):

```
gradient = context.createRadialGradient(355, 85, 0, 355, 85, 150)
```

Note   The second radius value of 150 pixels creates a circle with a diameter of 300 pixels. But note that although this circle extends beyond the area being filled and well into the previous rectangle, the other rectangle is not affected. This is because the gradient applies only to future fills, and not to any pre-existing fills.

The `addColorStop()` Function

Now that you've seen how to create two different types of gradient fills, let's look at how to modify these to stretch areas of a color and provide nonlinear fills, and to also incorporate colors.

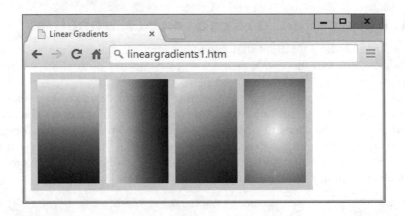

FIGURE 10-6 The radius of the gradient fill has been substantially increased.

The way to do this is to modify the values passed to the addColorStop() function, and to add more of them to create in-between steps. For example, here's the code that created the first rectangle in Figures 10-2 to 10-6:

```
gradient = context.createLinearGradient(55, 10, 55, 160)
gradient.addColorStop(0, '#FFF')
gradient.addColorStop(1, '#000')
context.fillStyle = gradient
context.fillRect(10, 10, 90, 150)
```

The two lines of importance are the second and third, in which the position is either 0 or 1 (for the start and the end) and the two colors of #FFF (for white) and #000 (for black), which I will now change as follows, to create the rectangle shown in Figure 10-7:

```
gradient.addColorStop(0, '#F00')
gradient.addColorStop(1, 'yellow')
```

FIGURE 10-7 This linear gradient smoothly changes from red to yellow.

Note I used both types of color values supported by the `addColorStop()` function; a hexadecimal string (in this instance three digits, but it could have been six), and a color name (in this case `yellow`).

Now let's modify the gradient applied to the second rectangle used in the previous examples, by keeping it grayscale, but adding an additional stop point and color value:

```
gradient.addColorStop(0.0, '#FFF')
gradient.addColorStop(0.2, '#555')
gradient.addColorStop(1.0, '#000')
```

Here, in the second line, a very dark gray color with the value #555 has been applied at position 0.2, which is only 20 percent into the gradient. This forces the left 20 percent to quickly fade from #FFF to #555, and then the remaining 80 percent fades more slowly from #555 to #000, as shown in Figure 10-8.

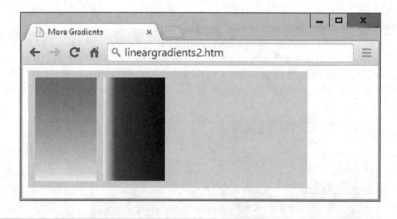

FIGURE 10-8 The first 20 percent of the gradient fades far more quickly than the final 80 percent.

You can include more stops if you like, and they can be any colors you like. So I have chosen to use a rainbow of colors for the third rectangle, like this, with the result shown in Figure 10-9:

```
gradient.addColorStop(0.00, 'red')
gradient.addColorStop(0.16, 'orange')
gradient.addColorStop(0.33, 'yellow')
gradient.addColorStop(0.50, 'green')
gradient.addColorStop(0.66, 'blue')
gradient.addColorStop(0.83, 'indigo')
gradient.addColorStop(1.00, 'violet')
```

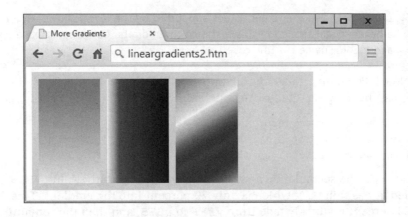

FIGURE 10-9 A rainbow of colors is applied to the third rectangle's gradient fill.

And remember that all these fills apply equally well to radial gradient fills, so I have chosen to reapply the same rainbow gradient used in the third rectangle to the fill in the final rectangle (but with a radius of 75 pixels to allow the circle to touch the top and bottom edges and show more of the fill), with the result shown in Figure 10-10.

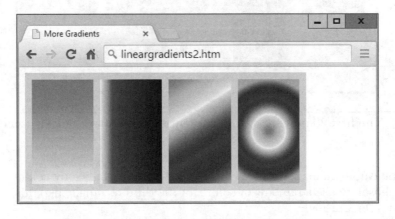

FIGURE 10-10 The rainbow gradient fill is applied radially to the final rectangle.

Using Patterns

In the final part of this lesson I'll show you how to use patterns on an HTML5 canvas, which you can apply instead of a plain or gradient fill by simply modifying the details you pass to the `fillStyle` property, and using the same `fillRect()` or other fill functions.

The `createPattern()` Function

To create a pattern, you need to supply a pre-existing image such as a *jpeg*, *png,* or *gif* file, and the type of repetition to use when applying the fill, out of the following options:

- **repeat**   Repeat the image both vertically and horizontally.
- **repeat-x**   Repeat the image horizontally.
- **repeat-y**   Repeat the image vertically.
- **no-repeat**   Do not repeat the image.

For example, the following code loads in the image *smiley-50.png* and then uses it as a fill for the first rectangle:

```
image     = new Image()
image.src = 'smiley-50.png'

image.onload = function()
{
  pattern = context.createPattern(image, 'repeat')
  context.fillStyle = pattern
  context.fillRect(10, 10, 90, 150)
}
```

This code requires some explaining (especially if you are new to JavaScript). What is happening is that in the first line a new object called `image` is created using the JavaScript `Image()` function and the keyword `new`. This new object then has the value of its `src` attribute set to `smiley-50.png`, which is a file already saved into the same folder.

Then the `onload` event of the image has a function attached to it. But what does this mean? Well, the `image` object has various attributes such as its width and height, the source from where it is loaded and, in this instance, `onload`. However, the `onload` attribute is known as an *event* because it is handled in a special manner such that only when the image has been fully loaded from its source is the event called.

To handle the event when it is called, a function is attached that will access the canvas and do the pattern filling. Within the function (inside its curly braces), there are three lines of code, and here you should be back in familiar territory, because the first one is simply a call to `createPattern()` specifying the `image` object and a value of `repeat`, indicating how the image should be used, the result of which is placed in the new object called `pattern`.

The final two lines simply apply this `pattern` object to the `fillStyle` property and then call the `fillRect()` function to use that fill on a rectangle (whose top-left corner is at 10,10) and with a width of 90 pixels and height of 150 pixels. The result is shown in Figure 10-11.

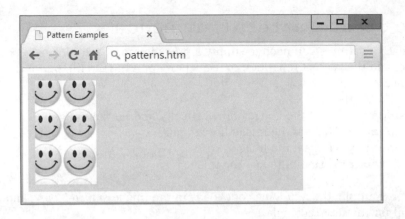

FIGURE 10-11 The rectangle has been filled with a repeating smiley image.

 If the function is not attached to the image's onload event, and the code is simply called from outside of the function, then you run the risk that the image may not be fully loaded when you make the call to the fill command, and therefore the call may fail. This is a standard issue with JavaScript and external images that you must always consider, and so wherever such an image is loaded in, you are recommended to attach the code that will use it to the onload event of the image.

In the figure you can see that the first smiley image is not fully within the rectangle. This is because the fill area is considered to be the entire canvas, and therefore the fill commences at the top left of the canvas (location 0,0), but is only revealed within the constraints of the fill area.

Using the value of repeat-x for the repetition results in Figure 10-12, repeat-y results in Figure 10-13, and no-repeat results in Figure 10-14.

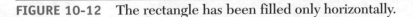

FIGURE 10-12 The rectangle has been filled only horizontally.

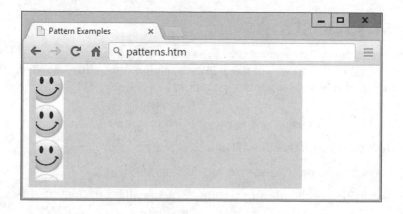

FIGURE 10-13 The rectangle has been filled only vertically.

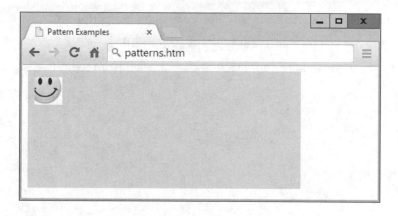

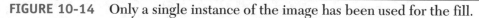

FIGURE 10-14 Only a single instance of the image has been used for the fill.

Summary

At this point you already have substantial ability to work with the HTML5 canvas, and will be able to draw on these concepts in the following lesson, which moves on to writing text (including using gradients and pattern fills), drawing lines and curves, drawing with images, and more.

Self-Test Questions

Test how much you have learned in this lesson with these questions. If you don't know an answer, go back and reread the relevant section until your knowledge is complete. You can find the answers in the appendix.

1. Which function is used to create a filled rectangle?

2. How can you change the fill color?

3. How can you draw a clear rectangle?

4. With which function can you draw a rectangular outline?

5. How can you create a linear gradient?

6. How do you create a radial gradient?

7. How do you specify the colors in a gradient?

8. With which function can you use an image for a pattern fill?

9. What are the four different types of pattern fill?

10. How do you ensure an image has been loaded before you use it?

Writing Text to the Canvas

 To view the accompanying video for this lesson, please visit mhprofessional.com/ nixonhtml5/.

This lesson continues our exploration of the HTML5 canvas by looking at how you can write text to it, including using a variety of fonts and styles, as well as incorporating the various fill styles covered in the previous lesson.

Many of these examples draw on those in Lesson 10, so you may wish to refer back to that from time to time as you work your way through this one.

Writing Text

HTML 4.01 provides some handy tags for setting font sizes, colors, and faces, and CSS gives you even more control over how these are applied, including using effects such as shadowing. But when you want absolutely precise control over how your text should display, the canvas has what you need. Also, although you can use CSS to overlay text on top of a canvas, you can't use it to layer text into a canvas, or to apply the gradient and pattern fill effects that the canvas supports.

The `font` Property

Let's look at the `font` property first, and see how to select the font face to use. As ever, I am assuming that if you follow these examples yourself, you have also included the `O()` and `S()` functions and the code to create a 2D context on the canvas in an object with the name `context`. To recap, your code should look something like this:

```
<canvas id='example' width='410' height='170'></canvas>

<script>
```

```
canvas               = O('example')
S(canvas).background = '#ddd'


// Enter the examples from this lesson
// so that they replace these comments


// The O() and S() functions go here,
// or in another script section
</script>
```

The width and height of 410 by 170 pixels shown will be suitable for all the examples, and this code will create a light gray background behind the canvas so that its position and dimensions are clearly visible. You must place the O() and S() functions somewhere in your document within a `<script>` section for these examples to work.

So, first, let's choose a font, like this:

```
context.font = '72pt Arial'
```

And that's it—when you write the text to the canvas, it will be in 72-point Arial.

Font Size Measurement Units

You can also use other measurement units for your font sizes, which can be either relative or fixed. Here's the full list of supported relative font units:

- **em** Ems: Based on the default preference set in the browser.
- **ex** X-height: Based on the height of the lowercase x character.
- **px** Pixels: Based on the resolution of the screen.
- **%** Percentage (similar to em): Based on the default preference of the browser.

And the fixed units are:

- **in** Inches: Imperial measurement.
- **cm** Centimeters: Metric measurement equivalent to one 100th of a meter.
- **mm** Millimeters: Metric measurement equivalent to one 10th of a centimeter.
- **pt** Points: A print unit.
- **pc** Picas: Another print unit.

Therefore the following examples are all valid:

```
context.font = '3em Helvetica'
context.font = '16px Impact'
context.font = '150% Courier'
context.font = '10mm Times'
context.font = '72pt Arial'
```

The `strokeText()` Function

Of course, you now need a way to write text in the newly selected font to the canvas, and you can do that using the `strokeText()` function, like this (which results in Figure 11-1):

```
context.strokeText('Hello!', 20, 120)
```

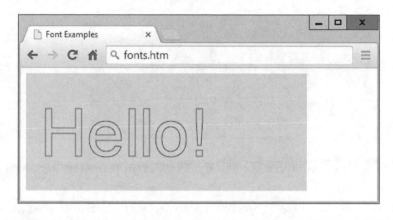

FIGURE 11-1   Seventy-two-point outlined text displayed on an HTML5 canvas

And that's how easy it is to get text onto a canvas. Simply set the font property to the font and size to use and then (for an outlined font) call `strokeText()`, passing the text to display and the location where the bottom-left corner of the text should appear by default, although you will see next how you can choose a different horizontal alignment with the `textAlign` property, and use the `textBaseline` property to specify the offset of the text relative to the vertical coordinate supplied.

The `textAlign` Property

But there's more to writing text to a canvas than that because there are three properties you can pass values to that will further customize the way text appears. For example, using the `textAlign` property, you can specify the alignment of the text out of the values `start`, `end`, `left`, `right`, and `center`. So, to center some text, you could set the property like this:

```
context.textAlign = 'center'
context.strokeText('Hello!', 205, 120)
```

As you may have noticed, in order to properly center the text, the call to `strokeText()` needed its horizontal offset changed from 20 in the previous example to 205, because that is half the width of the canvas (which is 410 pixels wide), and the result is shown in Figure 11-2.

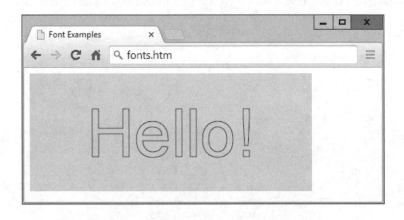

FIGURE 11-2 The text is centered using the `textAlign` property

Incidentally, with the `lineWidth` property, you can also change the width of any line drawn using any of the line-drawing functions (more about these in Lesson 12), and this also includes `strokeText()`. The following line of code increases the width to five pixels, as seen in Figure 11-3, where the previous example has been modified to create a very thick border.

```
context.lineWidth = 5
context.strokeText('Hello!', 205, 120)
```

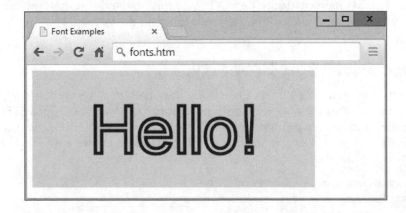

FIGURE 11-3 The border outline has been thickened to five pixels wide.

The `textBaseline` Property

When you draw text to the canvas, you must supply horizontal and vertical (x and y) coordinates for its top-left corner. Using the `textBaseline` property, you can choose the vertical offset (or y value) at which text will be displayed from this location.

- **top**   Aligns the top of the text to the y value.
- **middle**   Aligns the middle of the text to the y value.
- **bottom**   Aligns the bottom of the text to the y value.
- **alphabetic**   Aligns the alphabetic baseline of the text to the y value.
- **hanging**   Similar to `top`.
- **ideographic**   Similar to `alphabetic`.

Figure 11-4 illustrates using the first four preceding values for this property, as in the following lines of code, which write the word "top" using the `textBaseline` value of `top`. The hanging and `ideographic` values are offset by a tiny amount from `top` and `alphabetic` respectively   the best way to see whether you need these values is to try them for yourself.

```
context.textBaseline = 'top'
context.strokeText('top', 0, 100)
```

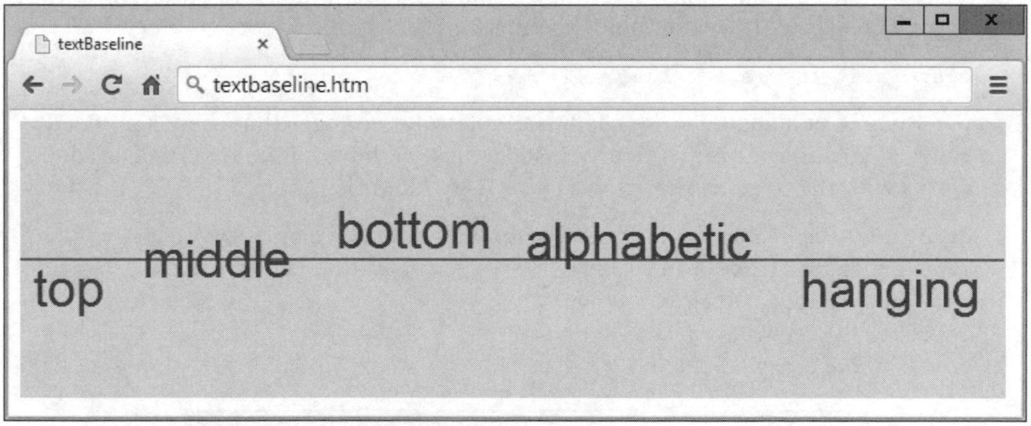

FIGURE 11-4   Vertically aligning text using the `textBaseline` property

The `fillText()` Function

In the same way that you can use `strokeText()` in a similar fashion to `strokeRect()` (as detailed in the previous lesson), you can also use `fillText()` to create solid, gradient, and pattern-filled text, just as you can provide those types of fills to rectangles with the `fillRect()` function.

To show how this works, here's some code to write the word HTML5 in a big and bold black color since no fill color has been specified (so the default of black is used), as shown in Figure 11-5:

```
context.font = '116pt Impact'
context.fillText('HTML5', 0, 150)
```

FIGURE 11-5   A 116-point font filled in with the color black

Now let's look at applying different colors, gradient fills, and patterns, starting by simply changing the text to blue, like this:

```
context.fillStyle = 'blue'
```

By now you should be so used to simple color changes that there's no need to show the result of this in a figure. Instead let's see how a simple vertical gradient works with the font (as shown in Figure 11-6), like this:

```
gradient = context.createLinearGradient(205,25, 205, 150)
gradient.addColorStop(0, '#FFF')
gradient.addColorStop(1, '#000')
context.fillStyle = gradient
context.fillText('HTML5', 0, 150)
```

FIGURE 11-6   The solid fill has been replaced with a gradient.

Note As explained in the previous lesson, you can set the start and end point of the gradient to any locations within (or even outside of) the canvas, allowing you to create a wider variety of effects than if they were limited to simply applying it under the object being drawn.

Using the rainbow color gradient from the previous lesson but applying it creatively as a radial gradient allows the effect of a real rainbow to be applied as the fill effect, like this, which displays as Figure 11-7:

```
gradient = context.createRadialGradient(205, 230, 120, 205, 230, 240)
gradient.addColorStop(0.00, 'red')
gradient.addColorStop(0.16, 'orange')
gradient.addColorStop(0.33, 'yellow')
gradient.addColorStop(0.50, 'green')
gradient.addColorStop(0.66, 'blue')
gradient.addColorStop(0.83, 'indigo')
gradient.addColorStop(1.00, 'violet')
context.fillStyle = gradient
context.fillText('HTML5', 0, 150)
```

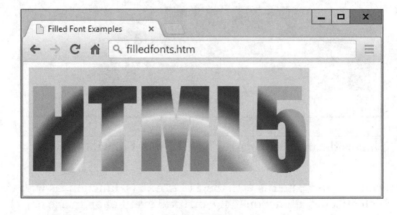

FIGURE 11-7 Creating a rainbow effect with a radial gradient

In this example, a vertical offset of 230 pixels from the top of the canvas was selected. This places the center of the radial gradients at a location 60 pixels below the bottom of the canvas. This allows only a top portion of the rainbow to be used for the fill. If you select radius values of 120 pixels for the inner gradient and 240 for the outer one, the rainbow is 120 pixels wide. However, due to the way the fill works, the areas inside and outside of this section are set to the initial and final color values, so that the inside is red and the outside is violet.

If this is not the effect required, it is a simple matter to surround the initial and final colors with white (or whichever colors you prefer), and make room for them by slightly adjusting the addColorStop values of the previous start and end colors, like this:

```
gradient.addColorStop(0.00, 'white')  // Clear inner to white
gradient.addColorStop(0.01, 'red')    // Changed from 0.00
gradient.addColorStop(0.16, 'orange')
gradient.addColorStop(0.33, 'yellow')
gradient.addColorStop(0.50, 'green')
gradient.addColorStop(0.66, 'blue')
gradient.addColorStop(0.83, 'indigo')
gradient.addColorStop(0.99, 'violet') // Changed from 1.00
gradient.addColorStop(1.00, 'white')  // Clear outer to white
```

As shown in Figure 11-8, this results in only the rainbow itself being displayed.

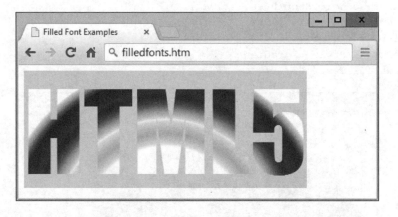

FIGURE 11-8 The inside and outside areas have been set to white.

You can also use patterns with the fillText() function, as with the following code, which attaches a function to the onload event of an image object called image that uses a marble pattern from the file *marble.jpg* (to ensure that the code runs only after the image has fully loaded):

```
context.font = '116pt Impact'
image        = new Image()
image.src    = 'marble.jpg'

image.onload = function()
{
  pattern            = context.createPattern(image, 'no-repeat')
  context.fillStyle = pattern
  context.fillText('HTML5', 0, 150)
}
```

The image is then processed using the `createPattern()` function with a setting of `no-repeat`, and passed to a new object called `pattern`. In turn, `pattern` is supplied as the value for the `fillStyle` property, which is then used to fill the text using the `fillText()` function. The result of this can be seen in Figure 11-9.

FIGURE 11-9   The text has now been filled with a pattern.

In this instance the image used for the fill pattern is larger than the canvas, so there is no need to repeat (or tile) it. But if you have a smaller image that will tile well, you can repeat it horizontally, vertically, or in both directions. See Lesson 10 for more details on how to create and use patterns.

Determining Text Width

Sometimes you need to know how wide some text will be in order to best position it. To find out this value, set all the properties as you would before writing the text and then issue statements such as the following, which creates an object called `metrics` into which information about the text is stored.

As illustrated by the following example (see Figure 11-10), the `width` property of `metrics` then holds the width of the text in pixels, which is displayed by the JavaScript `alert()` function (which pops up a small window containing the string in parentheses following the `alert` function name, namely some text surrounding the `width` property):

```
metrics = context.measureText('HTML5')
alert('Text width: ' + metrics.width + ' pixels')
```

The object returned by the `measureText()` function currently only supports the `width` property.

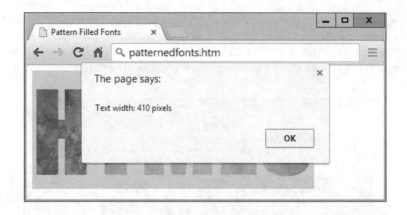

FIGURE 11-10   Displaying the width of some text

Summary

With creating text now in your toolkit, in the following lesson we will return to looking at some of the drawing tools, this time ones that use paths to create lines, so that you have fine control over all the straight lines, shapes, and curves you could want. And in the lesson after that, I'll show you how you can use an image as a paintbrush, how to add shadow effects, and how to manipulate each and any of the pixels (individual dots) in a canvas.

Self-Test Questions

Test how much you have learned in this lesson with these questions. If you don't know an answer, go back and reread the relevant section until your knowledge is complete. You can find the answers in the appendix.

1. How do you choose the font for writing to a canvas?

2. With which function can you write outlined text to a canvas?

3. What are the relative measurement units supported by the canvas?

4. What are the fixed measurement units supported by the canvas?

5. Which function allows you to write filled text to a canvas?

6. How could you center-align text on a canvas?

7. Which text alignment values are supported by `textAlign`?

8. How can you change the horizontal line about which text will be based?

9. Which values are supported for altering this base line?

10. How can you discover the width in pixels that a text-writing call will require?

12

Drawing Lines, Paths, and Curves

 To view the accompanying video for this lesson, please visit mhprofessional.com/nixonhtml5/.

I n this lesson I'll be showing you how you can customize all the functions that draw using lines, such as `strokeRect()` and `strokeText()` (which you've already seen), as well as the line-drawing functions, and how to use paths to create complicated patterns and curves. All example files used in this (and every other) lesson can be downloaded from 20lessons.com.

Drawing Lines

The HTML5 canvas supports line drawing using many different styles because you can precisely specify the width of lines with the `lineWidth` property (as you have previously seen), and can also set properties such as `lineCap`, `lineJoin`, and `miterLimit`.

The `lineWidth` Property

You previously encountered the `lineWidth` property in Lesson 11 where it was used to thicken the line width used in a call to the `strokeText()` function. What this property does is change the line width for future operations that use line drawing, including `strokeText()` and `stroke()` (detailed a little later).

For example, the following command sets the `lineWidth` property to 10 pixels, as seen in the horizontal and angled lines in Figure 12-1 (for comparison the thin, vertical lines in the figure are one pixel wide):

```
context.lineWidth = 10
```

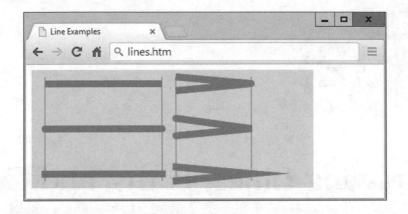

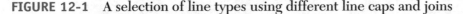

FIGURE 12-1   A selection of line types using different line caps and joins

The `lineCap` Property

Using the `lineCap` property, you can choose the way the starts and ends of lines are displayed. This is known as their *line cap*, and hence the `lineCap` property name, which can be any value out of `butt`, `round`, and `square`, as shown in the left half of Figure 12-1, and used like these examples:

```
context.lineCap = 'butt'
context.lineCap = 'round'
context.lineCap = 'square'
```

The top line on the left of the figure uses the `lineCap` value of `butt` in which the ends butt up exactly against the vertical lines I have drawn (for comparing the line cap types), indicating the start and end points of each line. If no value is given to the `lineCap` property, it assumes a default value of `butt`.

The middle line uses a `lineCap` property of `round` and, as you can see, it therefore extends past the left and right edges, with the center point of the rounded cap being the end points of the line.

The bottom line uses the value `square` for the `lineCap` property, which is almost the same as `round`, in that the centers of the squares are the end points of the line.

The `lineJoin` Property

The `lineJoin` property is similar to the `lineCap` property, but it applies only at the points at which lines are joined. It supports the values of `round`, `bevel`, and `miter`, as you can see by looking at the joins of the three right-hand pairs of lines in Figure 12-1, in which the end caps are the same as the lines on the left. Following are examples of setting this property:

```
context.lineJoin = 'round'
context.lineJoin = 'bevel'
context.lineJoin = 'miter'
```

However, the top pair of lines uses the value round for the lineJoin property, the middle pair uses the value bevel, and the bottom one uses the value miter.

The miterLimit Property

In order to achieve the sharp miter in the bottom-right pair of lines in Figure 12-1, it was necessary to use the miterLimit property, giving it a value of 12, in order to allow the quite sharp angle to extend far enough. Here is how you would set this property:

```
context.miterLimit = 12
```

 Note If miterLimit is not set to a sufficiently large enough value for a miter, then mitered joins will simply use the bevel value instead, so if you are having trouble with your miters, simply increase the value you supply for miterLimit until the miter displays.

Drawing with Paths

Figure 12-1 was created using a combination of line properties (as described in the previous section), along with a combination of path-handling functions. Using them, it is easy to move an imaginary pen to a start location, define a path it must follow, and then tell it to draw along that path using the properties already set up for it such as width, caps, joins, and color, as described next.

The beginPath() and closePath() Functions

Every path created for an HTML5 canvas must start with a call to beginPath(), and end with a call to closePath(), like this:

```
context.beginPath()
// Path instructions go here
context.closePath()
```

Think of them as being like opening and closing HTML tags. Once a path is created, you can make it display, but first let's look at how to create one.

The moveTo() and lineTo() Functions

The first step in a path is generally to move to a location on the canvas so, for example, to move to the location 20,20, you would issue this command:

```
context.moveTo(20, 20)
```

To then specify that a line should be drawn (once the path is completed), you can then issue a command such as the following, which will specify that the next part of the path is to draw a line from the current location 20,20 to 390,20:

```
context.lineTo(390, 20)
```

Let's look at the path used to draw a rectangle, including the opening and closing path function calls:

```
context.beginPath()
context.moveTo( 20,   20)
context.lineTo(390,   20)
context.lineTo(390,  150)
context.lineTo( 20,  150)
context.lineTo( 20,   20)
context.closePath()
```

The `stroke()` Function

Once you have a path created, you can draw it on the canvas using the `stroke()` function like this, which in the case of the current example displays as Figure 12-2:

```
context.stroke()
```

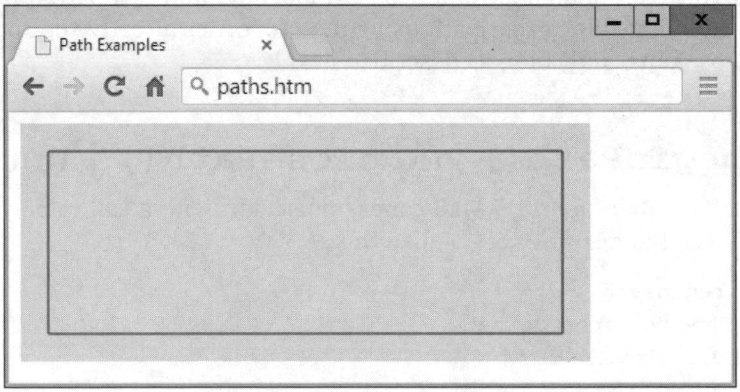

FIGURE 12-2 A rectangle drawn using a path

And there you have it. The path has been processed by the `stroke()` function and all the parts in the path are now drawn.

The `rect()` Function

If all you wanted to draw in the first instance was a rectangle, then there's a quicker way to do this than defining an entire path. Instead you can use the `rect()` function with a path, like this:

```
context.beginPath()
context.rect(40, 40, 330, 90)
context.closePath()
context.stroke()
```

The top left-hand corner of the rectangle is specified by the first two arguments in the function call, and the second two contain the width and height of the rectangle. The end result is shown in Figure 12-3, in which both rectangles (from the previous and current examples) have been combined and created within the same path, as follows:

```
context.beginPath()
context.moveTo( 20,  20)
context.lineTo(390,  20)
context.lineTo(390, 150)
context.lineTo( 20, 150)
context.lineTo( 20,  20)
context.rect(40, 40, 330, 90)
context.closePath()
context.stroke()
```

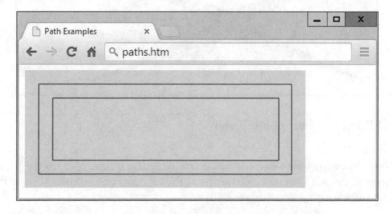

FIGURE 12-3   The two rectangles are created from a single path.

The `fill()` Function

Using the `fill()` function, you can fill in any area bounded by a path. For example, the following code creates a four-pointed star, which is then filled in, as shown in Figure 12-4:

```
context.beginPath()
context.moveTo(0,     0)
context.lineTo(205,   65)
context.lineTo(410,    0)
context.lineTo(225,   85)
context.lineTo(410,  170)
context.lineTo(205,  105)
context.lineTo(0,    170)
context.lineTo(185,   85)
context.lineTo(0,      0)
context.closePath()
context.fill()
```

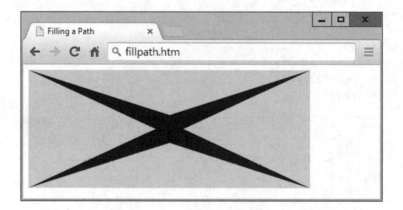

FIGURE 12-4   Filling in a four-pointed star

If you don't fully enclose the shape by drawing a line back to the start point, the function still does a very good attempt at filling only the shape by making that final link for you before performing the fill.

The `clip()` Function

When creating a path, you can choose to constrain the drawing area using the `clip()` function to select any area of the canvas, so that any part that would be drawn outside of this area will be ignored, and only parts of the path that fall inside the clipped area will be used.

The clip() function works on a path in the same way as the stroke() or fill() functions. For example, the following code creates a diamond-shaped path, which is then revealed with a simple call to stroke(), as shown in Figure 12-5, in which the diamond has been drawn over the star shape:

```
context.beginPath()
context.moveTo(0,     85)
context.lineTo(205,    0)
context.lineTo(410,   85)
context.lineTo(205,  170)
context.lineTo(0,     85)
context.closePath()
context.stroke()
```

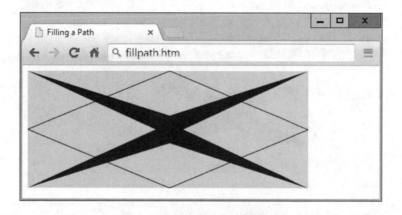

FIGURE 12-5   The diamond path is drawn on top of the star pattern.

However, by placing the diamond path before the star shape is drawn, and using the clip() function on it after the stroke() function, this path becomes a bounded area, outside of which future path-related functions cannot draw, as with the following code (the result of which is shown in Figure 12-6):

```
context.beginPath()
context.moveTo(0,     85)
context.lineTo(205,    0)
context.lineTo(410,   85)
context.lineTo(205,  170)
context.lineTo(0,     85)
context.closePath()
context.stroke()
context.clip()
```

```
context.beginPath()
context.moveTo(0,        0)
context.lineTo(205,     65)
context.lineTo(410,      0)
context.lineTo(225,     85)
context.lineTo(410,    170)
context.lineTo(205,    105)
context.lineTo(0,      170)
context.lineTo(185,     85)
context.lineTo(0,        0)
context.closePath()
context.fill()
```

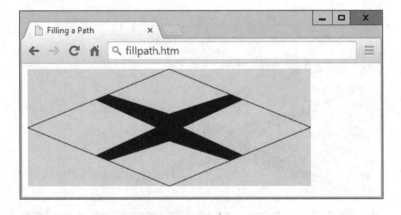

FIGURE 12-6 The diamond is both drawn and used in a `clip()` call.

If you want to use a path for constraint only, and not actually draw it, simply omit the call to `stroke()` from the previous example, and the result is Figure 12-7.

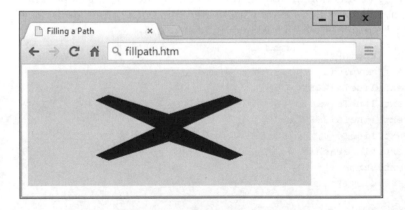

FIGURE 12-7 Only the star shape is drawn, constrained by the diamond area.

Or, perhaps you simply may wish to give the diamond shape a border, fill it with one color, and then fill the area of the star within that shape in another color, which is easily achieved by placing the relevant fillStyle assignments before the drawing commands, as shown in Figure 12-8. I'll leave it up to you to work out how to achieve this effect—it's very simple (or you can view the commented code in the accompanying example files, downloadable using the link at the start of this lesson).

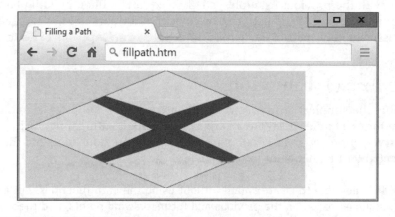

FIGURE 12-8   The diamond is filled, as is the portion of the star within it.

Note   You may, of course, use any types of fill on a path as well as the solid color fills, including linear and radial gradients and patterns. Simply assign the relevant value to the fillStyle property before making a fill.

The `isPointInPath()` Function

Sometimes you need to know whether a particular point lies in a path you have constructed. However, you will normally only want to use this function if you are quite proficient with JavaScript. You will generally call it as part of a conditional statement, like this:

```
if (isPointInPath(100, 123))
{
    // Do something here
}
```

If the location specified lies along any of the points in the path, the function returns the value true and the contents of the if() statement are executed. Otherwise, the value false is returned and the contents of the if() statement do not get executed.

Creating Curves

I leapt a little ahead of myself by showing you how to fill in and clip paths, but I wanted to show you some of the fun you could have with them and I couldn't resist. So now (slightly out of order), here are some more path functions you can use, this time for creating arcs, circles, and complex curves.

As with the previous examples, all of these can be filled in with plain colors, gradient or radial fills and patterns, or you can draw curves using stroke functions and their associated properties such as `lineWidth`, `lineCap`, and `lineJoin`.

The `arc()` Function

Probably the simplest form of curve is the arc, which is simply a segment of the perimeter of a circle. To create an arc, you include it within a path with the start of the curve connected to the final point on the path previous to it, and the curve's end connected to the next point in the path after it.

 It is possible to create an arc without using the path functions, but a path will be assumed based on the previous and future drawing points, and these will connect up to it. So for precise control, I recommend always using it inside a path.

You must provide six arguments to the function: a pair of coordinates representing the center of the circle upon which the arc is based, the radius required, the radian offset value for the start of the arc, a radiant offset value for the end of the arc, and then a value indicating whether to draw the arc clockwise or counterclockwise. Let's look at these in turn.

- **X and Y coordinates**   The coordinates for an arc are simply the horizontal and vertical offset from the top-left corner of the canvas for the center of the circle, such as 205,85, which is 205 pixels in from the left, and 85 pixels down from the top of the canvas.
- **Radius**   This is a value in pixels representing the distance from the center of the circle to its perimeter (or circumference). This is the location at which the arc will be drawn. For example, the value 75 states that the arc will be drawn at a distance of 75 pixels from the center of the circle.
- **Radian offsets**   These specify the start and end position on the circle's perimeter between which the arc should be created. A value of 0 radians specifies the three o'clock position directly to the right of the circle's center. A radian has the value 180 ÷ π (the equivalent of about 57 degrees), and so there are π × 2 radians in a complete circle of 360 degrees. This means that to draw a quarter circle (for example), from the three o'clock to six o'clock positions, you would use an initial value of 0 radians, and a second value of π ÷ 2 radians. For a semicircle, the second value would be π radians, and for a circle it would be π × 2 radians. Remember that π is the number of times the diameter of a circle fits into its circumference (or about 3.1415927 in decimal).

- **Direction**   To create a clockwise arc, the final argument must have a value of `false`, which is the default value if you omit this argument. For a counterclockwise arc, it should be `true`.

So, for example, the following code draws four segments of a pie, with the final one filled in using the `fill()` function, rather than drawn using the `stroke()` function, as shown in Figure 12-9:

```
context.beginPath()
context.moveTo(55, 85)
context.arc(55,  85, 45, 0, Math.PI / 2)
context.closePath()
context.stroke()

context.beginPath()
context.moveTo(155, 85)
context.arc(155, 85, 45, 0, Math.PI)
context.closePath()
context.stroke()

context.beginPath()
context.moveTo(255, 85)
context.arc(255, 85, 45, 0, Math.PI / 2 * 3)
context.closePath()
context.stroke()

context.beginPath()
context.moveTo(355, 85)
context.arc(355, 85, 45, 0, Math.PI * 2)
context.closePath()
context.fill()
```

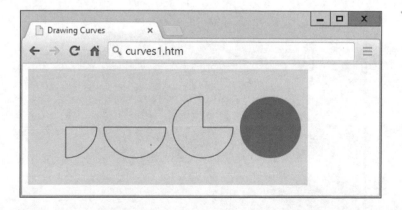

FIGURE 12-9   Arcs created with the `arc()` function

Math.PI is a convenient way to refer to the value of π using JavaScript. The first image in the figure uses radian values of 0 and Math.PI / 2, the second image, uses 0 and Math.PI, the third image, uses 0 and Math.PI / 2 * 3, and the fourth image uses Math.PI * 2. In each case, a call to moveTo() moves the path starting point to the center of the circle, then the next point in the path is the start of the arc, followed by the arc's end, and then the initial starting point again. By doing this, a slice of the circle is created to clearly show the arcs. In the final image the fill() function was used to illustrate how you can use that instead of stroke() if you wish, as well as the linear, gradient, and pattern fills.

If you wish to draw only the arc portion of the images in Figure 12-9, then you need to close the path *after* issuing the call to the stroke() function, and you do not need to first move the path start to the center of each circle. So you could use code such as this (which results in Figure 12-10):

```
context.beginPath()
context.arc(55,  85, 45, 0, Math.PI / 2)
context.stroke()
context.closePath()

context.beginPath()
context.arc(155, 85, 45, 0, Math.PI)
context.stroke()
context.closePath()

context.beginPath()
context.arc(255, 85, 45, 0, Math.PI / 2 * 3)
context.stroke()
context.closePath()

context.beginPath()
context.arc(355, 85, 45, 0, Math.PI * 2)
context.stroke()
context.closePath()
```

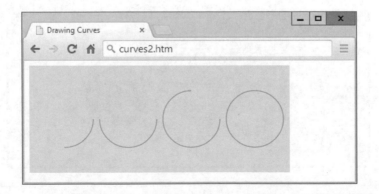

FIGURE 12-10 Only the arcs are now drawn.

For this example, I chose not to fill in the final circle so you can see how to draw a complete, outlined circle. Remember too that you can change the stroke width and other properties by assigning the relevant values to the `strokeStyle` property.

If you wish to draw the arcs in a counterclockwise direction, you can change the final argument in the call to `arc()` to `true`. The result is shown in Figure 12-11, in which you will note that you always get a full circle for image four, regardless of the direction of drawing.

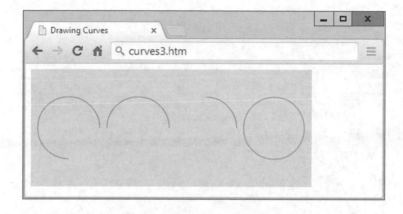

FIGURE 12-11   Drawing the arcs in a counterclockwise direction

The `arcTo()` Function

There's another way you can draw an arc, which is to use the `arcTo()` function, which draws a curve based on the current location the path has reached, and arguments that you supply to it representing a pair of imaginary tangent lines touching the circle's perimeter.

For example, let's assume that the current path position has been achieved using a `moveTo()` call, like this, which places the start position of the path at the bottom-left corner of the canvas:

```
context.beginPath()
context.moveTo(0, 170)
```

Now a curve can be created with its start point at this location and an end point at location 170,0, like this:

```
context.arcTo(0, 0, 170, 0, 170)
```

So, we have the start point of 0,170 from the `moveTo()` call, and end point of 170,0 being the third and fourth arguments to `arcTo()`, but what about the first two and final arguments in the `arcTo()` call?

Well, the first two arguments of 0,0 in the `arcTo()` call represent the end point of an imaginary tangent line starting at 0,170 and ending at 0,0. Then the third and fourth arguments (as well as being the end point for the arc) represent the end of a tangent line drawn from 0,0 to 170,0.

The points where these two tangents meet the circle's circumference are the arc's start and end points and, because a tangent must always be at a right angle to the radius of a circle, the arc to create can now be calculated. Let's see how this works by first drawing the imaginary lines, with the following code, as shown in Figure 12-12:

```
context.beginPath()
context.moveTo(0, 170)
context.lineTo(0,    0)
context.lineTo(170, 0)
context.stroke()
context.closePath()
```

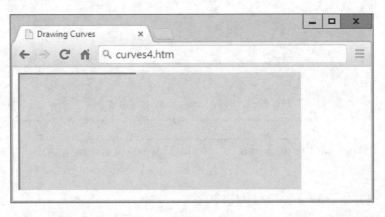

FIGURE 12-12 Two lines have been drawn, which are tangential to the circle.

The first line sets a green color to differentiate from the arc that will be drawn in a moment. Then a simple path is created to draw the two lines, which are simply to show where the imaginary tangents would be if they were displayed, so the preceding code is only for illustrative purposes. The arcTo() code is as follows, and results in Figure 12-13:

```
context.beginPath()
context.moveTo(0, 170)
context.arcTo(0, 0, 170, 0, 170)
context.stroke()
context.closePath()
```

Figure 12-13 also serves to illustrate the purpose of the final argument to the arcTo() function, which is the radius of the circle on which the arc is based. In this example the two tangents are sides of a square (at 90 degrees to each other), and the arc is a quarter circle with a radius of 170 pixels (whose origin—or center—is therefore at location 170,170).

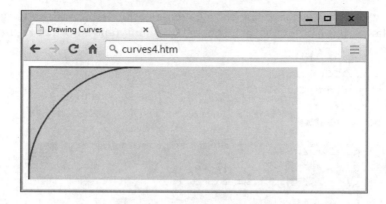

FIGURE 12-13 The arc has connected the end points of the pair of tangents.

 If this function baffles you, try playing with the examples on the companion website (at 20lessons.com), and you'll soon come to grips with how these tangents work.

The `quadraticCurveTo()` Function

In addition to arcs, you can even create the most fancy of curves using the function `quadraticCurveTo()`, which employs an imaginary attractor object that pulls the curve towards it. For example, let's draw a line between the left and right side of the canvas using a simple `stroke()` call, like this (as shown in Figure 12-14):

```
context.beginPath()
context.moveTo(0,    85)
context.lineTo(410,  85)
context.stroke()
context.closePath()
```

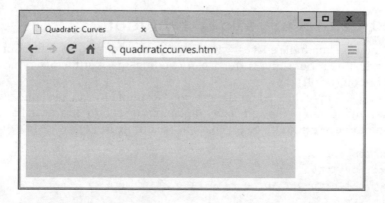

FIGURE 12-14 A simple horizontal line

Now let's draw a curved line between these positions, but with an imaginary attractor up in the top left-hand corner, at location 0,0, like this (and shown in Figure 12-15):

```
context.beginPath()
context.moveTo(0, 85)
context.quadraticCurveTo(0, 0, 410, 85)
context.stroke()
context.closePath()
```

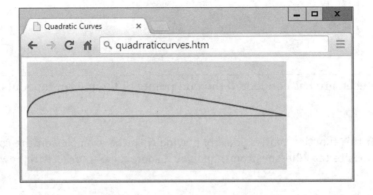

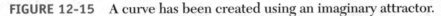

FIGURE 12-15 A curve has been created using an imaginary attractor.

As you can see from the figure, the entire curve has been pulled toward the attraction point as if the curve were made of an elasticized magnetic material being attracted toward a magnet. The further up the attractor is placed, the higher the curve will be pulled. Similarly, if the attractor is moved to the left or right, then the attraction will also move in that direction.

 Note Sometimes it takes a little trial and error to get just the curve you need, but you should soon get the hang of this function.

The `bezierCurveTo()` Function

If you thought quadratic curves were funky, then wait till you check out Bézier curves. These are similar but support the use of two imaginary attractors, which can be placed anywhere on (or off) the canvas.

For an example, let's adapt the previous example to add a second attractor at the bottom-right corner of the canvas by replacing the call to `quadraticCurveTo()` with one to `bezierCurveTo()`, like this (resulting in Figure 12-16):

```
context.beginPath()
context.moveTo(0, 85)
context.bezierCurveTo(0, 0, 410, 170, 410, 85)
context.stroke()
context.closePath()
```

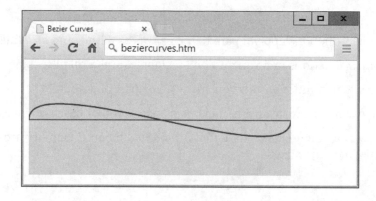

FIGURE 12-16 This curve has two imaginary attractors.

 Since you can place the pair of attractors anywhere you like (not necessarily at opposites sides of the curve), you can create any curve that is possible to draw using Bézier curves, although trial and error may again be required.

Summary

You now have all the line, curve, and path tools added to your toolkit. Remember that you may create as complicated and lengthy paths as you like, and you are not limited to the small snippets of examples I have shown you in this lesson. When your code is properly implemented, you can create sketches and logos, or use the functions as part of a design program you can write in JavaScript.

In the following lesson I'll continue our journey into the vast resource that is the HTML5 canvas by showing you how to write on the canvas using images, how to apply shadows, and even manipulate pixels directly.

Self-Test Questions

Test how much you have learned in this lesson with these questions. If you don't know an answer, go back and reread the relevant section until your knowledge is complete. You can find the answers in the appendix.

1. With which property can you change the width of line drawing on the canvas?

2. How can you change the way lines start and end, and the way lines join to each other? And how can you extend the limit of mitered line joins?

3. How do you start and end a path?

4. How do you move the drawing position of a path without creating a line?

5. How do you create a line within a path?

6. Which functions apply a path to the canvas as a line, and as a filled area?

7. Which functions draw an outlined rectangle, and a filled rectangle?

8. With which function can you create all or part of a circle?

9. How can you create an arc from one point to another based on imaginary tangents?

10. How can you create a curve that is modified by an imaginary attractor? And two imaginary attractors?

Manipulating Images, Shadows, and Pixels

 To view the accompanying video for this lesson, please visit mhprofessional.com/ nixonhtml5/.

In this lesson I'll begin to look into the more advanced aspects of the HTML5 canvas, including drawing using images, adding shadows, and even directly manipulating the pixels (individual dots) of the canvas by their constituent primary colors of red, green, and blue, and their transparency too.

Using Images

On top of all the other drawing functions available to you for manipulating the HTML5 canvas, you have also seen how you can import an image to use as a fill pattern. In fact, you can also use images to draw directly on the canvas.

The **drawImage()** Function

Using the drawImage() function, you can load in an image such as a *jpg*, *gif*, or *png*, and draw it directly on the canvas, like this code, which draws it with its top-left corner at location 10,10, as displayed in Figure 13-1:

```
image     = new Image()
image.src = 'html5.png'

image.onload = function()
{
  context.drawImage(image, 10, 10)
}
```

FIGURE 13-1   An image is loaded in and placed on the canvas.

As you will recall from previous lessons, the `onload` event of the `image` object is attached to a function, whose code is executed only when the image has been fully loaded. If this were not the case, the image might not display.

In this instance only the first three parameters the function accepts have been used. These are the image to use and the horizontal and vertical location at which it should be displayed, so the image is displayed full size. However, it is also possible to resize the image before it is placed on the canvas by passing additional arguments, as with these two examples (with the resizing values highlighted in bold), the result of which is shown in Figure 13-2:

```
context.drawImage(image, 152, 10, 62, 70)
context.drawImage(image, 152, 90, 62, 70)
```

FIGURE 13-2   Two copies of the reduced image have been added.

Here the image has been reduced to just under a quarter of its original size by more than halving its dimensions, and then two copies have been placed alongside the original, one above the other. This version of the function call takes arguments in this order: the image to display, the horizontal and vertical location to display it, and the width and height to use for displaying it.

 When using rescaling on an image, you may not always get the sharpest anti-aliased results you could otherwise achieve by first resizing them in a graphics program. However, the results aren't bad and they are fast, and if you understand writing loops in JavaScript, you can even use them for animation.

But, as they say in the infomercials, there's more. Not only can you resize an image down, you can resize it up too. What's more, you can also choose which area of the image to use when doing so, and you are therefore not restricted to using the entire image.

For example, the original *html5.png* image used in these examples has dimensions of 132 by 150 pixels. Using the following line of code, a rectangular subsection of this image has been selected, enlarged, and placed to the right of the two smaller images, as shown in Figure 13-3:

```
context.drawImage(image, 23, 26, 86, 98, 224, 10, 118, 150)
```

FIGURE 13-3 The image has been cropped and enlarged before use.

You must be wary when using this version of the function call because, rather than adding parameters to the existing ones, four new arguments are inserted between the image argument and the ones in the previous examples. For example, in this instance the first four numeric arguments of 23, 26, 86, and 98 are two pairs, the first of which is the location of the top-left corner of the part of the image to crop, and the second pair are the width and height for the crop.

These values result in clipping out the number 5 from the image. Then the remaining four values are the same as in the previous examples. They are the horizontal and vertical location at which to place the cropped image, and the width and height to use for displaying it.

Using the Canvas as a Source Image

You are not restricted to using only external images within a canvas because you can copy sections of the canvas itself and write them back to it, even after cropping and/ or reducing or enlarging them.

For example, in the following code the left half of the canvas is captured, reduced in size, and copied to the top right of the canvas, as shown in Figure 13-4:

```
context.drawImage(canvas, 10, 10, 205, 150, 352, 10, 48, 35)
```

FIGURE 13-4 A portion of the image has been grabbed and reused.

This code works by referring to the canvas object in the first argument, rather than one for an external image. As you can see, the reduced images are looking quite jagged now, so it's probably worth doing your own resizing in an editor for major changes like this, although, as I previously mentioned, as part of an animation or transition effect, this function works just great.

Note The HTML5 specifications also call for being able to use an HTML video element for drawing on a canvas, but this doesn't seem to work on any of the browsers I have tested it with. Hopefully this feature will be operational soon as it would be really useful. In the meantime, if you are skilled with JavaScript, there are more complicated ways you can google to find out how to place video on a canvas.

Adding Shadows

The HTML canvas supports the addition of a shadow to any element that you draw on it with the use of a group of four properties you can set to specify a vertical and horizontal offset, the shadow blur, and its color, as follows:

- **shadowOffsetX** The horizontal offset in pixels that the shadow should be shifted to the right by (or to the left if the value is negative).

- **shadowOffsetY**   The vertical offset in pixels that the shadow should be shifted down by (or up if the value is negative).
- **shadowBlur**   The number of pixels over which to blur the shadow's outline.
- **shadowColor**   The base color to use for the shadow. If a blur is in use, this color will blend with the background in the blurred area.

For example, in the following (somewhat longer than usual) example code, four elements are drawn on the canvas using slightly different shadow properties, as shown in Figure 13-5.

```
image1 = new Image()
image2 = new Image()
image3 = new Image()
image4 = new Image()

image1.src = 'html5.png'
image2.src = 'smiley-50.pnq'
image3.src = 'mom.jpg'
image4.src = 'dad.jpg'

image1.onload = function() // HTML5 logo
{
  context.shadowOffsetX = 8
  context.shadowOffsetY = 8
  context.shadowBlur    = 8
  context.shadowColor   = '#000'
  context.drawImage(image1,  10, 10)
}

image2.onload = function() // Smiley image
{
  context.shadowOffsetX = 6
  context.shadowOffsetY = 6
  context.shadowBlur    = 6
  context.shadowColor   = '#333'
  context.drawImage(image2,  152, 10)
}

image3.onload = function() // Mom image
{
  context.shadowOffsetX = 4
  context.shadowOffsetY = 4
  context.shadowBlur    = 4
  context.shadowColor   = '#666'
  context.drawImage(image3,  212, 10, 90, 73)
}
```

```
image4.onload = function() // Dad image
{
  context.shadowOffsetX = 2
  context.shadowOffsetY = 2
  context.shadowBlur    = 2
  context.shadowColor   = '#999'
  context.drawImage(image4,  312, 10, 90, 73)
}

context.shadowOffsetX = 3  // "Hello" text
context.shadowOffsetY = 3
context.shadowBlur    = 5
context.shadowColor   = '#444'
context.font          = '38pt Arial'
context.fillStyle     = 'blue'
context.fillText('Hello', 152, 135)

context.shadowOffsetX = 0  // Outlined rectangle
context.shadowOffsetY = 0
context.shadowBlur    = 6
context.shadowColor   = '#000'
context.strokeStyle   = 'red'
context.lineWidth     = 3
context.strokeRect(280, 95, 120, 65)
```

FIGURE 13-5   A variety of elements using different shadow properties

I used a variety of elements in this example as they illustrate a number of different points. So let's look at them in turn, starting with the HTML5 logo.

The first thing you may notice with this image is that, unlike the other external images, this one doesn't have a colored background but, instead, features a transparent one. Note how the shadow properties make use of this and draw the shadow only around the nontransparent areas. This image also has the largest shadow set, with vertical and horizontal offsets and a blur area of eight pixels, and the background color used for the shadow is black (#000).

The following three external images all have white backgrounds and so the shadow forms around the outside edges of each image. In turn these images use shadow offsets and blur areas of six, four, and two pixels respectively. At the same time the background color for the shadow uses increasingly lighter shades of gray (#333, #666, and #999).

The word "Hello" is drawn in blue, 38-point Arial text, has a vertical and horizontal shadow offset of three pixels, and a blur area of five pixels. See how the shadow lifts it from the background.

Finally, the rectangle uses a line width of three pixels and is drawn in red. The shadow offsets are both 0 but the blur area is six pixels, and black (#000) has been used for the shadow background color. This makes the shadow appear both inside and outside the rectangle.

 Note   The rectangle at the bottom right of Figure 13-5 illustrates how you can create inner shadows, which aren't directly supported by the HTML5 canvas. Simply draw an object and specify a shadow that will appear inside that shape. Then draw another shape to cover over the outside shadows in the places where you don't want them. Alternatively, it may be easier to simply create a clipped area using the `clip()` function, to prevent any drawing such as the shadows from being made outside of this area. If you do so, remember to reset the clipped area back to the entire canvas when you're done.

Pixel Editing

We've now covered just about every conceivable drawing tool you could want for getting creative with the HTML5 canvas, but there's one more trick remaining in the magician's hat, and that's direct pixel editing.

Using the `getImageData()`, `putImageData()`, and `createImageData()` functions, in conjunction with the `data[]` array, you can directly manipulate the canvas at pixel level, even down to the red, green, blue, and transparency constituents of a pixel.

The `getImageData()` Function

Let's start by creating an image on a canvas (as shown in Figure 13-6) and then grabbing a portion of it with `getImageData()`, like this:

```
image     = new Image()
image.src = 'boat.png'

image.onload = function()
```

```
{
  context.drawImage(image, 0, 0)
  imagedata = context.getImageData(0, 0, 205, 170)
}
```

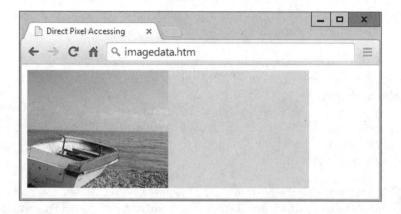

FIGURE 13-6 An image has been loaded, placed on the canvas, and copied.

This code uses the usual technique of loading in an image and then attaching a function to its `onload` event so that the code in the function is called only when the image is fully loaded. Within the function the image is then drawn on the canvas so that it takes up its left half. The final line then creates an object called `imagedata` by grabbing information from the canvas starting at location 0,0 and with a width of 205 and height of 170 pixels.

At this point the image data that constitutes the left half of the canvas is now loaded into the `imagedata` array and it can be accessed from JavaScript to read or write its pixel data. This is done using the `data[]` array, which is a property of `imagedata`.

The `data[]` Array

The canvas element supports millions of colors (as well as transparency) for each pixel, and these are managed by allocating four locations per pixel for its red, green, blue, and alpha (transparency) components, each accepting a value of between 0 and 255. These locations are stored contiguously in the `data[]` array so that the pixel at the top left of the canvas (at location 0,0) can be accessed as follows:

```
imagedata.data[0] // The red portion of:   0,0
imagedata.data[1] // The green portion of: 0,0
imagedata.data[2] // The blue portion of:  0,0
imagedata.data[3] // The alpha portion of: 0,0
```

Therefore the pixel one to the right of this at location 1,0 can be accessed like this:

```
imagedata.data[4] // The red portion of:    1,0
imagedata.data[5] // The green portion of: 1,0
imagedata.data[6] // The blue portion of:  1,0
imagedata.data[7] // The alpha portion of: 1,0
```

Once the end of the first row of pixels is reached, the array continues with the next line. So, for a 205-pixel-wide section (such as the one grabbed in this example), there are 4 × 205 locations (or 820) on each row. Therefore the pixels at location 204,0 are accessed like this:

```
imagedata.data[816] // The red portion of:    204,0
imagedata.data[817] // The green portion of: 204,0
imagedata.data[818] // The blue portion of:  204,0
imagedata.data[819] // The alpha portion of: 204,0
```

And the pixels at location 0,1 are accessed as follows:

```
imagedata.data[820] // The red portion of:    0,1
imagedata.data[821] // The green portion of: 0,1
imagedata.data[822] // The blue portion of:  0,1
imagedata.data[823] // The alpha portion of: 0,1
```

Or, if you don't mind using JavaScript expressions, you can address the array using code such as the following, where the JavaScript variables x and y contain the pixel to reference, and w is the width of the area in pixels × 4:

```
imagedata.data[x * 4 + y * w    ] // Red
imagedata.data[x * 4 + y * w + 1] // Green
imagedata.data[x * 4 + y * w + 2] // Blue
imagedata.data[x * 4 + y * w + 3] // Alpha
```

The `putImageData()` Function

So let's use the previous information to convert the image data grabbed from the left half of the canvas into grayscale, by averaging all the color values and setting them to the same value in each pixel. For example, if a pixel displays as yellow, which is a combination of red and green (color string #FFFF00), then we add up the FF, the FF, and the 00 to get a value of 1FE in hexadecimal (or 510 decimal, since FF hexadecimal is 255 in decimal, and twice that is 510).

Next, that value is divided by 3 (the number of different component colors) to return the value AA (or 170 in decimal), which is then assigned to all components of the pixel as the hexadecimal color #AAAAAA. Therefore the average brightness value of the color yellow (#FFFF00 in hexadecimal) is a gray tone with the value #AAAAAA, in which each color component has a value of AA in hexadecimal, or 170 in decimal.

Let's look at some code to do this for the pixel at location 0,0:

```
average = (imagedata.data[0] +
           imagedata.data[1] +
           imagedata.data[2]) / 3
```

The variable `average` now contains the average value of the red, green, and blue components of the pixel's color. In this instance the fourth constituent of the pixel (which is the transparency) is being ignored.

Assuming that all the pixels in the `imagedata` object's `data[]` array have been averaged in this manner, the updated image data can now be written back to the canvas like this, as shown in Figure 13-7 (although you won't see much difference when viewing this page in monochrome):

```
context.putImageData(imagedata, 205, 0)
```

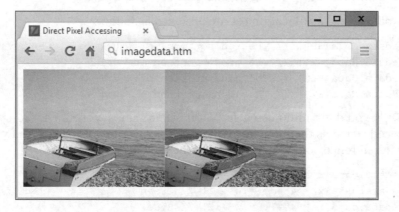

FIGURE 13-7 The left half has been copied, grayed, and pasted back to the right.

Following is the code that was used to perform this transformation. Be warned, though, that you may find it a little complicated, and use of techniques such as this is recommended only if you have an understanding of JavaScript programming:

```
image     = new Image()
image.src = 'boat.png'

image.onload = function()
{
  context.drawImage(image, 0, 0)
  imagedata = context.getImageData(0, 0, 205, 170)
  width     = 205
  height    = 170

  for (y = 0 ; y < height ; ++y)
  {
```

```
pos = y * width * 4

for (x = 0 ; x < width ; ++x)
{
  average = (imagedata.data[pos    ] +
             imagedata.data[pos + 1] +
             imagedata.data[pos + 2]) / 3

  for (j = 0 ; j < 3 ; ++j)
    imagedata.data[pos + j] = average

  pos += 4
  }
}


context.putImageData(imagedata, 205, 0)
}
```

By simply adding an extra line after the three lines of code that calculate the average, you can change the transformation to create a negative grayscale image, by subtracting the value in average from the hexadecimal value FF (255 in decimal), like this:

```
average = 0xFF - average
```

What this does is change the value 1 to 254, 17 to 238, 255 to 0, and so forth, inverting the image, as shown in Figure 13-8.

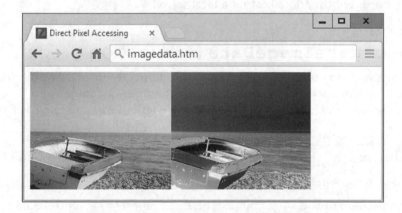

FIGURE 13-8   The image data is averaged, inverted, and pasted back.

You can do other things too, such as changing the overall brightness of the image instead of inverting it, for example, by using this line instead, which adds hexadecimal 50 (80 in decimal) to each color component, as displayed as Figure 13-9.

```
average + = 0x50
```

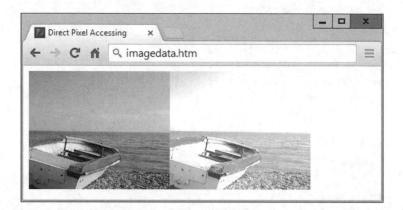

FIGURE 13-9 The grayscaled image has been lightened.

As you can see, once you have access to this data in the data[] array of the imagedata object, you can perform all manner of transformations on it. For example, you can mirror or flip the image, use matrixes (an advanced programming concept) to sharpen or blur the image, and so on. In fact, with a little ingenuity, you can do many of the things a professional graphic editing program like Photoshop can do.

For security reasons, some browsers will not allow examples such as the preceding to directly modify data this way unless they are served from a web server. That means the examples may not work on some browsers if you simply load them in from a file system for testing. Instead ensure you load them using a server domain name, or http://localhost for a local server.

The `createImageData()` Function

You don't have to create an imagedata object directly from a canvas. You can simply create a new one with blank data by calling the createImageData() function, like the following, which creates an object with a width of 320 and height of 240 pixels:

```
imagedata = createImageData(320, 240)
```

Alternatively, you can create a new object from an existing object, like this:

```
newimagedataobject = createImageData(imagedata)
```

It's then up to you what you do with these objects to add pixel data to them, and how you paste them on the canvas or create other objects from them.

Summary

You now have all the basic HTML5 canvas skills in your toolkit, but there are a few more advanced features yet to come, all of which are covered in the final lesson of this part of the book. In it you'll learn about compositing, transparency, and transformations, which you can use to create just the professional touch you need in your canvases.

Self-Test Questions

Test how much you have learned in this lesson with these questions. If you don't know an answer, go back and reread the relevant section until your knowledge is complete. You can find the answers in the appendix.

1. Which function is used to draw an image to the canvas?

2. How can you resize an image when it is drawn?

3. How can you ensure that an image is ready for use before drawing?

4. How can you easily copy one portion of a canvas to another?

5. Which four properties are used to add and modify shadows underneath drawn objects?

6. How can you grab all the pixel data from an image into a form that is editable?

7. Once image data has been grabbed from a canvas and placed in an object, what sub-object of that object contains the actual data?

8. What are the four components of each pixel?

9. Which function is used to write image data to the canvas?

10. How can you create a new object containing blank image data?

LESSON 14

Compositing, Transparency, and Transformations

 To view the accompanying video for this lesson, please visit mhprofessional.com/nixonhtml5/.

In this final lesson on the HTML5 canvas, I show you how to use the remaining advanced graphical features not yet introduced, including compositing, transparency, and transformations, as well as how to save and restore context between operations.

Compositing and Transparency

Compositing is the method used for placing an element on the canvas, and there are 12 different available types, which have the effect of placing new elements in front of or behind existing ones, only on top of an existing element, never over an existing element, and so forth.

This is achieved using a property called globalCompositeOperation, providing it with the required value for the compositing you require.

The globalCompositeOperation Property

This property drastically affects the way new elements are added to the canvas. It supports 12 different values such as source-over, which is the default, and is applied like this:

```
context.globalCompositeOperation = 'source-over'
```

Following is a breakdown of all 12 types and the way they work. You should read them in conjunction with looking at Figure 14-1, which displays an example of each type:

- **source-over** The default. The source image is copied over the destination image.
- **source-in** Only parts of the source image that will appear within the destination are shown, and the destination image is removed. Any alpha transparency in the source image causes the destination under it to be removed.
- **source-out** Only parts of the source image that do not appear within the destination are shown, and the destination image is removed. Any alpha transparency in the source image causes the destination under it to be removed.

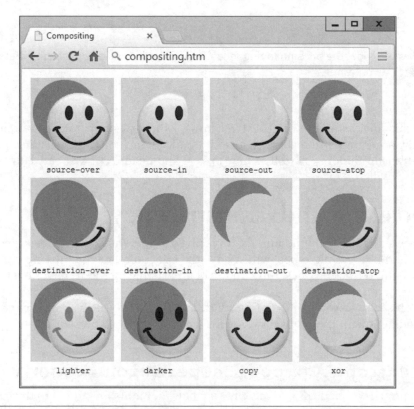

FIGURE 14-1 The 12 different compositing types

- **source-atop**   The source image is displayed where it overlays the destination. The destination image is displayed where the destination image is opaque and the source image is transparent. Other regions are transparent.
- **destination-over**   The source image is drawn under the destination image.
- **destination-in**   The destination image displays where the source and destination image overlap, but not in any areas of source image transparency. The source image does not display.
- **destination-out**   Only those parts of the destination outside of the source image's nontransparent sections are shown. The source image does not display.
- **destination-atop**   The source image displays where the destination is not displayed. Where the destination and source overlap, the destination image is displayed. Any transparency in the source image prevents that area of the destination image being shown.
- **lighter**   The sum of the source and destination is applied such that where they do not overlap they display as normal, but where they overlap, the sum of both images is shown, but lightened.
- **darker**   The sum of the source and destination is applied such that where they do not overlap they display as normal, but where they overlap, the sum of both images is shown, but darkened.
- **copy**   The source image is copied over the destination. The destination image is ignored.
- **xor**   Where the source and destination images do not overlap, they display as normal. Where they overlap their color values are exclusive ored.

 Compositing can be really tricky to get right, so my advice is to use trial and error, and you may prefer to choose a compositing type based on the examples shown in Figure 14-1, rather than on the descriptions given here.

The `globalAlpha` Property

When drawing an element to the canvas, you can choose how much transparency to give it by providing a floating-point value to the `globalAlpha` property of between 0 and 1 inclusive, with 0 signifying no transparency, 1 being totally transparent, and (for example) 0.5 being half transparent, and so on, like this:

```
context.globalAlpha = 0.5
```

In Figure 14-2 a value of 0.5 has been applied to the `globalAlpha` property of the previous compositing example by adding the preceding line of code.

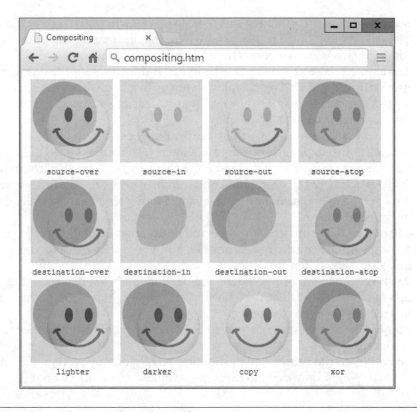

FIGURE 14-2   These elements have been drawn using 50 percent transparency.

Using Transformations

There are four functions available for applying transformations to elements when drawing them to the HTML5 canvas. They are: `scale()`, `rotate()`, `translate()`, and `transform()`, and with them, if your element is not quite at the right angle, the correct size, or at the right perspective, you can tweak it until you get it just right.

The `scale()` Function

As you've already seen, there are various ways you can scale different objects, such as by specifying the width and height at which to draw them on the canvas. But you can also use the `scale()` function to apply a global scaling factor to all future elements drawn on the canvas, like the following, which sets the scaling of horizontal dimensions to 1.8 times, and vertical to 1.5 times the original size:

```
context.scale(1.8, 1.5)
```

Let's look at this in practice with the following code, which draws a rectangle, increases the scaling factors, and then redraws the rectangle, as shown in Figure 14-3:

```
context.strokeStyle = 'red'
context.strokeRect(20, 20, 195, 75)

context.scale(1.8, 1.5)

context.strokeStyle = 'blue'
context.strokeRect(20, 20, 195, 75)
```

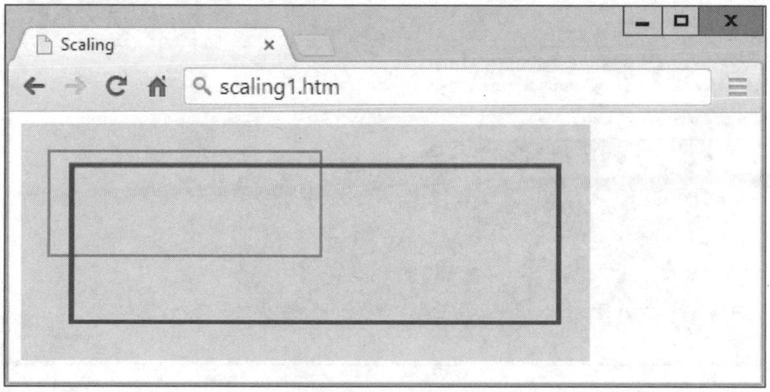

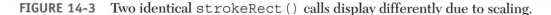

FIGURE 14-3   Two identical `strokeRect()` calls display differently due to scaling.

To help show the difference between the rectangles, the original (smaller) one is displayed in red, and the second (larger) one in blue. The arguments used in the parameters to the calls for drawing the rectangles are identical to each other, but the `scale()` call between the two ensures that the second rectangle is 1.8 times wider and 1.5 times deeper.

As well as modifying the dimensions, this scaling is applied to the origin of the rectangles (their top-left corners), and so the larger one is offset to a location 1.8 times the original rectangle's horizontal offset of 20 pixels (to a new coordinate of 36), and 1.5 times the original vertical offset of 20 pixels (to a new coordinate of 30). Thus the new origin for the larger square is at location 36,30, rather than 20,20.

Here's an example of using the `scale()` function more than once on the same rectangle (but changing the colors so you can see the difference), as shown in Figure 14-4:

```
context.fillStyle = 'red'
context.fillRect(10, 10, 80, 30)

context.scale(1.6, 1.6)
context.fillStyle = 'yellow'
```

```
context.fillRect(10, 10, 80, 30)

context.scale(1.6, 1.6)
context.fillStyle = 'blue'
context.fillRect(10, 10, 80, 30)

context.scale(1.6, 1.6)
context.fillStyle = 'green'
context.fillRect(10, 10, 80, 30)
```

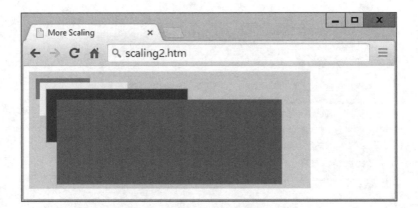

FIGURE 14-4 The same rectangle scaled up three times

 In this lesson I have selected colors that are reasonably different to each other when viewed in greyscale (as with the print version of this book). You can easily tell which grey represents which color, by comparing the example source code for each figure with the image.

The `save()` and `restore()` Functions

After drawing elements using a changed scaling, if you then wish to draw some using their original dimensions, you'll need to issue the correct `scale()` call with negative values to get the scaling back down to a ratio of 1:1. But in the preceding example where the scaling ratio was increased upward three times, you would have to reduce the scaling ratio back three times by using values lower than 1 that achieve the same amount of reduction, like this (where 0.625 is the inverse of 1.6):

```
context.scale(0.625, 0.625)
context.scale(0.625, 0.625)
context.scale(0.625, 0.625)
```

Obviously, this is somewhat fiddly in that it involves calculating the inverse value, and also repeating a function call unnecessarily. Or, you could calculate the full inverse value for a single call to `scale()`, which happens to be 0.24414 (arrived at by multiplying 0.625 by itself three times), like this:

```
context.scale(0.24414, 0.24414)
```

But there's a much simpler method for returning the scale to the default (along with many other properties too), and that's to issue a call to `save()` before making any changes to properties or calling functions such as `scale()`, and then calling `restore()` afterward to reset all the properties to the way they were, like this code, which uses the functions to restore the scaling before drawing a final rectangle in orange on top of the very first red one, as shown in Figure 14-5:

```
context.save()

context.fillStyle = 'red'
context.fillRect(10, 10, 80, 30)
context.scale(1.6, 1.6)
context.fillStyle = 'yellow'
context.fillRect(10, 10, 80, 30)
context.scale(1.6, 1.6)
context.fillStyle = 'blue'
context.fillRect(10, 10, 80, 30)
context.scale(1.6, 1.6)
context.fillStyle = 'green'
context.fillRect(10, 10, 80, 30)

context.restore()

context.fillStyle = 'orange'
context.fillRect(10, 10, 80, 30)
```

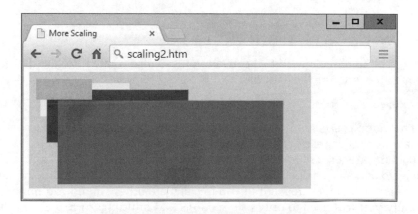

FIGURE 14-5   The scaling is saved, and then restored for a final rectangle.

As well as the scaling ratio, several other properties are saved and restored by these functions, as follows:

- `fillStyle`
- `font`
- `globalAlpha`
- `globalCompositeOperation`
- `lineCap`
- `lineJoin`
- `lineWidth`
- `miterLimit`
- `shadowBlur`
- `shadowColor`
- `shadowOffsetX`
- `shadowOffsetY`
- `strokeStyle`
- `textAlign`
- `textBaseline`
- `scale()` properties
- `rotate()` properties
- `translate()` properties
- `transform()` properties

This process of using `save()` and `restore()` is known as saving and restoring the drawing context. You can call the `save()` method as often as you like and each time the current context will be saved. For each call to `save`, you can issue a matching `restore()` call to return the context to the previous state. This enables you to save the state as you perform more steps and then "unwind" the state backward as each step completes.

The `rotate()` Function

Before applying an element to a canvas, you can also rotate it to just the right angle with a call to `rotate()`, like this:

```
context.rotate(Math.PI / 2)
```

The value passed to the function is in radians, each of which has a value of $180 \div \pi$ (or about 57.3 degrees). There are $\pi \times 2$ radians in a complete circle.

Radians are a sensible unit of measurement because $\pi \div 2$ radians is a quarter circle, π radians is a half circle, $\pi \times 3 \div 2$ radians is three-quarters of a circle, and $\pi \times 2$ radians is a full circle. I leave it to you to calculate other values you might require, but generally you will need to only use fractions and multiples of π, whose value you can get by using the JavaScript property of `Math.PI`.

Therefore the previous example line will rotate all future elements placed on the canvas by a quarter turn (or 90 degrees). Here's an example in action, as seen in Figure 14-6, in which a square has been rotated nine times:

```
context.fillStyle = 'green'
context.fillRect(75, 0, 75, 75)

context.rotate(Math.PI / 20)
context.fillStyle = 'pink'
context.fillRect(75, 0, 75, 75)

context.rotate(Math.PI / 20)
context.fillStyle = 'blue'
context.fillRect(75, 0, 75, 75)

context.rotate(Math.PI / 20)
context.fillStyle = 'yellow '
context.fillRect(75, 0, 75, 75)

context.rotate(Math.PI / 20)
context.fillStyle = 'red'
context.fillRect(75, 0, 75, 75)

context.rotate(Math.PI / 20)
context.fillStyle = 'violet'
context.fillRect(75, 0, 75, 75)

context.rotate(Math.PI / 20)
context.fillStyle = 'purple'
context.fillRect(75, 0, 75, 75)

context.rotate(Math.PI / 20)
context.fillStyle = 'lime'
context.fillRect(75, 0, 75, 75)

context.rotate(Math.PI / 20)
context.fillStyle = 'plum'
context.fillRect(75, 0, 75, 75)

context.rotate(Math.PI / 20)
context.fillStyle = 'brown'
context.fillRect(75, 0, 75, 75)
```

Because the `rotate()` function is called prior to each call to `fillRect()`, the rotation factor is increased for each one. The place around which the rotation takes place is the origin of the canvas, at location 0,0.

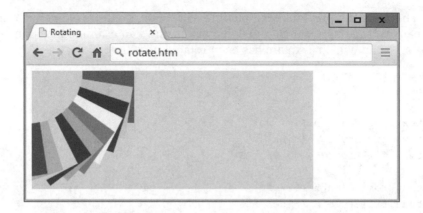

FIGURE 14-6 A square is rotated nine times.

Working with Degrees

If you prefer working with degrees rather than radians, you can convert degrees to radians using the formula *radians = degrees × 0.01745324* (because 0.01745324 is π ÷ 180). For example, if you want a quick way to supply a value of 90 degrees to a function that requires radians, just pass the expression `90 * 0.01745324` as the argument. Or you can create a function to do this to JavaScript's maximum level of accuracy, like this:

```
degToRad(val)
{
  return val * Math.PI / 180
}
```

Then (for example) just supply the expression `degToRad(90)` to the function.

The `translate()` Function

If you prefer to rotate an object around another axis such as its center, you need to also call the `translate()` function to move the origin of the canvas to a new location, around which the elements can rotate, like this line for example (which sets it to the coordinates 100,100):

```
context.translate(100, 100)
```

Let's use this in a simple example similar to the previous one, but in which the squares will rotate around their centers, like this (as shown in Figure 14-7):

```
context.translate(280, 85)
context.fillStyle = 'green'
context.fillRect(-60, -60, 120, 120)
```

```
context.rotate(Math.PI / 10)
context.fillStyle = 'pink'
context.fillRect(-60, -60, 120, 120)

context.rotate(Math.PI / 10)
context.fillStyle = 'blue'
context.fillRect(-60, -60, 120, 120)

context.rotate(Math.PI / 10)
context.fillStyle = 'yellow'
context.fillRect(-60, -60, 120, 120)

context.rotate(Math.PI / 10)
context.fillStyle = 'violet'
context.fillRect(-60, -60, 120, 120)
```

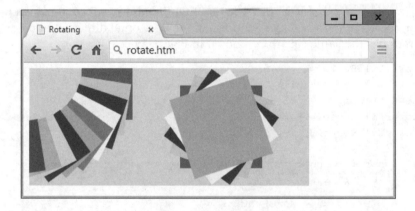

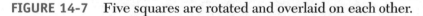

FIGURE 14-7   Five squares are rotated and overlaid on each other.

If you look closely at the code in this example, you'll see some negative values. This is because the origin of the canvas is no longer at location 0,0—it has been translated to the location 280,85. Therefore all function calls that address the canvas must now bear this new origin in mind and, since the squares are 120 pixels wide and deep, to place their centers over the new origin position, they must be located at a point relative to the origin of -60,-60.

 After translating the origin of the canvas, you may wish to restore it to 0,0 for future access of the canvas, or you can use the `save()` and `restore()` functions in appropriate places to automatically restore the context.

The `transform()` Function

Finally, in this part of the book on the HTML5 canvas, comes the most complicated and possibly the most powerful feature of all, the `transform()` function, with which you can stretch and transform elements in many different ways using matrixes.

Interestingly, the previous functions that manipulate elements all actually use matrixes to achieve their effects, and you can do the same yourself using the `transform()` method to either emulate or improve the built-in functions, or create your own new transforms. For example, you can emulate the `scale()` function by issuing the following command:

```
context.transform(1.6, 0, 0, 1.6, 0, 0)
```

This is equivalent to the following call because the first and fourth parameters represent the horizontal and vertical scaling respectively:

```
context.scale(1.6, 1.6)
```

Here's some code using the function that first draws a 50 × 50-pixel square in green, then applies a scaling factor of 2 in the horizontal direction and 1.5 vertically and redraws the same square, as shown in Figure 14-8.

```
context.fillStyle = 'green'
context.fillRect(35, 35, 50, 50)
context.transform(2, 0, 0, 1.5, 0, 0)
context.fillStyle = 'blue'
context.fillRect(35, 35, 50, 50)
```

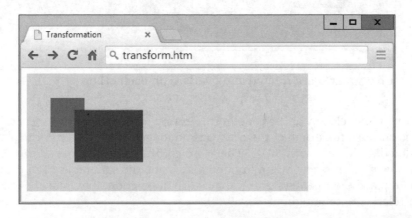

FIGURE 14-8   The original square is redrawn with scaling of 2 and 1.5.

This is the same as using the following command:

```
context.scale(2, 1.5)
```

The second and third parameters to the `transform()` function control shearing of the element. For example, to shear the original square downward (and not use any scaling), you could issue a command such as this:

```
context.transform(1, 0.7, 0, 1, 0, 0)
```

To shear to the right, you might use a command like this:

```
context.transform(1, 0, 0.7, 1, 0, 0)
```

And to shear in both directions, you might use a command such as this:

```
context.transform(1, 0.7, 0.7, 1, 0, 0)
```

In fact, here's some example code that illustrates all three of these shears at once, as shown in Figure 14-9:

```
context.fillStyle = 'green'
context.fillRect(35, 35, 50, 50)

context.restore()
context.save()
context.transform(1, 0.7, 0, 1, 0, 0)
context.fillStyle = 'orange'
context.fillRect(35, 35, 50, 50)

context.restore()
context.save()
context.transform(1, 0, 0.7, 1, 0, 0)
context.fillStyle = 'violet'
context.fillRect(35, 35, 50, 50)

context.restore()
context.save()
context.transform(1, 0.7, 0.7, 1, 0, 0)
context.fillStyle = 'red'
context.fillRect(35, 35, 50, 50)
```

The first section of code creates the initial square. Then `save()` and `restore()` are used for the following sections to ensure the context is returned for reuse after each. In the first `transform()` call, the bottom-left shape is created. The top-right one is created next, and then the bottom-right shape is created out of a combined horizontal and vertical shear.

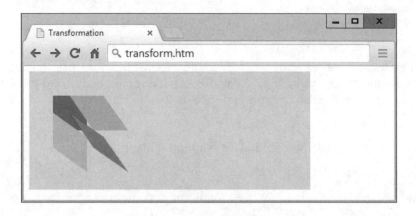

FIGURE 14-9 Three different shears have been applied to the square.

 You may use different values than 0.7 in these functions, and that includes negative values to shear in the other direction.

The final two arguments to the function are the horizontal and vertical offset to apply to the element when it is drawn on the canvas. These may be negative as well as positive values. Therefore the following three lines of code modify the `transform()` calls in the previous example to move the bottom-left shape to the left by 30 and down by 20 pixels, the top-right shape to the right by 20 and up by 30 pixels, and the bottom-right shape both down and to the right by 25 pixels, as shown in Figure 14-10:

```
context.transform(1, 0.7,   0, 1, -30,  20)
context.transform(1,   0, 0.7, 1,  20, -30)
context.transform(1, 0.7, 0.7, 1,  25,  25)
```

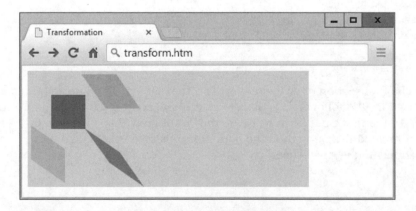

FIGURE 14-10 The sheared shapes have been offset away from the original.

The `setTransform()` Function

As well as using the `save()` and `restore()` functions, you can reset the transform matrix at any time by issuing this call:

```
context.transform(1, 0, 0, 1, 0  0)
```

Then you are ready to issue a new transform of your choosing, like this, for example:

```
context.transform(1, 1.2, -1.2, 1, -20, 20)
```

However, rather than issuing two separate calls, you can make just one call to the `setTransform()` function instead. This has the effect of resetting the transform matrix and then applying the requested new transform. So, in place of the two preceding calls, for example, you can simply make the following call:

```
context.setTransform(1, 1.2, -1.2, 1, -20, 20)
```

 For more information about transformation matrixes, there's a comprehensive article at: *wikipedia.org/wiki/Transformation_matrix*.

Summary

This concludes your introduction to the world of the HTML5 canvas. I hope you have found it enlightening and will use the functions it provides to create some weird and wonderful and compelling web pages. In the next lesson we'll move on to seeing how a browser can identify your location, and what you can use this information for.

Self-Test Questions

Test how much you have learned in this lesson with these questions. If you don't know an answer, go back and reread the relevant section until your knowledge is complete. You can find the answers in the appendix.

1. With which property can you change the type of compositing used to draw to the canvas?

2. How can you set the transparency of future drawing operations?

3. Which function lets you change the scale for future drawing operations?

4. How can you easily resume previous settings after changing the scaling one or more times?

5. Which function lets you rotate the angle of future drawing operations?

6. How many radians are there in 360 degrees?

7. How can you move the origin of future drawing operations from its default location at 0,0?

8. What is the procedure to rotate an object around its center before drawing it to the canvas?

9. With which function can you scale, rotate, and skew, all at the same time?

10. Which function can you use to create absolute transformations (as opposed to relative ones from the current transform settings)?

PART III

Advanced HTML5

Supporting Geolocation

 To view the accompanying video for this lesson, please visit mhprofessional.com/ nixonhtml5/.

With the incredible rise in popularity of smartphones, the ability to determine the location of a device has become almost essential, particularly for running interactive maps and navigation software, and even for finding local Wi-Fi hotspots, or services such as restaurants or cash dispensing machines, and so on.

Geolocation is also being used more and more to try to sell you services by offering promotions in stores that are near to you, and a little more benevolently in enabling you to know whether friends or acquaintances are within your near vicinity. Thankfully, you are in control of when you allow your location information to be revealed, so you can minimize any privacy or security risks the technology could create.

In this lesson I will show you how to use JavaScript to determine the location of any geolocation-enabled device, as long as the user allows you.

Accessing Geolocation with JavaScript

There are no two ways about it; many of the HTML5 features are so advanced that they cannot be accessed by simple HTML. Instead you do have to learn a little JavaScript.

So far in this course I have done my best to teach you only the fewest parts of JavaScript you need in order to work through the examples. And the same goes for this lesson. However, there is no substitute for getting a good book (such as my book *JavaScript: 20 Lessons for Successful Web Development*) or taking a course on JavaScript, if you wish to make full and professional use of features such as geolocation.

The `geolocation` Property

The first thing you must do when accessing geolocation is to determine whether or not it is available by testing the `geolocation` property, like this (preceding the property with the `navigator` object name):

```
if (typeof navigator.geolocation == 'undefined')
{
    alert("Sorry, no Geolocation support.")
}
else
{
    // Geolocation code goes here
}
```

This code uses a JavaScript `if()` statement in which the first part of the code is executed if geolocation is not supported. Typically you will inform the user that their browser doesn't support geolocation, provide some other kind of message, or perhaps simply do nothing. In this instance I have chosen to pop up an `alert()` message window with a short message.

If geolocation is supported, the part of code after the `else` statement is executed, and that's where your code that uses the geolocation information goes, as follows.

The `getCurrentPosition()` Function

Once you know that a browser supports geolocation, you may ask it for its current position using the `getCurrentPosition()` function, like this:

```
navigator.geolocation.getCurrentPosition(granted, denied)
```

This line of code calls the browser's geolocation software, passing it the names of two new functions called `granted()` and `denied()`. Because the function names (and not the actual function contents) are being passed to the `getCurrentPosition()` function, no parentheses are placed after the names.

One or the other of these two functions will be called back by the browser according to whether the user grants or denies you the use of its location data. Therefore both of these routines must be written.

A `granted()` Function

Here's what an example `granted()` function might look like:

```
function granted(position)
{
  alert('You are at location: '
    + position.coords.latitude + ','
    + position.coords.longitude)
}
```

In this instance I have opted to simply display the returned location information in an `alert()` message window. You will be more likely to display a map or perform other functions based on this information. As for the user's location, this is returned in the following two properties:

```
position.coords.latitude
position.coords.longitude
```

The former property holds the latitude value and the latter the longitude.

A `denied()` Function

If the user has chosen not to allow the browser's location data to be revealed to your code, then your `denied()` function will be called, and an error code will be given to state why.

Here's an example `denied()` function:

```
function denied(error)
{
  var message

  switch(error.code)
  {
    case 1: message = 'Permission Denied';    break
    case 2: message = 'Position Unavailable'; break
    case 3: message = 'Operation Timed Out';  break
    case 4: message = 'Unknown Error';        break
  }

  alert('Error with Geolocation: ' + message)
}
```

This code is a little longer because it processes the value in `error.code`, which can be a number between 1 and 4, as follows:

1. Permission Denied

2. Position Unavailable

3. Operation Timed Out

4. Unknown Error

Again, I have chosen a simple `alert()` message to provide this information. In your code (if you choose to give a message at all), you may wish to display a simpler and more friendly phrase such as "Geolocation request denied."

In the Real World

Here's a complete document you can use to display a Google map of a user's current location in a `<div>` element, based on the coordinates returned by the browser's geolocation code. If permission is not given or the browser doesn't support geolocation, then a message stating that is provided by writing directly into the contents of the `<div>` tag with the id of `status` using its `innerHTML` property.

```
<!DOCTYPE html>
<html>
  <head>
    <title>Geolocation Example</title>
  </head>
  <body>
    <p>This example will ask your browser for its location if it
    supports this feature.</p>

    <div id='status'></div>
    <div id='map'></div>

    <script src="https://maps.googleapis.com/maps/api/js?sensor=false">
    </script>
    <script>
      if (typeof navigator.geolocation == 'undefined')
        alert('Geolocation not supported.')
      else
        navigator.geolocation.getCurrentPosition(granted, denied)

      function granted(position)
      {
        O('status').innerHTML = 'Permission Granted'
        S('map').border       = '1px solid black'
        S('map').width        = '640px'
        S('map').height       = '320px'

        var lat  = position.coords.latitude
        var long = position.coords.longitude

        var gmap  = O('map')
        var gopts =
        {
          center: new google.maps.LatLng(lat, long),
          zoom: 10, mapTypeId: google.maps.MapTypeId.SATELLITE
        }
        var map = new google.maps.Map(gmap, gopts)
      }
```

```
function denied(error)
{
  var message

  switch(error.code)
  {
    case 1: message = 'Permission Denied';     break
    case 2: message = 'Position Unavailable'; break
    case 3: message = 'Operation Timed Out';   break
    case 4: message = 'Unknown Error';         break
  }

  O('status').innerHTML = message
}

function O(obj)
{
  if (typeof obj == 'object') return obj
  else return document.getElementById(obj)
}

function S(obj)
{
  return O(obj).style
}
    </script>
  </body>
</html>
```

When a web page containing this code is loaded into a browser, the first thing that happens is a request is made to the user. Depending on the browser and operating system in use, this may be presented in a variety of different ways. On Google Chrome, for example, it looks like Figure 15-1.

If permission is not given, then only a short message will be displayed, but if it is given, then the result will be similar to Figure 15-2.

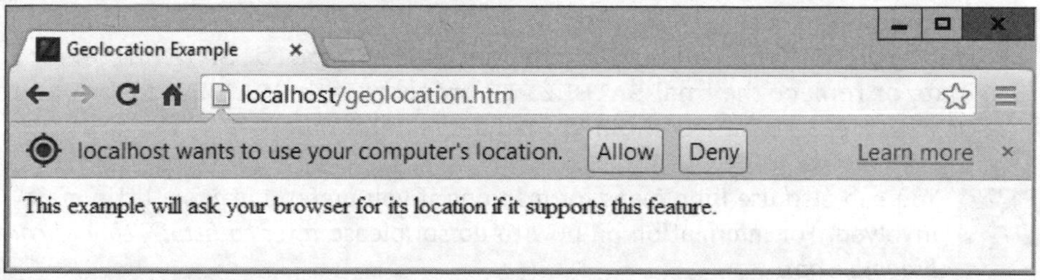

FIGURE 15-1 The geolocation request displayed by Google Chrome

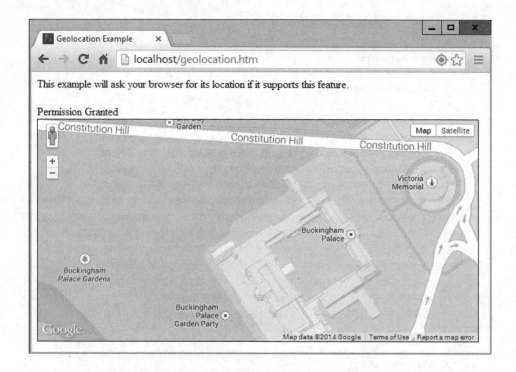

FIGURE 15-2 Permission has been granted and a map is displayed.

When using the Google Maps service, you can modify the arguments to the `gopts` object (highlighted in bold in the following code) to modify the type of map displayed:

```
center: new google.maps.LatLng(lat, long),
zoom: 10, mapTypeId: google.maps.MapTypeId.SATELLITE
```

The variables you can alter are:

- **Lat** and **long** These can be as retrieved from the user's device through geolocation, or coordinates you have determined and wish to supply (perhaps to provide a map of your employer's place of work)
- **zoom** This can be a value between 1 for fully zoomed out and 20 for fully zoomed in.
- **mapTypeId** This can be `google.maps.MapTypeId.SATELLITE` for a satellite map, or replace the final `SATELLITE` property with `ROADMAP` for a road map, or with `HYBRID` for a combined road and satellite map.

 Note You can also use Bing maps for mapping if you prefer, but it's a little more involved. For information on how to do so, please refer to *http://tinyurl.com/bingmapsapi*.

The GPS Service

The GPS (Global Positioning System) service consists of multiple satellites orbiting the earth whose positions are very precisely known. When a GPS-enabled device tunes in to these satellites, the different times at which signals from these various satellites arrive enable the device to know where it is to within just a few feet.

This is achieved by the fact that the speed of light (and radio waves) is a known constant, and the time it takes a signal to get from a satellite to a GPS device precisely indicates the satellite's distance. By making a note of all the different times at which signals arrive from different satellites, a simple calculation lets the device derive each of the satellite's positions relative to each other, and therefore very closely triangulate the position of the device relative to them.

Many mobile devices such as phones and tablets have GPS chips and can provide this information. But some don't, others have them turned off, and others may be used indoors where they are shielded from the GPS satellites, and therefore cannot receive any signals. In these cases, additional techniques may be used to attempt to determine your location.

Other Location Methods

First, if your device has mobile phone hardware, it may attempt to triangulate its location by checking the timings of signals received from the various communications towers with which it can communicate (and whose positions are very precisely known). If there are a few towers, this can get almost as close to your location as GPS. But where there's a single tower, the signal strength is used to determine a radius around the tower, and the circle it creates represents the area in which you are likely to be located. This could place you anywhere within a mile or two of your actual location, down to within a few tens of feet.

Failing that, there may be known Wi-Fi access points within range of your device whose positions are known, and since all access points have a unique identifying address called a MAC (Media Access Control) address, a reasonably good approximation of location can be obtained, perhaps to within a street or two.

And if that fails, the IP (Internet Protocol) address used by your device can be queried and used as a rough indicator of your location. Often though, this provides only the location of a major switch belonging to your Internet provider, which could be dozens or even hundreds of miles away. But at the very least, your IP address can narrow down the country, and sometimes the region you are in.

 Your IP address is commonly used by media companies that restrict playback of their content by territory. However, some people are able to set up proxy servers that use a forwarding IP address in the country that is blocking them to fetch and pass content through the blockade back to their browser. Therefore, you should be aware that if you locate someone by IP address, the country identification may not necessarily be reliable.

Using geolocation will enable you to improve the features you offer to your mobile device web visitors, but not so much for desktop users, whose locations will remain difficult to ascertain.

Nevertheless, used sensibly and perhaps even in conjunction with asking your users directly to correct any such misinformation in order for you to provide better service, geolocation is a great feature. And if you know your user has an iPhone, Android, or Windows phone, you can be almost certain that you're receiving the right data.

Summary

And that's all there is to geolocation, so this is a short and sweet lesson, but hopefully one you have found very useful. In the next lesson I'll take you through the extensions that HTML5 has made to HTML forms.

Self-Test Questions

Test how much you have learned in this lesson with these questions. If you don't know an answer, go back and reread the relevant section until your knowledge is complete. You can find the answers in the appendix.

1. What is the most common form of geolocation positioning hardware?

2. How can you determine whether a browser supports geolocation?

3. Which method do you call to request location data from a browser, and what values should be passed to this function?

4. If the user grants permission for you to access their location, how will that data be supplied?

5. If the user doesn't grant permission to access their location, what information is supplied instead?

6. If you are using location data to display a Google Map, what is the URL of the API (Application Programming Interface) you should call in a <script> tag?

7. How do you pass the latitude and longitude to display to the Google Maps API?

8. What values can you supply to the Google Maps zoom property to choose the zoom level?

9. What types of Google Maps can be displayed, and how?

10. Why are IP addresses not a very accurate form of geolocation?

Building Advanced Forms

 To view the accompanying video for this lesson, please visit mhprofessional.com/
nixonhtml5/.

If you've ever used HTML forms, you'll be aware of how limiting they can be. Yes,
they do provide the facility to create different types of fields and buttons, but that's
about it.

There are no date pickers for easy selection of dates from pop-up menus. There's no
built-in verification of data types such as numbers, strings, or e-mail addresses, and
there's no built-in ability to match patterns in regular expressions.

But with HTML5 all these problems and several more have been addressed, making
completing forms easier than ever for users, and also much simpler for web developers
to create.

New Form Attributes

HTML5 is still very much an evolving specification that browsers are implementing
only piecemeal. Therefore some features are available in some browsers, and others in
different ones.

And it's not always the same browsers that haven't yet caught up with the spec
because, as of this writing, all of the latest versions of all the main browsers omit at
least three of these attributes, and some omit as many as ten.

Nevertheless, as time passes, browsers will implement more and more of the
HTML5 spec, and therefore this lesson provides the information you need for using
these features.

The `autocomplete` Attribute

The autocomplete attribute can be applied to the <form> tag or any of the color, date, email, password, range, search, telephone, text, or url types of the <input> tag. Valid arguments for this attribute are on (the default) and off.

When autocomplete is on, any field with an id that has previously had an input entered will remember its value and offer it as a suggested value, saving you from having to enter it again.

When autocomplete is off, this behavior is disabled. When applied to a <form> tag, the attribute affects all relevant fields within a form. When applied to an <input> tag, only that field is affected. Here are two examples of using the attribute:

```
<form action='prog.php' method='post' autocomplete='on'>
  <input type='text' name='field1' autocomplete='off'>
</form>
```

The `autofocus` Attribute

The autofocus attribute can be applied to any <input> tag to give its field automatic focus when a page loads. This has the effect of placing the cursor in an input field ready to type, or selecting any other type of field ready to change it, and is activated like this:

```
<input type='text' name='field' autofocus='autofocus'>
```

 This feature is supported by the latest versions of all major browsers, but not mobile browsers, as it would be a distraction calling up the onscreen keyboard when often it wouldn't be wanted.

To achieve the same effect in older browsers, you can add some JavaScript to the <body> tag of your web page, like this:

```
<body onload='document.forms.myform.myfield.focus()'>
```

Then make sure your form looks something like this:

```
<form id='myform' action='prog.php' method='post' autocomplete='on'>
  <input id='myfield' type='text' name='field' autofocus='autofocus'>
</form>
```

To make this work, both the <form> and the <input> tags must each be given a unique id. In this case I chose the name myform for the form and myfield for the field. These are then easily referenced in the argument to the onload event of the <body> tag, which calls the focus() function on the field when the web page has loaded.

The `form` Attribute

With the form attribute, it is not necessary for you to place <input> tags within the form to which they apply. Instead, as long as you give a form an id, you can specify that value as the argument for a form attribute.

For example, the following code opens and then closes a form with the `id` of `myform`, and the `<input>` tag `field` is attached to it only after the form is closed:

```
<form id='myform' action='form.php' method='get'>
  <input type='submit'>
</form>


<input form='myform' type='text' name='field'>
```

This feature is not supported by Internet Explorer at the time of writing.

Form Overrides

Several new attributes have been added to HTML in version 5 that allow you to override various form settings such as the `action` and `enctype` properties, but so far only a few browsers have implemented them.

Form overrides work with either of the `submit` or `image` types of the `<input>` tag, and are supported in the latest versions of all major browsers.

The `formaction` Attribute

The `formaction` attribute is a form override that lets you change the `action` attribute to a different destination. For example, in the following code, the form will not post to the program *prog.php* as specified in the `<form>` tag, and will instead post to *prog2.php*:

```
<form action='prog.php' method='post'>
  <input type='text' name='field'>
  <input type='submit' formaction='prog2.php'>
</form>
```

This attribute can be particularly useful when you wish to provide more than one submit button, each with a different destination program to which the form should submit.

The `formenctype` Attribute

The `formenctype` attribute is a form override that lets you change the encoding type of a form (the `enctype` attribute), in a similar manner to the `formaction` override.

The `formmethod` Attribute

The `formmethod` attribute is a form override that lets you change the posting method (the `post` or `get` value of the `method` attribute), in a similar manner to the `formaction` override.

The `formnovalidate` Attribute

The `formnovalidate` attribute is a form override that lets you change the `novalidate` attribute, in a similar manner to the `formaction` override.

The `formtarget` Attribute

The `formtarget` attribute is a form override that lets you change the `target` attribute, in a similar manner to the `formaction` override.

The `height` and `width` Attributes

The `height` and `width` attributes can be applied to the `image` type of the `<input>` tag to change its height and width. You use the attributes like this, with a result such as that in Figure 16-1:

```
<input type='image' src='finger.png' width='117' height='100'>
```

FIGURE 16-1 Resizing an image used in an input

The `list` Attribute and `<datalist>` and `<option>` Tags

Some input fields support lists and the `list` attribute can be used to reference them. For example, the following HTML uses this attribute, along with the new `<datalist>` tag, to offer a selection of URLs from which to choose:

```
Choose a web page: <input type='url' name='site' list='links'>

<datalist id='links'>
  <option label='Google' value='http://google.com'>
  <option label='Yahoo!' value='http://yahoo.com' >
  <option label='Bing'   value='http://bing.com'  >
  <option label='Ask'    value='http://ask.com'   >
</datalist>
```

The value supplied to the `list` attribute should be the id name of a `<datalist>` tag. This feature works a bit like the `autocomplete` attribute, except that you define the list of suggested choices that appear when the input is given focus.

 Currently this feature is not supported in Safari, but you can still use it in your web pages (as shown in Figure 16-2) because Safari will simply not display the list of suggestions, but for other browsers, your web forms that use it will be quicker to fill in.

FIGURE 16-2   Prepopulating input using the `list` attribute and `<datalist>` tag

The `min` and `max` Attributes

The `min` and `max` attributes are used to specify minimum and maximum value for input types that contain numbers or dates. Here is an example (the result of which can be seen in Figure 16-3, in which the up and down selectors can be seen to the right of the input):

```
<input type='time' name='deliver' value='09:00' min='09:00' max='17:00'>
```

FIGURE 16-3   Using the `min` and `max` properties

In addition to using the mouse to change the input up or down (within the minimum and maximum values), a valid input between these values can be directly entered, or the up and down keyboard buttons can be used to scroll through the supported values.

Note I don't recommend you rely on this type of validation yet, though, since neither Firefox nor Internet Explorer support its use (the attributes will be ignored).

The `multiple` Attribute

The `multiple` attribute allows you to accept multiple values for an `<input>` tag that uses any of the `email`, `range`, or `file` types. It works in the latest versions of all major browsers except for Internet Explorer and Opera. You will enable it like this:

```
<input type='file' name='images' multiple='multiple'>
```

Then, when the browse box pops up, multiple files can be selected at a time (normally in conjunction with the CTRL key). On browsers that don't yet support this feature, only single files can be selected.

Note Because browsers that don't support this feature will only allow single items to be selected, until all browsers support it, this feature is not safe to use if you are requiring multiple inputs (rather than simply allowing them).

The `novalidate` and `formnovalidate` Attributes

These Boolean attributes specify that a form should not be validated when it is submitted. The `novalidate` attribute is applicable to the `<form>` tag and the `formnovalidate` attribute is applicable to only the `submit` and `image` types of the `<input>` tag. You use `novalidate` like this:

```
<form novalidate='novalidate'>
  // Various inputs...
  <input type='submit'>
</form>
```

And you use `formnovalidate` like this:

```
<form>
  // Various inputs...
  <input type='submit' formnovalidate='formnovalidate'>
</form>
```

Note At the time of writing Safari does not yet support this feature, but once it is implemented across all browsers, you may well choose to use it all the time, at least until the validation features in HTML5 are much better than those currently offered. If you are looking for reliable in-browser form validation, there are many libraries available, such as the open source tool at *livevalidation.com*.

The `pattern` Attribute

The `pattern` attribute lets you specify a regular expression with which an input field should be evaluated. It can be applied to any `<input>` tag that uses any of the `email`, `password`, `search`, `telephone`, `text`, or `url` types. For example, to allow only alphanumeric characters, the dash, and underline in a field, you might use the following HTML:

```
<input type='text' name='username' pattern='[\w\-]{6,16}'>
```

The pattern `'[\w\-]{6,16}'` tells the browser to accept only the following:

- `\w`   The letters a-z and A-Z, the digits 0-9, and the underline character
- `\-`   The dash character
- `{6,16}`   Between 6 and 16 characters inclusive

 Currently this feature is not supported by Safari, and therefore it cannot be relied upon for reliable in-browser validation. I would also add that Chrome simply refuses to submit a form when a pattern doesn't match—giving you no idea why, while Opera says "[input] is not in the format this page requires!" Therefore I recommend ignoring this feature until such time as it is available on all browsers, and has matured to the point of actually informing users what they need to enter.

The `placeholder` Attribute

The `placeholder` attribute lets you place a helpful hint in any blank input field, with which you can help explain to users what they should enter. You use it like this:

```
<input type='text' name='username' size='35'
  placeholder='Enter your 6-16 character username'>
```

The `size` attribute value of 35 ensures that there's enough room for the placeholder text which, as long as nothing has yet been entered into a field, is displayed in a light color, as shown in Figure 16-4.

FIGURE 16-4   Displaying a placeholder

As soon as the field is given focus and a user starts typing, the prompt disappears. This attribute can be applied to any of the `email`, `password`, `search`, `telephone`, `text`, and `url` types of the `<input>` tag.

The `required` Attribute

The `required` attribute is used to ensure that a field has been completed before a form is submitted. You use it like this:

```
<input type='number' name='age' required='required'>
```

The `step` Attribute

The `step` attribute is used to specify a step value for input types that contain numbers or dates. Here's how you might use it in conjunction with the `min` and `max` attributes:

```
<input type='time' name='deliver' value='09:00' min='09:00'
  max='17:00' step='3600'>
```

The value can be any positive integer and, in the case of times, its value is in seconds. The result of using the preceding HTML is shown earlier in Figure 16-3. By clicking on the up and down icons, or by using the up and down cursor keys, it is possible to scroll through the hours to make a selection.

 Note At the time of writing, this feature is not yet supported by Firefox or Internet Explorer.

New Form Input Types

Over the years, it has been discovered that there are many more types of input a website might ask for than the simple selection types supported by HTML 4.01. In fact, there are now 16 new types of input available in HTML5.

What they provide is tighter control over user input, along with built-in validation. The only drawback is that these input types are not widely implemented. Nevertheless, you can still use all of them, even on unsupported browsers, as they will fall back to being regular text fields. If you use these types over time, then as other browsers catch up, your forms will automatically become easier to complete.

 Note Mobile devices should generally be aware of some of these input types in the sense that they will change the keyboard type presented to you accordingly. For example, the `email` input type will ensure that an @ symbol is included in the main set of characters, the `number` type ensures that number keys are visible, and the `tel` type displays a telephone keypad.

The `color` Input Type

The `color` input type calls up a color picker so you can simply click on the color of your choice. You use it like this:

```
Enter your preferred color <input type='color' name='favcolor'>
```

 Note This feature is only available in Chrome and Opera at the time of writing.

Date and Time Pickers

Date and time pickers are similar to the `color` input type in that eventually you'll be able to click on one and a calendar will pop up, from which you can select a date or time, as shown in Figure 16-5.

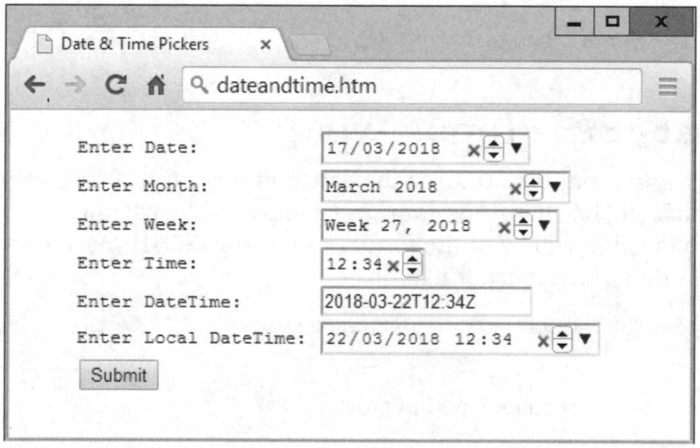

FIGURE 16-5   Date pickers in Google Chrome

 Note Currently these pickers do not work in Firefox or Internet Explorer, so my advice is to ignore these features until they mature and work properly on all the main browsers; in the meantime, there are plenty of JavaScript date picker libraries you can find via search engines.

The `date` Input Type

The `date` input type selects a date and is used like this:

```
<input type='date' name='thedate'>
```

The returned value will be of the form YYYY-MM-DD.

The month Input Type

The month input type selects a month and is used like this:

```
<input type='month' name='themonth'>
```

The value returned is of the form YYYY-MM.

The time Input Type

The time input type returns a time in the 24-hour form HH:MM. You use it like this:

```
<input type='time' name='thetime'>
```

The week Input Type

The week input type returns the week in the form YYYY-WNN (for example 2018-W06). You use it like this:

```
<input type='week' name='theweek'>
```

The datetime Input Type

The datetime input type returns the date and time in UTC (Coordinated Universal Time), which will be almost the same as Greenwich Mean Time, give or take a second. The returned value will be of the form YYYY-MM-DDTHH:MMZ (for example 2018-10-15T15:35Z). You use it like this:

```
<input type='datetime' name='dateandtime'>
```

 This type is not supported in Chrome.

The datetime-local Input Type

The datetime-local input type returns the user's local date and time. The returned value will be of the form YYYY-MM-DDTHH:MM (for example, 2018-10-15T15:35) and will contain no time zone information. You use it like this:

```
<input type='datetime-local' name='localdateandtime'>
```

The `email` Input Type

The `email` validation type ensures that the browser knows an e-mail address is expected and if necessary can cater to it (for example, by including the @ character on the pop-up keyboard of a mobile phone):

```
<input type='email' name='emailaddress'>
```

 This type is not supported by Safari.

The `number` Input Type

The `number` validation type ensures that only numbers can be entered. You use it like this:

```
<input type='number' name='age'>
```

Small up and down icons appear next to the input to allow changing a default value by clicking them, or by using the up and down cursor keys.

The `range` Input Type

The `range` input type causes a range widget to be displayed that you can slide to select any value between a minimum and maximum, and with a specified start and step value.

It is used like this, and the result is shown in Figure 16-6.

```
<input type='range' name='num' min='0' max='255' value='128' step='1'>
```

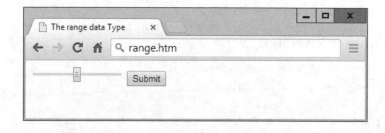

FIGURE 16-6   A range widget in Google Chrome

The `search` Input Type

When you specify the `search` type, browsers are supposed to tailor the input box to provide features that might include search suggestions (in a similar way to Google Search), an icon with which to empty the field, and possibly styling changes to alert you to the type of input.

The only enhancements are an X icon for clearing the input, and a rounded input field (on Mac Safari only). But there's no harm in you using this input type right now, as other browsers simply display the default text field, and when they support the feature, your web pages will already be enhanced for it.

You use the attribute like this:

```
<input type='search' name='searchphrase'>
```

Note   As of writing, this has been implemented only on Safari and Chrome.

The `tel` Input Type

The `tel` input type informs the browser that a telephone number is to be expected. Currently it is used by iOS devices when the field is selected to bring up a telephone number keypad in place of a keyboard:

```
<input type='tel' name='phone'>
```

The `url` Input Type

As with the `tel` input type, the `url` type is also there to tell the browser about the type of data to be expected. In the case of the iPhone and other iOS devices, this ensures that the `.`, `/` and `.com` buttons are displayed.

Other browsers may also offer enhancements for this type in the future, which is created with the following HTML:

```
<input type='url' name='webpage'>
```

Summary

As you will have noticed, forms are probably the subsection of the HTML5 specification that have been the least worked on by the browser developers. This is a shame because submitting data is one of the most common and important tasks people do on the web. Still, HTML5 browser support is improving, and you can keep up with the latest developments at *tinyurl.com/h5forms*. In the next lesson we'll take a look at local storage and cross document messaging.

Self-Test Questions

Test how much you have learned in this lesson with these questions. If you don't know an answer, go back and reread the relevant section until your knowledge is complete. You can find the answers in the appendix.

1. How can you provide access to typing into an input field without the user first having to click it?

2. With which attribute can you allow previous values that have been entered for the current input field's name to be selected by the user?

3. What is the purpose of the `list` attribute?

4. How can you set minimum and maximum limits for an input?

5. Which attribute enables uploading of more than one file at a time via a form?

6. How can you place text in an empty input field to prompt the user for the type of input expected?

7. Which attribute can you use to ensure that an input must be completed before a form is submitted?

8. What does the attribute `pattern='[\w]{5,10}'` do to the input to which it is applied?

9. How can you offer a color picker in an input (to browsers that support it)?

10. How can you call up a calendar date picker in an input (for browsers that support it)?

Implementing Local Storage and Cross-Document Messaging

 To view the accompanying video for this lesson, please visit mhprofessional.com/nixonhtml5/.

You are probably quite familiar with cookies: small units of data that are stored locally by your browser, which contain information helpful to using a website, such as your login details (to save you from continuously re-entering them), and which are often also used somewhat more intrusively to track your surfing habits.

Local storage is similar to cookies, but it supports storing much larger amounts of data and also supplies a local database engine to make saving and retrieving data much easier.

The benefits of this are more powerful web apps, with more data residing on your computer, rather than on servers somewhere else in the world. For example, a website that manages your TV viewing could store all your favorite programs in a local database, so that when you open the app, it only has to check a website of listings to see when these programs are on next, and on which channels. This takes a strain off the web server by leaving the data distributed among users.

Another benefit is that such local databases can be accessed from a local web page using JavaScript, meaning that the data can be used by the app even where there is no Internet connection (in this example case, as long as the TV listings have also been downloaded).

Using Local Storage

In the past the only way you could store data on a user's computer was with cookies, which were limited in number and could hold only 4K each. They also have to be passed back on every page load or reload and, unless your server uses SSL (Secure Sockets Layer) encryption (like with HTTPS), each time a cookie is transmitted it travels in the clear.

But with HTML5 you have access to a much larger local storage space (typically between 5MB and 10MB per domain depending on the browser) that remains over page loads and between website visits (and even after powering a computer down and back up again), and which is not sent to the server on each page load.

You handle the data in pairs consisting of a key and its value. The key is the name assigned for referencing the data and the value can hold any type of data, but it is saved as a string.

All data is unique to the current domain. Any local storage created by websites with different domains is separate from the current local storage for security reasons, and is not accessible by any domain other than the one that stored the data.

 For security reasons, local storage will work only when a web document is viewed after being sent via a web server. You cannot test documents that implement this feature from a local file system.

Storing and Retrieving Local Data

To access local storage, you use methods of the `localStorage` object such as `setItem()`, `getItem()`, `removeItem()`, and `clear()`. For example, to locally store a user's username and password, you might use code such as this:

```
localStorage.setItem('username', 'BObama')
localStorage.setItem('password', 'IAmThePrez')
```

If the size of the value is larger than the disk quota remaining for the storage area, an "Out of memory" exception is thrown. Otherwise, when another page loads or when the user returns to the website, these details can be retrieved to save the user entering them again, like this:

```
username = localStorage.getItem('username')
password = localStorage.getItem('password')
```

If the key doesn't exist, then the `getItem()` function returns a value of `null`.

You don't have to use these function names if you don't want to, because you can access the `localStorage` object directly as the two following statements are equivalent to each other:

```
localStorage.setItem('key', 'value')
localStorage['key'] = 'value'
```

And the two following statements are therefore also equivalent to each other:

```
value = localStorage.getItem('key')
value = localStorage['key']
```

Figure 17-1 shows an `alert()` message window displaying these values being retrieved from local storage, using the following code:

```
if (typeof localStorage == 'undefined')
{
  document.write("Local storage unavailable.")
```

```
    }
    else
    {
      document.write("Local storage available.")

      localStorage.setItem('username', 'BObama')
      localStorage.setItem('password', 'IAmThePrez')

      username  = localStorage.getItem('username')
      password  = localStorage.getItem('password')

      alert("Data retrieved: username = '" + username +
                  "', password = '" + password + "'.")
    }
```

> The page at localhost says:
>
> Data retrieved: username = 'BObama', password =
> 'IAmThePrez'.
>
> [OK]

FIGURE 17-1   Data has been saved to and retrieved from local storage.

The first part of code within the `if ()` statement writes an error message to the web page if local storage is not supported in the browser. This is determined by examining the `localStorage` object and, if it is undefined, then local storage is unavailable.

In the `else` part of the code, a message is first written to the web page indicating that local storage is supported. Then the username and password are saved to local storage with the `setItem()` function. Next, these values are retrieved from local storage into the variables `username` and `password`. Finally, an `alert()` message window is popped up, which displays the retrieved values.

 Note   Until they are erased, these values will remain in the local storage once saved, and you can verify this by trying the preceding code for yourself, running it once, commenting out the two lines of code that call `setItem()`, and then running it again—the alert window will still report the same values.

Removing and Clearing Local Data

To remove an item of data from the local storage, all you need to do is issue a command such as this:

```
username = localStorage.removeItem('username')
```

This serves to retrieve the item of data and place it into a variable (in this case username), and then deletes the data from local storage. If you don't need to first read the data you are removing, you can simply call the function on its own, like this:

```
localStorage.removeItem('username')
```

You can also completely clear the local storage for the current domain by issuing this command:

```
localStorage.clear()
```

 Try any of these methods on the preceding example and run it again, and you'll find that the values have been erased.

Saving and retrieving data is starting to take us into the realms of much more complicated JavaScript programming, somewhat beyond the scope of this book. So the information in this lesson is mostly of use to programmers working with large amounts of JavaScript program code.

If you are a beginner to JavaScript, then it's best to simply be aware of the possibilities of local storage, and come back here to refresh your memory about how it works when your programming is sufficiently advanced and you find the need for it.

Cross-Document Messaging

Cross-document messaging (also known as web messaging) allows scripts in different documents to interact with each other through use of the postMessage() function. The code to send messages is just a single instruction, in which you pass the message to be sent and the domain to which it applies, as follows:

```
<!DOCTYPE HTML>
<html>
  <head>
    <title>Web Message Sender</title>
  </head>
<body>
    <iframe id='frame' src='listen.htm' width='360' height='75'></iframe>

    <script>
    count = 1

    setInterval(function()
    {
      document.getElementById('frame').contentWindow.
        postMessage('Message ' + count++, 'http://localhost')
    }, 1000)
```

```
    </script>
  </body>
</html>
```

In this example an `<iframe>` element with the ID of `frame` is created, that loads in the web document *listen.htm* (see the following code listing). Then, within the `<script>` section, the variable `count` is initialized to 1 and a repeating interval is set up to occur every second to post the string `'Message '` (using the `postMessage()` function) along with the current value of `count`, which is then incremented, and the message is posted only to listeners in the domain *http://localhost*.

The file *listen.htm* looks like this:

```
<!DOCTYPE HTML>
<html>
  <head>
    <title>Web Message Listener</title>
  </head>
  <body>
    <div id='output'></div>

    <script>
      window.onmessage = function(event)
      {
        document.getElementById('output').innerHTML = event.data
      }
    </script>
  </body>
</html>
```

This example creates a `<div>` element with the ID `output`, in which the contents of received messages will be placed. In the `<script>` section there's a single anonymous function attached to the `onmessage` event of the window. In this function the `event`.`data` property (the contents of the message) is then displayed, as shown in Figure 17-2.

FIGURE 17-2   The iframe is displaying messages from the parent frame.

For security reasons web messaging works only with domains, and so you cannot test it by loading files in from a file system—a web server must be used. The origin used in this example is http://localhost, because these examples are running on a local development server.

As it stands, the *listen.htm* document displays any and all messages it receives, which is also not very secure because malicious documents also present in the browser can attempt to send messages that unwary listener code might access. Therefore you can restrict the messages your listener reacts to using an if() statement to test the origin property, like this:

```
window.onmessage = function(event)
{
  if (event.origin == 'http://localhost')
    document.getElementById('output').innerHTML = event.data
}
```

Summary

That concludes this part of the course on some of the more advanced aspects of HTML5 that you can use right now. In the next two lessons I'll show you how to add HTML5 audio and video to your web pages, without having to resort to using plug-ins such as Microsoft Silverlight or Adobe Flash.

Self-Test Questions

Test how much you have learned in this lesson with these questions. If you don't know an answer, go back and reread the relevant section until your knowledge is complete. You can find the answers in the appendix.

1. Why is local storage a better solution than cookies?

2. How can you determine whether local storage is available in a browser?

3. How do you store an item of local storage data?

4. How do you retrieve an item of local storage data?

5. How can you remove an item from local storage?

6. How do you clear all the data relating to your domain in local storage?

7. How can you post a message to another document loaded into the browser?

8. How can you listen for messages from other loaded documents?

9. What should you do to ensure that you post messages only to the documents you want to receive them?

10. What should you do to ignore any message received from documents from which you do not wish to receive them?

Playing Audio

 To view the accompanying video for this lesson, please visit mhprofessional.com/ nixonhtml5/.

In this section of the course, I introduce two of the most popular additions to HTML5, the <audio> and <video> tags. In fact, they are probably going to be even more used than the <canvas> tag due to the ability to play media directly within the browser, without the need for an external plug-in such as the Flash Player.

So in this lesson I'll show you how easy it is to add HTML5 audio to your pages, which I think you'll find is a remarkably easy thing to do, as long as the browser is a recent one.

As you work through this lesson, please remember that the technology is still young and the file formats supported are constantly evolving (and vary by browser for patent reasons), but the following explains all you need to know to embed audio using HTML5.

 Flash is a programming environment best suited for creating animations and games, which has mostly been adopted for playing video. But it is likely that HTML will supersede it, partly due to Apple not including it by default on new Macs and banning it from iOS devices, and also because the <canvas> tag provides almost everything a programmer previously would have needed Flash for.

Understanding Codecs

The term *codec* stands for enCOder/DECoder and describes the functionality provided by software that encodes and decodes media such as audio and video. In HTML5 there are currently a number of different sets of codecs available, depending on the browser used.

Here are the codecs currently in use by the HTML5 `<audio>` tag (and also when audio is attached to HTML5 video):

- **AAC**   This audio codec, which stands for Advanced Audio Coding, is the one used by Apple's iTunes store. It was originally proprietary, patented technology, but has since been standardized as part of the MPEG-2 and MPEG-4 specifications, and is supported by Apple, Google, and Microsoft.
- **MP3**   This audio codec, which stands for MPEG Audio Layer 3, has been available for many years and the term is often (incorrectly) used to refer to any type of digital audio. It's an open proprietary format (but subject to patents in some countries) that is supported by Apple, Google, and Microsoft.
- **PCM**   This audio codec, which stands for Pulse Coded Modulation, stores the full data as encoded by an analog to digital converter, and is the format used for storing data on audio CDs. Due to not using compression, it is called a *lossless codec*, and its files are generally many times larger than AAC or MP3 files. It is supported by Apple, Mozilla, and Opera.
- **Vorbis**   Sometimes referred to as Ogg Vorbis, because it generally uses the *.ogg* file extension, this audio codec is unencumbered by patents and free of royalty payments. It is supported by Google Chrome, Mozilla Firefox, and Opera.

The following list details the major operating systems and browsers, along with the audio types they support by default:

- **Apple iOS**   AAC, MP3, PCM
- **Apple Safari**   AAC, MP3, PCM
- **Google Android 2.3 +**   AAC, MP3, Vorbis
- **Google Chrome**   AAC, MP3, Vorbis
- **Internet Explorer**   AAC, MP3
- **Mozilla Firefox**   MP3, PCM, Vorbis
- **Opera**   PCM, Vorbis

If you study this list, you'll see that none of these codecs are shared by all browsers and platforms, which is rather inconvenient. The problem occurs particularly because some browsers choose to not employ the licensable codecs.

 Apple Safari for Windows requires the Apple QuickTime media player to be installed in order for HTML5 audio and video to play, so you may wish to use JavaScript browser detection software to alert your Windows Safari users of this, particularly since the only error they may otherwise get is any message you include inside the `<audio>` tags.

The <audio> and <source> Tags

However, there's a simple (if inconvenient) solution, which is to record your content using multiple codecs and then list them all within <audio> and </audio> tags, as in the following example. The result of running this code in all the main browsers can be seen in Figure 18-1:

```
<audio controls>
  <source src='audio.m4a' type='audio/aac'>
  <source src='audio.mp3' type='audio/mpeg'>
  <source src='audio.ogg' type='audio/ogg'>
</audio>
```

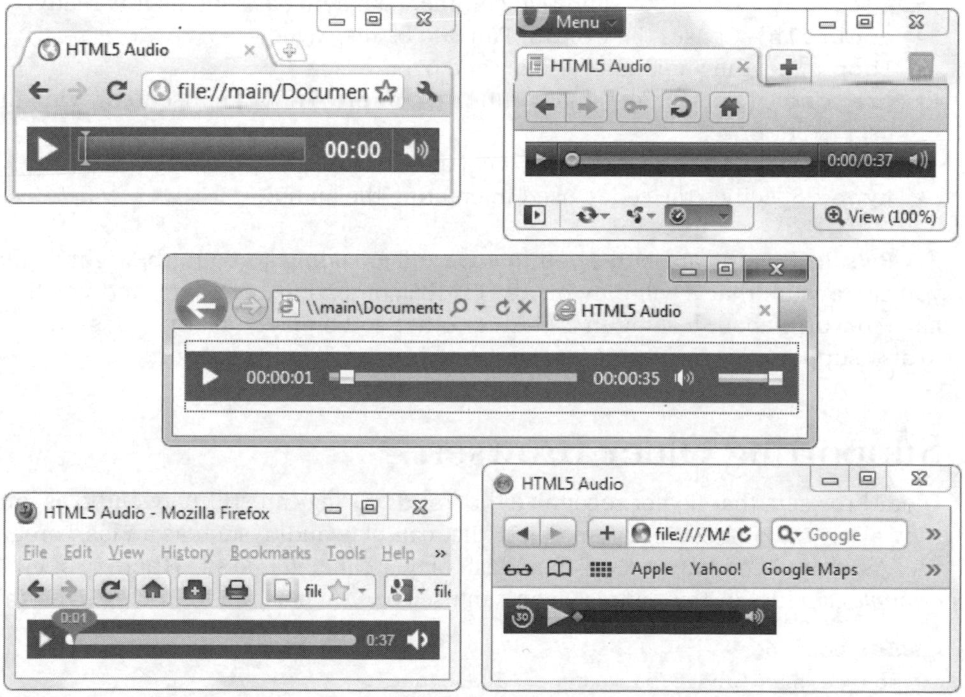

FIGURE 18-1 How the five main browsers display HTML5 audio

In the preceding example, three types of audio are made available, but nowadays you generally only need to encode in two formats: OGG, and either AAC or MP3 to ensure you cover all the bases.

Perform an Internet search to find suitable programs to create the file types you need—there are plenty of them, both paid and free.

The `<audio>` and `<source>` Tag Attributes

In the preceding example you may have noticed that I applied an attribute with the name `controls` to the `<audio>` tag. This had the effect of causing a set of controls to appear, as displayed in Figure 18-1. If that attribute is omitted, then the controls will not display (and you'd either have to use another attribute called `autostart` or some JavaScript to make the audio play).

Here's a list of audio attributes supported by HTML5:

- `autoplay`   Causes the audio to commence playing as soon as it is ready.
- `controls`   Causes the Control Panel to be displayed.
- `loop`   Sets the audio to play over and over.
- `preload`   Hints at how much buffering (or preloading) to use to provide the best user experience.
- `src`   Specifies the source location of an audio file.
- `type`   Specifies the codec used in creating the audio.

By selecting the attributes you require and encoding audio in the right formats, you can ensure that it will play on all HTML5-compatible browsers, and you'll never have to worry about loading in a Flash or other audio player again, unless you intend to also support older browsers, as described in the following section.

Supporting Older Browsers

Older browsers that do not recognize the `<audio>` tag can still play audio as long as they allow the embedding of an object that can play audio, such as a Flash program file. Assuming you have access to a Flash player called *audio.swf* (there is one in the *examples.zip* file for this course), you can use code such as the following to do this:

```
<audio controls>
  <source src='audio.m4a' type='audio/aac'>
  <source src='audio.mp3' type='audio/mpeg'>
  <source src='audio.ogg' type='audio/ogg'>
  <object type="application/x-shockwave-flash"
    data="audioplayer.swf" height="30" width="300">
    <param name="FlashVars"
      value="mp3=audio.mp3&amp;showstop=1&amp;showvolume=1">
  </object>
</audio>
```

On a non-HTML5 audio-enabled browser, the code within the `<object>` and `</object>` tags will load in the Flash program file *audio.swf*, and pass it the MP3 file *audio.mp3*, which can then be played by selecting the Play button. Figure 18-2 shows what the player looks like—not bad compared to the HTML5 ones, so it's a pretty good fallback.

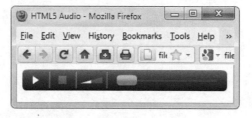

FIGURE 18-2   The fallback Flash audio player

Summary

You now have all the tools you need in order to play audio in your web pages, whether or not the browser supports HTML5 (but as long as it at least supports Flash). In the next lesson I'll show you how to do the same with video.

Self-Test Questions

Test how much you have learned in this lesson with these questions. If you don't know an answer, go back and reread the relevant section until your knowledge is complete. You can find the answers in the appendix.

1. Which HTML5 tag embeds audio in a document?

2. Name the four types of audio format supported by HTML5 browsers.

3. Which two audio formats used together will ensure that your audio will play on all major browsers and platforms?

4. What is the purpose of the `<source>` tag?

5. Which two attributes does the `<source>` tag require?

6. Which attribute makes audio play on page load?

7. How can you control whether or not the audio controls are displayed?

8. How can you set a piece of audio to play over and over?

9. How can you cause audio to begin loading even before the user selects Play?

10. How can you support older browsers that do not recognize HTML5 audio?

Displaying Video

 To view the accompanying video for this lesson, please visit mhprofessional.com/ nixonhtml5/.

Adding HTML5 video to your pages is almost as easy as adding audio, but there are some differences, and I'll point out the things you need to concern yourself with.

The main thing to realize, though, is that HTML5 video is still in its infancy and that specifications and codecs may change over time, as may the best ways to code and display your video. Still, following the advice in this lesson, you'll be able to add video to any HTML5-enabled browser that supports the `<video>` tag, and also some other or earlier browsers that do not (as long as they support the Flash plug-in).

The Video Codecs

As explained in the previous lesson, the term *codec* stands for enCOder/DECoder and describes the functionality provided by software that encodes and decodes media such as audio and video.

For video, though, codecs are placed within containers, which may be any of the following:

- **MP4** A license-encumbered multimedia container format standard specified as a part of MPEG-4, supported by Apple, Microsoft and, to a lesser extent Google, since it has its own WebM container format.
- **OGG** A free, open container format maintained by the *Xiph.Org* Foundation. The creators of the OGG format state that it is unrestricted by software patents and is designed to provide for efficient streaming and manipulation of high-quality digital multimedia.

- **WebM**   An audio-video format designed to provide a royalty-free, open video compression format for use with HTML5 video. The project's development is sponsored by Google.

In the HTML5 <video> tag there are currently a number of different sets of codecs available, depending on the browser used:

- **H.264**   A patented proprietary video codec for which playback is free for the end user, but which may incur royalty fees for all parts of the encoding and transmission process.
- **Theora**   This is a video codec unencumbered by patents, and which is free of royalty payments at all levels of encoding, transmission, and playback. This codec is supported by Google Chrome, Mozilla Firefox, and Opera.
- **VP8**   This video codec is similar to Theora but is owned by Google, which has published it as open source, making it royalty-free. It is supported by Google Chrome, Mozilla Firefox, and Opera. There is also a newer VP9 codec.

The following list details the major operating systems and browsers, along with the video containers and video types they support by default:

- **Apple iOS**   MP4 / H.264
- **Apple Safari**   MP4 / H.264
- **Google Android 2.3 +**   MP4, OGG, WebM / H.264, Theora, VP8
- **Google Chrome**   MP4, OGG, WebM / H.264, Theora, VP8/VP9
- **Internet Explorer**   MP4 / H.264
- **Mozilla Firefox**   MP4, OGG, WebM / H.276, Theora, VP8/VP9
- **Opera**   OGG, WebM / Theora, VP8

As with HTML5 <audio>, there is no single container and/or codec for the <video> tag common to all browsers and platforms. However, the dominant format is MP4 / H.264, so if you encode in that and then OGG / VP8 too, you'll cover all the major browsers.

The <video> and <source> Tags

In the following example three different video formats are offered to the browser, as shown in Figure 19-1:

```
<video width='560' height='320' controls>
  <source src='video.mp4'  type='video/mp4'>
  <source src='video.webm' type='video/webm'>
  <source src='video.ogv'  type='video/ogg'>
</video>
```

FIGURE 19-1 Playing an HTML5 video

 If you don't have access to any, you can search the Internet for a range of free and paid video conversion and compression tools.

The `<video>` and `<source>` Tag Attributes

In the preceding example I applied the attribute with the name `controls` to the `<video>` tag. This had the effect of causing a set of controls to appear, as displayed in Figure 19-1. If that attribute is omitted, then the controls will not display (and you'd either have to use the `autostart` attribute, or use some JavaScript to make the video play).

Here's a list of video attributes supported by HTML5:

- **autoplay** Causes the video to commence playing as soon as it is ready.
- **controls** Causes the Control Panel to be displayed.
- **height** Specifies the height at which to display the video.
- **loop** Sets the video to play over and over.
- **poster** Lets you choose an image to display prior to playback.
- **preload** Hints at how much buffering (or preloading) to use to provide the best user experience.
- **src** Specifies the source location of a video file.
- **type** Specifies the codec used in creating the video.
- **width** Specifies the width at which to display the video.

By selecting the attributes you require and encoding video in the right formats, you can ensure that it will play on all HTML5-compatible browsers, and you'll never have to worry about loading in a Flash or other video player again, unless you intend to also support older browsers, as follows:

```
<video width='560' height='320' controls>
  <source src='video.mp4'  type='video/mp4' >
  <source src='video.webm' type='video/webm'>
  <source src='video.ogv'  type='video/ogg' >
  <object width='560' height='320' type='application/x-shockwave-flash'
    data='flowplayer.swf'>
    <param name='movie'      value='flowplayer.swf'>
    <param name='flashvars' value='config={"clip": {"url":
      "http://robinnixon.com/media/video.mp4",
      "autoPlay":false, "autoBuffering":true}}'>
  </object>
</video>
```

Using the code in the `<object>` and `</object>` tags, you can ensure that non-HTML5-enabled browsers can still play your MP4 videos as long as they have the Flash plug-in loaded. The *flowplayer.swf* files required to do this are included in the *examples.zip* file on the accompanying website, but you can check for newer versions at the *flowplayer.org* website. If you download a newer version, ensure you match the code to the filenames, which will have numeric extensions such as -3.2.7, and so on.

The preceding code displays like Figure 19-2 in browsers that do not support the `<video>` tag, but do have Flash installed.

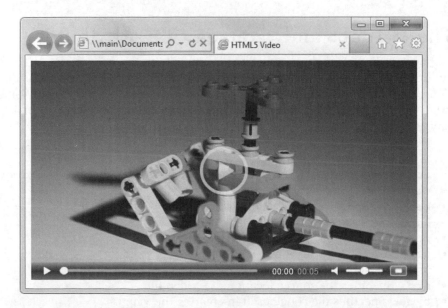

FIGURE 19-2   Displaying the same video using a Flash player

The *flowplayer.swf* file restricts the playing of files directly from a local folder on a computer, therefore you must supply it with the full Internet URL of a file, as in the example.

Summary

Now that you've completed this lesson, you will have all the audio and video tools you need in order to play media in your web pages, whether or not the browser supports HTML5 (but as long as it at least supports Flash). You have now learned almost everything that is currently usable in HTML5. In the next lesson I'll explain the features that are included in HTML5 but which have so far been poorly implemented (if at all), but which you should know about because they will probably be adopted by the major browsers over the coming months and years.

Self-Test Questions

Test how much you have learned in this lesson with these questions. If you don't know an answer, go back and reread the relevant section until your knowledge is complete. You can find the answers in the appendix.

1. Which HTML5 tag embeds video in a document?

2. Name the three types of video format supported by HTML5 browsers.

3. Which two video formats used together will ensure that your video will play on all major browsers and platforms?

4. What is the purpose of the `<source>` tag?

5. Which two attributes does the `<source>` tag require?

6. Which attribute makes video play on page load?

7. How can you control whether or not the video controls are displayed?

8. How can you set a video's width and height?

9. How can you display an image of your choice as a placeholder for where the video will play?

10. How can you support older browsers that do not recognize HTML5 video?

Working with Microdata, Web Workers, and Web Applications

 To view the accompanying video for this lesson, please visit mhprofessional.com/nixonhtml5/.

HTML5 is an extension of HTML that is proceeding gradually. Many of its tags and features have already been implemented by the major browsers, while, as you've seen, others are only partially developed on some browsers.

So I have reserved the final lesson in this course for discussion of the remaining advanced HTML5 features, some of which have yet to be fully (or even properly) implemented, but are going to turn out extremely powerful when they become available, and some of which it may benefit you to start using already.

I show you how they work (or are planned to work), although aspects of some parts of the implementation could develop or be improved over time, as HTML5 is really more of a bundling of a group of unrelated features that developers want to add to HTML.

Microdata

The first of these features is called *microdata*, which is a subset of HTML designed for making a document have meaning to machines by providing metadata, just as it has meaning to a reader of the document.

What it does is make available the following new tag attributes: `itemscope`, `itemtype`, `itemid`, `itemref`, and `itemprop`. Using them you will be able to clearly define the properties of an item such as a book, providing a range of information that a computer can use to understand, for example, its authors, publishers, contents, and so on.

Here's how HTML code looks that incorporates microdata, and Figure 20-1 shows how this HTML displays:

```
<section
  itemscope itemtype='http://data-vocabulary.org/Person'>

  <img itemprop='photo' src='robin.jpg'
    alt='Robin Nixon' style='float:left; margin-right:10px'>

  <h2 itemprop='name'>Robin Nixon</h2>

  <p>I am a <span itemprop='role'>Book Author</span>, and
    online <span itemprop='title'>Instructor</span>.
    Some people call me <span itemprop='nickname'>Rob</span>,
    and my website is: <a itemprop='url'
    href='http://robinnixon.com'>robinnixon.com</a>.

    My address is:</p>

  <address
    itemscope itemtype='http://data-vocabulary.org/Address'
    itemprop='address'>

    <span itemprop='street-address'>123 My Street</span>,
    <span itemprop='locality'>Anytown</span>,
    <span itemprop='region'>Anystate</span>,
    <span itemprop='postal-code'>AB12 3CD</span>,
    <span itemprop='country-name'>Great Britain</span>.

  </address>
</section>
```

As you might expect, the adding of microdata has done nothing to alter the format of the HTML in any way. But it has provided a wealth of information to any browsers or search engines that can read the microdata and understand what it represents.

If you study the example code, you'll see a couple of references to URLs at the *data-vocabulary.org* web server. That's because this is where all the information you need for using microdata can be found, and from which you can choose the microdata types to use in your HTML. I strongly recommend you check it out, especially since that website is now saying that *schema.org* is likely to supersede it.

The in-browser DOM (Document Object Model) functions for managing microdata appear not to have been implemented yet by many major browser publishers.

When the API is incorporated into the major browsers, the microdata scripts will be able to use the microdata to expose information to the user, for example offering it in a form that can be used by other applications. Very likely there will also be mouseover and other information revealed when mousing over text that has microdata attached. So from that point of view there's not a lot of reason to use microdata; not yet, anyway.

FIGURE 20-1   Packed with microdata, the HTML displays quite normally.

Because the API will use the function getItems(), you can test whether a browser supports it or not using the following code, which pops up a message telling you:

```
<script>
  if (!!document.getItems)
      alert("Microdata supported")
  else alert("Microdata not supported")
</script>
```

The specs for microdata are available at *tinyurl.com/microdataspecs*, so take a look if you want to know what to expect, and how to use the getItems() function when browsers start to support it.

 The first big users of microdata will actually be the search engines, and it has been reported that some microdata information is already turning up in Google's index. Therefore you do have a very good reason to start using microdata immediately, because anything you can do to legitimately improve your website rankings in the search engines is important to implement.

Web Workers

Normally, to achieve background processing in JavaScript, you need to set up a timer that is called repeatedly, supplying slices of processor time to one or more functions, and these functions must then quickly do a small piece of work and return, in order to not slow down the browser and make it seem sluggish.

Web workers, however, provide a standard way for browsers to run multiple JavaScript threads in the background that can pass messages to each other, in much the same manner as the threads running in an operating system. You simply call up a new worker script, which will sit there in the background waiting for messages to be sent to it, which it will then act upon.

The aim of this is to achieve a speed increase of two to three times over regular background JavaScripts, although getting to grips with programming them is likely to require a longer rather than shorter learning curve.

Here's how to find out if a browser supports web workers:

```
<script>
  if (!!window.Worker)
      alert("Web workers supported")
  else alert("Web workers not supported")
</script>
```

This script simply alerts you as to whether or not web workers are supported by the browser you are using. Once you have determined that the browser will use them, then you can run code such as the following, which calculates prime numbers in the background:

```
<p>The highest prime number discovered so far is:
  <output id='result'></output></p>
<script>
  var worker = new Worker('worker.js')

  worker.onmessage = function(event)
  {
    document.getElementById('result').innerHTML = event.data;
  }
</script>
```

This script displays some text and creates an element with the id of result into which the highest prime number found so far is continuously written. This is achieved by creating the new object called worker by calling the Worker() function, passing it the name of an external JavaScript file called *worker.js* (explained shortly).

The onmessage event of the worker object is then attached to by an anonymous function. This triggers only when there is a new message to display, and the code that is called copies the data in event.data into the innerHTML property of the result element. After the code exits, it will not be called again until another message is ready to display.

The code that does the prime number calculation is saved separately in the *worker.js*, and looks like this:

```
var n = 1

search: while (true)
{
```

```
   n += 1

   for (var i = 2; i <= Math.sqrt(n); i += 1)
     if (n % i == 0) continue search;

   postMessage(n)
}
```

This is a simple iterative piece of code that increases the value of n, starting from 1. After each increase, all values of 2 up to the square root of n are tested to see if they are a factor of n. If any of them is, then n cannot be prime and so the `continue` keyword forces execution to go back to the start of the `search:` loop to see if n+1 is prime, and so on.

But if n is found to have no factors, then it is prime and the `continue` keyword is not encountered, so program flow drops through to the `postMessage()` call, which posts the value n, creating an `onmessage` event on the `worker` object in the preceding code. The result of running this code is a line of text at the top of the browser that continuously updates and looks like this:

```
The highest prime number discovered so far is:  42737
```

Working together, an HTML page and associated JavaScript file can work away in the background performing all manner of tasks, something which was achievable in the past only by manually creating events to run the code a few instructions at a time before returning to allow the web page to have some processor cycles, after which the event is then created to let the program code run a few more cycles, and so on.

As you might imagine, the old way is rather tricky and can be cumbersome. It can also mess with smooth animations on your web page if you don't get the event timings and time sharing exactly right. But with web workers, you can forget all about these things and simply place your background code into its own file, and just ensure that the code calls the `postMessage()` function whenever it has something to say.

For full details on the web worker specifications, you can check out the official website at *tinyurl.com/webworkerspecs*.

Offline Web Applications

The idea of offline web applications is that once you visit a website, the website tells your browser about all the files it uses so that the browser can download them all and you can then run the web application locally, even without an Internet connection.

Offline web applications require a web server to set up with the correct MIME types (originally known as Multipurpose Internet Mail Extensions, but the word *Mail* has since been replaced with *Media*), in order for a browser that understands offline web applications to make use of the feature and fetch the files it needs.

If you are using a web server that is not Apache, consult your manuals for how to add the `text/cache-manifest` MIME type in order for your server to send the manifest file using the correct type. Otherwise, there's a neat shortcut you can use, which is to create a file called *.htaccess* in the same folder as the files to be made available offline, with the following contents:

```
AddType text/cache-manifest .appcache
```

 On Windows (at least in Windows Explorer), you cannot create a filename that starts with a period, so, if needed, call the file something like *a.htaccess* and then rename it to *.htaccess* after uploading it. On some FTP programs the file will then seem to disappear because it becomes a system file.

Here's how offline apps work. You start with a manifest file that contains all the files you'd like to offer for offline use, like the following, which is saved with the filename *clock.appcache*:

```
CACHE MANIFEST
clock.htm
clock.css
clock.js
```

The three files detailed in the manifest are then as follows, starting with *clock.htm*:

```
<!DOCTYPE html>
<html manifest='clock.appcache'>
  <head>
    <title>Offline Web Apps</title>
    <script src='clock.js'></script>
    <link rel='stylesheet' href='clock.css'>
  </head>
  <body>
    <p>The time is: <output id='clock'></output></p>
  </body>
</html>
```

Here's *clock.css*:

```
output { font-weight:bold; }
```

And this is *clock.js*:

```
setInterval(function ()
{
  document.getElementById('clock').innerHTML = new Date()
}, 1000)
```

Thanks to the manifest, all these files will be downloaded and made available for use offline to use in any environment. Between them, they create a simple clock that looks like Figure 20-2.

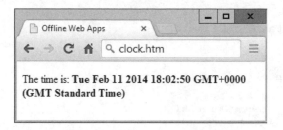

FIGURE 20-2   The clock web app running in Google Chrome

The code that does the work is in the *clock.js* file. It sets up a regular interval with `setInterval()` such that the code within it is called every 1,000 milliseconds (or once a second). This code simply copies the date into the `innerHTML` property of the `output` element.

For full details on the specifications for offline web applications, you can check out the official website at *tinyurl.com/offlinewebapps*.

Drag and Drop

You can support dragging and dropping of objects on a web page by setting up event handlers for the `ondragstart`, `ondragover`, and `ondrop` events, as follows:

```
<!DOCTYPE HTML>
<html>
  <head>
    <title>Drag and Drop</title>
    <style>
      #dest {
        background:lightblue;
        border    :1px solid #444;
        width     :320px;
        height    :100px;
        padding   :10px;
      }
    </style>
  </head>
  <body>
    <div id='dest' ondrop='drop(event)'
      ondragover='allow(event)'></div><br>
    Drag the image below into the above element<br><br>
```

```
    <img id='source' src='ball.gif' draggable='true'
      ondragstart='drag(event)'>

  <script>
    function allow(event)
    {
      event.preventDefault()
    }

    function drag(event)
    {
      event.dataTransfer.setData('image/png', event.target.id)
    }

    function drop(event)
    {
      event.preventDefault()
      var data=event.dataTransfer.getData('image/png')
      event.target.appendChild(document.getElementById(data))
    }
  </script>
  </body>
</html>
```

In the `<body>` of this example, a `<div>` element is created, and its `ondrop` and `ondragover` events have the event handler functions `drop` and `allow` attached to them. After this there's some text, and then an image is displayed, which has its `draggable` property set to `true`, and the function `drag` is attached to its `ondragstart` event.

In the `<script>` section, the `allow` event handler function simply prevents the default action of dragging (which is to disallow it) from occurring, while the `drag` event handler function calls the `setData` method of the `dataTransfer` object of the event, passing it the MIME type `image/png` and the `target.id` of the event (which is the object being dragged). The `dataTransfer` object holds the data that is being dragged during a drag-and-drop operation.

Finally, the `drop` event handler function also intercepts its default action so that dropping is allowed, then it fetches the contents of the object being dragged from the `dataTransfer` object, passing it the mime type of the object. Then the dropped data is appended to the target using its `appendChild` method.

When you load this example into a browser, you can drag and drop the image into the `<div>` element, as shown in Figure 20-3.

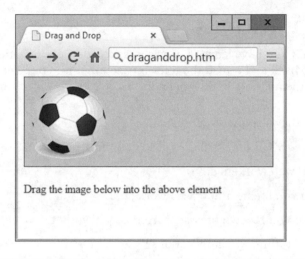

FIGURE 20-3   An image has been dragged and dropped.

Other HTML5 Tags

There are a number of other new HTML5 tags that have not yet been implemented in any browser (or have poor or limited support), and which I therefore won't detail (particularly since their specs could change).

But, for the sake of completeness, these tags are: `<article>`, `<aside>`, `<details>`, `<figcaption>`, `<figure>`, `<footer>`, `<header>`, `<hgroup>`, `<keygen>`, `<mark>`, `<menuitem>`, `<meter>`, `<nav>`, `<output>`, `<progress>`, `<rp>`, `<rt>`, `<ruby>`, `<section>`, `<summary>`, `<time>`, and `<wbr>`. You can get more information on these and all other HTML5 tags at the following URL: *http://whatwg.org/html*.

Summary

Congratulations! You've just completed this course on HTML5. Thanks for taking it! I hope you've enjoyed the process and have learned plenty of useful things from this course but, before you go, you may be interested in visiting my website at *robinnixon.com* to see my other books and courses, which cover both web technology and motivational and personal improvement topics.

If you feel so motivated, I would be very grateful for any review of this book you choose to leave at your preferred online website. And thanks once again for taking the course!

Self-Test Questions

Test how much you have learned in this lesson with these questions. If you don't know an answer, go back and reread the relevant section until your knowledge is complete. You can find the answers in the appendix.

1. What is the purpose of microdata?

2. What are two of the attributes used to denote microdata?

3. What do web workers do?

4. How do you create a new web worker?

5. How can you receive messages from a web worker?

6. What are offline web applications?

7. What MIME time is required by offline web applications for the manifest file?

8. To which events should you attach in order to implement drag and drop in a document?

9. What is the purpose of calling the `preventDefault()` function?

10. Which two functions handle the passing of dragged-and-dropped items?

A

Answers to the Self-Test Questions

This appendix contains the answers to all the questions posed at the end of the lessons in this book. To ensure you have understood everything, try to refrain from checking these answers until you have attempted to answer all the questions in a lesson.

If you don't know an answer, try to find it in the book before you look here if you can, as this will help you to remember it next time.

Lesson 1 Answers

1. The acronym HTML stands for HyperText Markup Language.

2. A web browser is used by someone surfing the Internet to view content that is sent by web servers.

3. The acronym HTTP stands for HyperText Transfer Protocol. This is the method used for transferring unencrypted web documents from a server to a browser (HTTPS is used for transferring encrypted documents).

4. A web proxy fetches data from a web server on behalf of a web browser. Generally, proxies store local copies of web data in a cache, and then serve up the copies to a web browser to provide faster response.

5. HTML documents often have the file extension *.html* or simply *.htm*.

6. A 404 page is so called because 404 is the HTTP error code returned by a web server when a document cannot be located, so "not-found" pages are often referred to as 404 pages.

7. An IP address is a set of numbers allocated to each unique Internet-connected device. A domain is an alphanumeric string used to refer to an IP address in a more memorable fashion. For example, at the time of writing, instead of remembering and entering *http://74.125.224.72*, you can simply type *http://google.com* into a browser.

8. A query string is a set of alphanumeric data after a URL that starts with a ? character. This data may contain form input that is being sent to a web server via a Get request.

9. An HTML tag is the name of an element enclosed within angle brackets, such as `<i>`, which represents italic text. Many tags also have matching closing tags such as `</i>`, which turns italics off again. Some tags such as `<img>` do not have a matching closing tag because they are self-closing (empty).

10. A tag attribute is additional data supplied to a tag, such as the URL of the image in `<img src='myimage.jpg'>`. Here `src` is the attribute name and *myimage.jpg* is its value.

Lesson 2 Answers

1. The declaration `<!DOCTYPE html>` should be at the start of all HTML5 documents.

2. The `<html>` and `</html>` tags are used to contain HTML. The `<html>` element represents the root of an HTML document.

3. The `<head>` tag is used (along with `</head>`) to denote a document's head section, which includes items such as its title.

4. To title a document, place the title between `<title>` and `</title>` tags.

5. The `<title>` tag should appear within `<head>` and `</head>` tags.

6. To denote the body of an HTML document, place it within `<body>` and `</body>` tags.

7. CSS rules should be placed within `<style>` and `</style>` tags in the `<head>` section.

8. You include a style sheet in an HTML document using the `<link>` tag, with appropriate attributes.

9. To embed JavaScript into an HTML document, place it between `<script>` and `</script>` tags.

10. You can run an external JavaScript file from an HTML document by calling it up from a `<script>` tag with its location provided as the value for its `src` attribute. You will also need a `</script>` tag following.

Lesson 3 Answers

1. To place a comment in an HTML document, preface it with the characters `<!--` and follow it with `-->`. Whatever is between these strings will not display.

2. A `<div>` element occupies a rectangular area in a web browser which, by default, extends to the browser's right-hand edge, and is often used as a container for groups of objects (such as creating a newspaper-style column). A `<span>` element flows with text and is intended mainly for adjusting the styling of text.

3. The six pairs of tags you can use to create different levels of headings are `<h1>` and `</h1>` for the largest size of heading, through `<h6>` and `</h6>` for the smallest.

4. To denote the start and end of a paragraph, you use the `<p>` and `</p>` tags.

5. To issue a line break in an HTML document, use the `<br>` tag.

6. To format HTML text in bold without using CSS, place it within `<b>` and `</b>` tags.

7. To display italic text in HTML, place it within `<i>` and `</i>` tags.

8. To display text in italics with CSS, you can place a rule inline, like this: `<span style='font-style:italic;'>Italic text</span>`, or you can create a class in the `<style>` section of a document, such as `.italic { font-style:italic; }`. You can then apply this class as follows: `<span class='italic'>Italic text</span>`.

9. To make an element display as line-through using CSS, you can use an inline rule such as: `<span style='text-decoration:line-through;'>Line-through</span>`, or you can create a class in the `<style>` section of a document, such as `.line { text-decoration:line-through; }`. You can then apply this class as follows: `<span class='line'>Line-through</span>`.

10. The term *deprecated* is applied to parts of HTML that should no longer be used and may become obsolete and removed from HTML at a later date—the developers of HTML are giving you warning that you should stop using such deprecated tags now while they still work, and that you shouldn't wait until they stop working, because your documents may then break if you don't update them in time.

Lesson 4 Answers

1. The `<font>` tag supports manipulating fonts with HTML.

2. The `color` attribute of the `<font>` tag is used to change color. For example: `<font color='green'>Green text</font>`.

3. To change the face of a font, use the `face` attribute. For example: `<font face='Arial'>Arial text</font>`.

4. To change a font's size in HTML, use the `size` attribute. For example: `<font size='6'>Size 6</font>`.

5. To change the background of a document's body without using CSS, you can apply a value to its `bgcolor` attribute, in the following manner: `<body bgcolor='black'>`.

6. The hexadecimal number #FF0000 is red, #FFFFFF is white, and #888888 is mid-grey.

7. To change font face using CSS, you can apply a style, either with a class or an ID, or inline like this: `<span style='font-family:Arial;'>Arial font</span>`.

8. To display images in HTML, use the `<img>` tag, like this: `<img src='photo.jpg'>`.

9. In HTML you can left-align an element such as an image by applying a value to its `align` attribute such as `left`, `right`, or `center`, like this: `<img src='photo.jpg' align='left'>`.

10. The CSS way of left-aligning an element is to use the `float` rule, like this: `<img src='photo.jpg' style='float:left'>`, or by applying a class, or an ID using this rule, and so on.

Lesson 5 Answers

1. You begin an ordered list with the `<ol>` tag, and close it with `</ol>`.

2. You denote a list element by placing it within `<li>` and `</li>` tags.

3. Unordered lists are specified in HTML with the `<ul>` and `</ul>` tags.

4. To change the start value of an ordered list, you apply a value to its `start` attribute. For example: `<ol start='20'>`.

5. To change the bullet type of an unordered list, apply the value `disc`, `circle`, or `square` to its `type` attribute, like this: `<ul type='square'>`. To change the case of an alphabetic ordered list, apply either *A* or *a* to its `type` attribute, or apply either *I* or *i* to change a roman numeral list, like this `<ol type='A'>`, or this `<ol type='i'>`.

6. Definition lists use the `<dl>` and `</dl>` tags, in conjunction with `<dt>` and `</dt>`, and `<dd>` and `</dd>`.

7. HTML tables are created with the `<table>` and `</table>` tags.

8. Table rows are created with `<tr>` and `</tr>` tags, table data cells with `<td>` and `</td>` tags, and table heading cells with `<th>` and `</th>` tags.

9. To add a caption to an HTML table, place the caption text between `<caption>` and `</caption>` tags, right after the `<table>` tag.

10. The two attributes that allow cells to spread out over more than one row or column are `rowspan` and `colspan`. For example: `<td rowspan='2'>`.

Lesson 6 Answers

1. To preface secure Internet URLs, you use the https:// prefix in a link (as long as the target web server supports secure web pages).

2. You can access a subfolder called *folder* from the root of mydomain.com using the URL http://mydomain.com/folder/.

3. To link to the website mydomain.com in HTML, you would use the following syntax: `<a href='http://mydomain.com'>Click here</a>`.

4. To link to the root of the current domain, simply use the relative URL / in a link, like this: `<a href='/'>Home</a>`.

5. To make a destination URL from a hyperlink load into a different frame or window, apply a value to the `target` attribute of the link, as follows: `<a href = 'http://mydomain.com' target = 'otherframe'>Click me</a>`. To always open a link in a new window (or tab if the user has this setting), assign the value `_blank` to `target`.

6. To hyperlink directly to a section within a web document, first create an anchor to that place like this: `<a name='subsection'></a>`, and then you can link to the HTML immediately following this anchor as follows: `<a href='#subsection'>Click me</a>`. If you are not linking to the current page, also include the other page's URL, like this: `<a href = 'http://mydomain.com/news.htm#subsection'>Click me</a>`.

7. To create an HTML form, use the `<form>` and `</form>` tags.

8. To request a single text input line from a user, you can use an `<input>` tag from within a form, like this: `<input type='text' name='firstname'>`.

9. To provide more than a single line of space to input text, you can use a `<textarea>` tag, like this: `<textarea name='bio' cols='40' rows='5'></textarea>`. This creates an input box with five lines of 40 characters per line.

10. To embed another document, you can use an iframe, like this: `<iframe src='http://othersite.com/news.html'></iframe>`.

Lesson 7 Answers

1. In conjunction with an `<img>` tag, the `<map>` tag is used to create an image map, consisting of one or more areas within the map defined by `<area>` tags.

2. To denote text as a citation, place it within `<cite>` and `</cite>` tags.

3. To change the direction of text flow from left-to-right to right-to-left, use the following HTML: `<bdo dir='rtl'>`, and use `</bdo>` when done.

4. *The Mark of the Web* is a use that Microsoft's Internet Explorer browser makes of HTML comments to set the security level of a document.

5. To display text as if it has been deleted, use HTML such as the following: `<del>deleted text</del>`.

6. To display text as if it has been inserted, use HTML such as the following: `<ins>inserted text</ins>`.

7. To display text in a superscript font, place it within `<sup>` and `</sup>` tags, like this: `July 23<sup>rd</sup>`.

8. A good way to display short quotations is between the `<q>` and `</q>` tags.

9. Long quotations can be displayed by placing them within `<blockquote>` and `</blockquote>` tags.

10. To display preformatted text in which the spaces and line feeds in the HTML are kept, enclose the relevant section within `<pre>` and `</pre>` tags.

Lesson 8 Answers

1. To create an HTML5 canvas, you use the `<canvas>` and `</canvas>` tags.

2. In non-HTML5-compatible browsers, `<canvas>` tags are ignored, and any text or HTML placed inside the tags is displayed.

3. Once an HTML element has been given an ID, it can be referenced from JavaScript by passing that ID to the `getElementById()` function.

4. GPS stands for Global Positioning System.

5. Local Storage is a new HTML5 technology that is superior to cookies in that it provides far greater storage space and much easier access.

6. The tags `<audio>` and `<video>` have been added to HTML5 to handle multimedia.

7. To allow fallback to Flash for playing media, you can pull in a player using the `<embed>` and `</embed>` tags.

8. Microdata is the new HTML5 technology that helps to provide additional information about the contents of a document by describing its parts very precisely.

9. With HTML5, programmers can now offload background JavaScript tasks to web workers, which are then maintained automatically by the browser.

10. MIME used to stand for Multipurpose Internet Mail Extensions, but that has since changed to Multipurpose Internet Media Extensions (more simply referred to as Internet Media Types these days).

Lesson 9 Answers

1. The DOM is the Document Object Model used by HTML and consists of all the elements and sub-elements as objects and properties that can be accessed from JavaScript.

2. To change a web document's title, you can assign a new value to the `document` `.title` property, like this: `document.title = 'New title'`.

3. You can create a JavaScript object from an HTML element by giving the element a unique ID, which you can then pass to the `getElementById()` function, which will return an object based on that element.

4. A canvas must be given an ID in order for JavaScript to access it, like this: `<canvas id='mycanvas'></canvas>`. This ID will generally be turned into an object by the `getElementById()` function.

5. You can access an object's style properties from JavaScript by appending `.style.` to the object, followed by the property's name to be read or set, like this: `object.style.width = '100px'`.

6. The purpose of the `O()` function is to be a typing shortcut because it is much shorter than `document.getElementById()`, and it supports the passing of either an ID or an object.

7. The purpose of the `S()` function is to provide quick and easy access to an object's style properties, either by an element's ID or by object.

8. In order for drawing functions to operate correctly on a canvas, it is first necessary to create a 2D context object from the canvas, like this: `context = canvas.getContext('2d')`. This context object has properties and methods that are used to write to and read from the canvas.

9. To copy canvas data into an image, you can use the `toDataURL()` function, which extracts all the image data from a canvas and reformats it in such a way that it can be directly provided as the value for the `src` attribute of an image.

10. To create a single-line comment in JavaScript, place the character pair `//` before the code to be commented out.

Lesson 10 Answers

1. You create a filled rectangle using the `fillRect()` function. For example, the following draws a square that is 100 pixels wide and 100 pixels high at the top left of the canvas: `context.fillRect(0, 0, 100, 100)`.

2. To change the fill color, assign a value to the `fillStyle` property. For example: `context.fillStyle = 'green'`.

3. To draw a clear rectangle, you can use the `clearRect()` function, like this: `context.clearRect(0, 0, 100, 100)`.

4. To draw a rectangular outline, use the `strokeRect()` function, in this manner: `context.strokeRect(0, 0, 100, 100)`.

5. Use the `createLinearGradient()` function to create a linear gradient, like this: `gradient = context.createLinearGradient(0, 0, 100, 100)`.

6. Use the `createRadialGradient()` function, like this: `gradient = context.createRadialGradient(100, 100, 0, 100, 100, 50)` to create a radial gradient.

7. To specify the colors in a gradient, use the `addColorStop()` function, like this: `gradient.addColorStop(0, 'yellow')`.

8. To use an image for a pattern fill, call the `createPattern()` function, like this: `pattern = context.createPattern(image, 'repeat')`.

9. The four different types of pattern fill are `repeat`, `no-repeat`, `repeat-x`, and `repeat-y`, which are passed as string values in the second argument to the `createPattern()` function.

10. To ensure an image has been loaded before you use it, you must attach a function to the image object's `onload` event. Place the code that uses this image in the function.

Lesson 11 Answers

1. To choose the font for writing to a canvas, you assign values to the `font` property, like this: `context.font = '16px Times'`.

2. To write outlined text to a canvas, you call the `strokeText()` function, like this: `context.strokeText('Text', 100, 100)`.

3. The relative measurement units supported by the canvas are em, ex, px, and %.

4. The fixed measurement units supported by the canvas are in, cm, mm, pt, and pc.

5. You write filled text to a canvas with the `fillText()` function, like this: `context.fillText('Text', 100, 100)`.

6. To center-align text on a canvas, you would use a command such as this: `context.textAlign = 'center'`.

7. The full list of values supported by the `textAlign` property includes `start`, `end`, `left`, `right`, and `center`.

8. To change the horizontal line about which text will be based, assign a value to the `textBaseline` property, like this: `context.textBaseline = 'top'`.

9. The values supported by the `textBaseline` property are `top`, `middle`, `alphabetic`, `hanging`, and `bottom`.

10. You can determine the width in pixels that a text-writing call will require by calling the `measureText()` function. The `width` property of the object it returns contains the text width.

Lesson 12 Answers

1. You can change the width of subsequent lines drawn on the canvas by assigning a value to the `lineWidth` property, like this: `context.lineWidth = 8`.

2. To change the way lines start and end, assign any of the values `butt`, `round`, or `square` to the `lineCap` property, like this: `context.lineCap = 'round'`. To change the way lines join to each other, assign any of the values `round`, `bevel`, or `miter` to the `lineJoin` property, like this: `context.lineJoin = 'bevel'`. To extend the limit of mitered line joins, you can assign a numeric value to the `miterLimit` property, like this: `context.miterLimit = 7`.

3. To start and end a path, call the `beginPath()` and `closePath()` functions of the canvas context.

4. To move the drawing position of a path without creating a line, use the `moveTo()` function, like this: `context.moveTo(100, 100)`.

5. To create a line within a path, you can use the `lineTo()` function, like this: `context.lineTo(100, 100)`.

6. To apply a path to the canvas as a line, use the `stroke()` function, like this: `context.stroke()`. To apply a path to the canvas as a filled area, use the `fill()` function, like this: `context.fill()`.

7. To draw an outlined rectangle, call the `strokeRect()` function, like this: `context.strokeRect(0, 0, 100, 100)`. To draw a filled rectangle, call the `fillRect()` function, like this: `context.fillRect(0, 0, 100, 100)`.

8. You can create all or part of a circle using the `arc()` function, like this (which creates a circle): `context.arc(100, 100, 50, 0, Math.PI * 2)`.

9. To create an arc from one point to another based on imaginary tangents, call the `arcTo()` function, like this: `context.arcTo(0, 0, 100, 0, 100)`.

10. To create a curve that is modified by one imaginary attractor, you can call the `quadraticCurveTo()` function, passing the coordinates of the attractor and destination, like this: `context.quadraticCurveTo(0, 0, 100, 100)`. To create a curve that is modified by two imaginary attractors, call the `bezierCurveTo()` function, passing the two sets of attractor coordinates and the destination, like this: `context.bezierCurveTo(0, 0, 0, 100, 100, 100)`.

Lesson 13 Answers

1. To draw an image to the canvas, you use the `drawImage()` function, like this: `context.drawImage(image, 20, 20)`.

2. To resize an image when it is drawn, you can add an additional pair of arguments to the `drawImage()` function for its new width and height in pixels, like this: `context.drawImage(image, 20, 20, 100, 100)`.

3. To ensure that an image is ready for use before drawing, attach a function to the image object's `onload` event, and place your image-using code in that function.

4. To easily copy one portion of a canvas to another, use the canvas itself as the image, like this: `context.drawImage(canvas, 200, 200)`.

5. The four properties used to add and modify shadows underneath drawn objects are `shadowOffsetX`, `shadowOffsetY`, `shadowBlur`, and `shadowColor`.

6. To grab all the image pixel data from an image into a form that is editable, you can call the `getImageData()` function, in this way: `imagedata = context.getImageData(0, 0, 100, 100)`.

7. Once image data has been grabbed from a canvas and placed in an object, the object's `data` sub-object is an array containing the pixel data.

8. The four components of each pixel are its red, green, blue, and alpha transparency values. These appear sequentially in image data, with four elements to a pixel.

9. The function used to write image data to the canvas is `putImageData()`, like this: `context.putImageData(imagedata, 0, 0)`.

10. To create a new object containing blank image data, you can call the `createImageData()` function, as in this example: `imagedata = createImageData(320, 240)`.

Lesson 14 Answers

1. To change the type of compositing used to draw to the canvas, assign one of the following values to the `globalCompositeOperation` property: `source-over`, `source-in`, `source-out`, `source-atop`, `destination-over`, `destination-in`, `destination-out`, `destination-atop`, `lighter`, `darker`, `copy`, or `xor`, like this: `context.globalCompositeOperation = 'lighter'`.

2. To set the transparency of future drawing operations, assign a value between 0.0 (fully transparent) and 1.0 (no transparency) to the `globalAlpha` property, like this: `context.globalAlpha = 0.3`.

3. To change the scale for future drawing operations, call the `scale()` function, in the following manner (which scales horizontal values up by 50 percent, and vertical ones down by 50 percent): `context.scale(1.5, 0.5)`.

4. You can easily resume previous settings after changing the scaling one or more times by first calling `save()`, like this: `context.save()`, issuing all your scaling and drawing commands, and then calling `restore()`, like this: `context.restore()` to return scaling to its previous state.

5. To rotate the angle of future drawing operations, call the `rotate()` function, like this (which rotates by 90 degrees): `context.rotate(Math.PI/2)`.

6. There are $2 \times \pi$ radians (or just over 6) in 360 degrees, and one radian is about 57 degrees. The best way to use radians is as fractions and multiples of π. One degree is $\pi/180$, and the value of π is about 3.1415927, but you can use the JavaScript alternative of `Math.PI` so that you don't have to remember the value. Conversion between the two can be achieved in JavaScript as follows: `radians = Math.PI / 180 * degrees`.

7. To move the origin of future drawing operations from its default location at 0,0, call the `translate()` function, like this: `context.translate(100, 100)`.

8. To rotate an object around its center before drawing it to the canvas, first call the `translate()` function to move the origin, passing the center of where you intend to place the object as a pair of coordinates. Next, issue the call to `rotate()`, and then draw the object on the canvas with its top-left corner 50 percent of its width to the left of the new origin, and 50 percent of its height up from the new origin. For example, if the object is a square that is 100 pixels wide and high, the destination location should be at -50,-50 (since the new origin is at the object's center).

9. You can scale, rotate, and skew all at the same time by using the `transform()` function, like this: `context.transform(1.5, 0.5, 0.5, 1.5, 10, 10)`.

10. To create absolute transformations (as opposed to relative ones from the current transform settings), you can call the `setTransform()` function, which is the same as `transform()` except that the scaling and other factors are first reset before the supplied values are applied.

Lesson 15 Answers

1. The most common form of geolocation positioning hardware is called GPS (for Global Positioning System). It uses a number of orbiting satellites to triangulate a device's location very accurately, including height above sea level.

2. To determine whether a browser supports geolocation, test whether the type of the `geolocation` property is a value of `undefined` (if so, geolocation is not available), like this: `if (typeof navigator.geolocation == 'undefined')` ....

3. To request location data from a browser, call the `getCurrentPosition()` function, passing it the names of two functions—one to be called if permission to access the user's location is granted, the other to be called if it isn't, like this: `navigator.geolocation.getCurrentPosition(granted, denied)`.

4. If the user grants permission for you to access their location, the data will be supplied to the function you created to receive it in the form of a position object. This object will have two properties for the latitude and longitude: `position.coords.latitude` and `position.coords.longitude`.

5. If the user doesn't grant permission to access their location, an `error` object is supplied to the function you created to handle this instance. This object will have a `code` property containing a number between 1 and 4 indicating the error type.

6. The API at *https://maps.googleapis.com/maps/api/js?sensor=false* will give you access to Google Maps if you supply it as the value to the `src` attribute of a `<script>` tag.

7. To pass the latitude and longitude to display to the Google Maps API, you should supply them as arguments to the `LatLng()` function, like this: `new google.maps.LatLng(lat, long)`.

8. The Google Maps `zoom` property accepts values between 1 for fully zoomed out, and 20 for fully zoomed in.

9. The types of Google Maps that can be displayed are satellite, road map, or hybrid, by attaching one of the constants `SATELLITE`, `ROADMAP`, or `HYBRID` to the `MapTypeId` object, like this: `google.maps.MapTypeId.HYBRID`.

10. IP addresses are not a very accurate form of geolocation for a number of reasons, including the fact that an IP address can apply to a proxy server anywhere in the world. But even if not, a local ISP might share the same IP numbers among its customers over a wide geographical area. At best, IP numbers should be used to offer just a hint as to a user's very rough location when a better location method is not available.

Lesson 16 Answers

1. To provide access to typing into an input field without the user first having to click it, use the `autofocus` attribute, like this: `<input type='text' name='name' autofocus='autofocus'>`.

2. You can allow previous values that have been entered for the current input field's name to be selected by the user with the `autocomplete` attribute, like this: `<input type='text' name='name' autocomplete='on'>`.

3. The `list` attribute supplies a list id to an input from which a selection can be made by the user, like this: `list='items'`. The list itself should be a collection of `<option>` elements inside a `<datalist>` element given the id name supplied as the value for the `list` attribute, like this: `<datalist id='items'>`.

4. To set minimum and maximum limits for an input, assign values to the `min` and `max` attributes, like this: `<input type='number' name='age' min='13' max='99'>`.

5. To enable uploading of more than one file at a time via a form, use the `multiple` attribute, like this: `<input type='file' name='files' multiple='multiple'>`.

6. You can place text in an empty input field to prompt the user for the type of input expected, by assigning that text to the `placeholder` attribute, like this: `<input type='text' name='username' placeholder='Enter Username'>`.

7. To ensure that an input must be completed before a form is submitted, you use the `required` attribute, like this: `<input type='password' name='pass' required='required'>`.

8. The attribute `pattern='[\w]{5,10}'` tells the web browser not to allow the form to be submitted unless this input field consists of between 5 and 10 (inclusive) uppercase and/or lowercase letters, and/or digits, and/or the underline character (\w means any word character).

9. You can offer a color picker in an input (in browsers that support it) by using an input type of `color`, like this: `<input name='background' type='color'>`.

10. You can call up a calendar date picker in an input (in browsers that support it) by using an input type of `date`, like this: `<input name='meeting' type='date'>`.

Lesson 17 Answers

1. Local storage is a better solution than cookies because it provides over a thousand times the storage capacity per domain, and it is easily accessed as key and value pairs.

2. You can determine whether local storage is available in a browser by testing the type of the `localStorage` object, like this: `if (typeof localStorage == 'undefined')`. If it is undefined, then local storage is not available.

3. To store an item of local storage data, use the `setItem()` function, like this: `localStorage.setItem('key', 'value')`.

4. To retrieve an item of local storage data, use the `getItem()` function, like this: `value = localStorage.getItem('key')`.

5. To remove an item from local storage, use the `removeItem()` function, like this: `localStorage.removeItem('key')`.

6. To clear all the data relating to your domain in local storage, use the `clear()` function, like this: `localStorage.clear()`.

7. To post a message to another document loaded into the browser, call the `postMessage()` function, like this: `window.postMessage('Message text', 'http://domain.com')`.

8. To listen for messages from other loaded documents, attach a function to the onmessage event of the window, like this: `window.onmessage = function(event) {}`. Within the curly braces you can access `event.data` to read the message.

9. To ensure that you post messages only to the documents you want to receive them, pass the correct domain as the second argument to `postMessage()`.

10. To ignore any message received from documents from which you do not wish to receive them, discard those that do not originate from your domain by checking the `origin` property of the onmessage event object, like this: `if (event.origin == 'http://domain.com')`.

Lesson 18 Answers

1. To embed audio in an HTML5 document, you use the `<audio>` tag.

2. The four types of audio format supported by HTML5 browsers are *AAC*, *MP3*, *PCM*, and *OGG Vorbis*.

3. To ensure that your audio will play on all major browsers and platforms, you need to provide your audio in two formats. One of these should be *OGG Vorbis*, and the other can be either *AAC* or *MP3*.

4. The purpose of the `<source>` tag is to offer an audio file to the browser. If the browser supports the audio type and it is the first audio file supported, then it will be selected for playing.

5. For playing audio, the `<source>` tag requires two attributes to be supplied to it: the URL of the audio file in the src attribute, and the type of the audio file in the type attribute, like this: `<source src='music.mp3' type='audio/mpeg'>`.

6. To make audio play on page load, supply the `autoplay` attribute to the `<audio>` tag, like this: `<audio autoplay>`.

7. You can control whether or not the audio controls are displayed by either including or omitting the `controls` attribute from the `<audio>` tag, like this: `<audio controls>`.

8. To set a piece of audio to play over and over, add the `loop` attribute to the `<audio>` tag, like this: `<audio loop>`.

9. To cause audio to begin loading even before the user selects Play, add the `preload` attribute to the `<audio>` tag, like this: `<audio preload>`.

10. You can support older browsers that do not recognize HTML5 audio by embedding a Flash audio player within the `<audio>` and `</audio>` tags. HTML5 browsers will ignore it, while older ones will ignore the `<audio>` tags and will run the Flash plug-in.

Lesson 19 Answers

1. To embed video in an HTML5 document, you use the `<video>` tag.

2. The three types of video format supported by HTML5 browsers are *MP4/H.264*, *OGG/Theora*, and *WebM/VP8*.

3. To ensure that your video will play on all major browsers and platforms, you need to provide your video in two formats. One of these should be *MP4*, and the other should be *OGG*.

4. The purpose of the `<source>` tag is to offer a video file to the browser. If the browser supports the video type and it is the first video file supported, then it will be selected for playing.

5. For playing audio, the `<source>` tag requires two attributes to be supplied to it: the URL of the video file in the `src` attribute, and the type of the video file in the `type` attribute, like this: `<source src='video.mp4' type='video/mp4'>`.

6. To make video play on page load, supply the `autoplay` attribute to the `<video>` tag, like this: `<video autoplay>`.

7. You can control whether or not the video controls are displayed by either including or omitting the `controls` attribute from the `<video>` tag, like this: `<video controls>`.

8. To set a video's width and height, assign values to the `width` and `height` attributes of the `<video>` tag, like this: `<video width='640' height='480'>`.

9. To display an image of your choice as a placeholder for where the video will play, use the `poster` attribute in the `<video>` tag, like this: `<video poster='myimage.jpg'>`.

10. You can support older browsers that do not recognize HTML5 video by embedding a Flash video player within the `<video>` and `</video>` tags. HTML5 browsers will ignore it, while older ones will ignore the `<video>` tags and will run the Flash plug-in.

Lesson 20 Answers

1. Microdata makes text that is easily understandable by people due to context equally understandable to machines, by explaining each part.

2. Two attributes used to denote microdata are `itemtype` for the type of microdata, and `itemprop` for each property. Other microdata attributes include `itemid`, `itemref`, and `itemscope`.

3. Web workers are JavaScript programs that are set to work in the background under the control of the browser to undertake tasks separate from the main foreground program.

4. You create a new web worker by calling the `Worker()` function, passing it the URL of a JavaScript program to run, like this: `worker = new Worker ('program.js')`.

5. You receive messages from a web worker by attaching a function to the `onmessage` event of the `worker` object that is returned by the call to `Worker()`. The `data` property of the object passed to this function contains the message.

6. Offline web applications are online web applications that can also run offline because all their associated files get downloaded locally by the browser.

7. Offline web applications use the MIME type `text/cache-manifest`. When a web browser encounters a file of this type, it knows that it contains information about the files it should download to enable an app to run offline.

8. In order to implement drag and drop in a document, you need to attach handler functions to the `ondragstart` event of any object to be dragged. You must also attach to the `ondragover` and `ondrop` events of any element into which items can be dropped.

9. The purpose of calling the `preventDefault()` function in the drag-and-drop handlers is to override the default action of disallowing drag-and-drop operations, thus making these operations available.

10. The functions that handle the passing of dragged-and-dropped items are `setData()` and `getData()`, which are methods of the `dataTransfer` property of the events being handled.

Index